P9-BIW-645

"Lighting up the Terrain": The Poetry of Margaret Avison

"Lighting up the terrain": The Poetry of Margaret Avison

EDITED BY DAVID KENT

ECW PRESS

CANADIAN CATALOGUING IN PUBLICATION DATA

Main entry under title:

"Lighting up the terrain": The poetry of Margaret Avison

Includes index.
ISBN 0-920763-94-4 (bound). — ISBN 0-920763-93-6 (PBK.)

1. Avison, Margaret, 1918– — *Criticism and interpretation.* I. Kent, David A., 1948– .

PS8501.V57Z752 1987 C811'.54 C87-093310-8
PR9199.3.A92Z752 1987

"Lighting up the terrain" has been published with the help of a grant from the Canadian Federation for the Humanities, using funds provided by the Social Sciences and Humanities Research Council of Canada. Additional grants have been provided by The Canada Council and the Ontario Arts Council.

Designed and typeset by ECW Production Services, Oakville, Ontario. Printed and bound by University of Toronto Press, Toronto, Ontario. Cover illustration by Linda Walker.

Published by ECW PRESS, 307 Coxwell Avenue, Toronto, Ontario M4L 3B5.

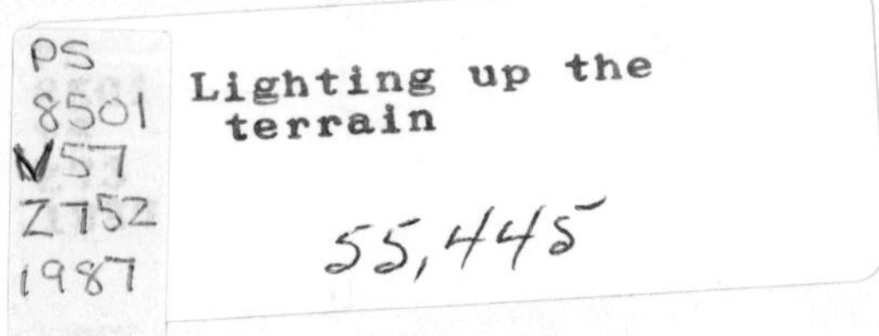

ACKNOWLEDGEMENTS

"Caedmon" (copyright 1984 by Denise Levertov) was first published as a broadside by William B. Ewert, *Publisher.* It is reprinted by permission of the author and the publisher.

"Neverness or The One Ship Beached on One Far Distant Shore" and "On Believing the Bible" are reprinted with the permission of Margaret Avison. "Not the Sweet Cicely of Gerardes Herball" and "Jael's Part" are reprinted with the permission of McClelland and Stewart. "The Bible to be Believed" is reprinted with the permission of Lancelot Press.

Abbreviated References

All references to Margaret Avison's collected poetry in this volume are noted as follows: from *Winter Sun* by *WS* and page number and from *The Dumbfounding* by *D* and page number (the page references are to the combined edition published in 1982 by McClelland and Stewart as *Winter Sun/The Dumbfounding: Poems 1940–66*); from *sunblue* (Hantsport, N.S.: Lancelot Press, 1978) by *s* and page number.

For my mother and in memory of my father

Contents

Introduction

DAVID A. KENT

MARGARET AVISON has often been described as an 'important' poet.[1] She is certainly one of Canada's most respected poets, nationally and internationally. Few other Canadian writers, for example, could claim to have recently been the subject of study in seminars directed by Denise Levertov at Stanford University. It is therefore remarkable that her reputation is based on just three published volumes of poetry, which appeared over a period of eighteen years. A poet of intense locality and yet one who has always been anxious to test the highest international standards, during the 1950s Avison published her work in such prestigious poetry magazines as *The Kenyon Review* and *Poetry* [Chicago]. She was also the recipient of a Guggenheim Fellowship in 1956–57, and this opportunity allowed her the time to prepare her first collection. However, after *Winter Sun* was rejected a dozen times in Canada, it was at last accepted by Routledge and Kegan Paul in London.[2] Subsequently, she sent her second volume, *The Dumbfounding*, to Norton in New York, while the third was given to a small Nova Scotia publisher, Lancelot Press in Hantsport, unknown to most of us prior to the publication of *sunblue* in 1978. Her standing as a significant contemporary writer and, latterly, a notable religious poet has, in effect, been achieved almost in spite of herself. Not many poets have, apparently, so assiduously avoided most of the means of systematic self-promotion available during the recent ascendancy of "Can. Lit." For example, she seldom gives public readings and is rarely interviewed. When Kenneth McRobbie inscribed *Eyes Without a Face* (Toronto: Gallery Editions, 1960) for her, he wrote: "To Margaret: the mysterious – the missed / with affection Kenneth June '60."[3] The essential purpose of the present volume is to throw light on the mystery of Margaret Avison, especially on her achievement as a Christian poet. This intention has evolved (naturally enough, perhaps) into something of a celebration of that person and that achievement. The contributors are therefore a mixture of critics and poets, with both Canadians and Americans among the latter. All the contributors share an admiration for Avison's fundamental integrity as person and poet.

Margaret Avison's well-known reticence is not simply the manifestation of a temperamental shyness. It is also partly based on a principled (and, ultimately, religious) distrust of certain aspects of the phenomenon known as the 'Can. Lit.' industry.[4] Highly trained in academic habits of mind (B.A., M.A. and ABD, English, University of Toronto), she nevertheless recognizes how the conceptual cravings of the systematizing intellect are, in so many respects, antithetical to the perceptual ways of the imagination as it bodies itself forth in language. Equally sceptical about the value of biographical data in the interpretation of poems, she has therefore been reluctant to disclose herself to curious academics.[5] On the other hand, she has generously helped and advised younger poets (as Gail Fox, bpNichol, and Gwendolyn MacEwen testify) whenever such attention did not compromise her high standards of poetic achievement or her sense of ethics and her perception of providence.

Paradoxically, despite her relatively reclusive stance, Avison has become something of a legendary presence haunting Canadian literature, her poetry a powerful influence on the past generation of writers. As Francis Mansbridge's recent bibliography so dramatically helps to demonstrate, her career has been unusually varied while being uncommonly dedicated.[6] She has devoted an otherwise itinerant, irregular working life to examining – from every conceivable angle – that central human miracle, articulation through language. We discover through Mansbridge's work that Avison has been, astonishingly enough, a bibliographer, an editor, a literary adviser to more than one student publication (as well as other periodicals), a writer of an elementary-school textbook, a ghost writer of a biography, a writer-in-residence, briefly an autobiographer, an academic critic and scholar, a book reviewer, a researcher, a translator, and a poet. This rich variety of linguistic experience has reinforced her conviction about the individuating process generated through the act of using language.[7] The same sense of personal identity is reflected in her achievement of a distinctive, individual, poetic voice. When Richard Tillinghast, for example, remarked in a 1967 commentary on some of her poems, "Who else could have written that?", he was testifying to the power of her particular style and manner and confirming her success in the quest for what she once called the poet's "scuffle to find his own words, his own idiom."[8]

We can recognize the Avison manner even in the following early poem,[9] written while Avison was a teenager and published in the literary periodical at Victoria College, *Acta Victoriana*:

BACK PEW

A small head bristles with short black hair;
A sleek head flows into ringlets fair;
An enormous swirl
Is the mad-cap girl
Attempting a modern sprightly curl.
One bald head, fuzzy, is drooped to doze,
One high and shining, with fervour glows
At one old nape
Where a knot should shape
A wisp is jubilant with escape.
The grey tufts stray, the one bald is gay,
The other nods, and the young heads sway
And yearn for the preacher from far-away
To shout and flourish and plunge and pray
And let them sit in the yard to play.

Here is a delightfully sardonic perspective on a church congregation. It is a panoramic view of head shapes and hair-styles, almost a kind of phrenological survey of personality types conducted by someone whose mind ought to be occupied by other things but whose vision, from the rear pew, is distracted by the spectacle of human variety. Avison's nascent poetic identity – her wit, her mastery of rhythm, her insight and compassion – is evident here, even as its mature, fully realized version has recently been seen in a "clutch of poems" published in the 1984 triple issue of *Exile*.[10] Avison's idiom, a compound of her sometimes stunning technical virtuosity and elusive rhetoric, is what readers must confront and with which they must wrestle, thereby engaging in the imaginative struggle she herself relishes when reading a challenging poet. She once said about the poetry of Dylan Thomas, for instance: "There is matter enough to absorb . . . and complexity to stun them [the readers] and hold them pleasurably agape in the doorway."[11]

Avison's presence in the world of Canadian letters was known long before *Winter Sun* was published in 1960, thanks largely to the support and promotion of A. J. M. Smith, who included her work in *The Book of Canadian Poetry* as early as 1943. Smith first championed Avison as a modern metaphysical poet (much as Robert Creeley, in his contribution here, praises the union of thought and feeling he finds in her poetry). Later, Smith hailed her as a Christian poet whose poems "have a validity as firm as the religious poetry of Hopkins or Eliot."[12] With the publication of *Winter Sun* and the praise it won (including the Governor-General's Award for poetry), Avison emerged from the shadows of what Milton Wilson had termed "a kind of negative legend" to rank "among the best two or three poets that Canada has produced since 1940."[13] Avison's *The Dumbfounding* (1966), her first post-conversion volume, brought further critical superlatives but also, significantly enough, the first murmurs of qualification. Keith Harrison was one reviewer who did not "think that the specifically religious poems . . . came off very well" (although he did look forward to more from "a very rich talent").[14] The rather muted response to *sunblue* tends to confirm what the reaction of Harrison and a few others hinted at: that Avison's sudden conversion to Christianity in 1963 and her commitment to being a Christian artist (with all that that entails) have effectively divided her audience into those readers who accept her stance and those who regard this commitment as damaging to her art, turning it into dogma and ideology.

This latter view seems well represented in a review by Rod Willmot.[15] He claims that Avison's Christianity has meant "intellectual and linguistic diminution" as well as "closure of word, in the uninventive illustration of Biblical themes, and closure of mind, in the too-pat reaching of foregone conclusions." The same sceptical, agnostic sensibility presents itself in reviews by Stephen Scobie and Sandra Djwa. For example, Djwa criticizes Avison for subordinating "her poetry to her faith" and remarks in dismay: "it may be that the struggle to find religious certitude is more conducive to poetry than its achievement," an observation that would doubtless come as a surprise to a number of writers firmly established in the English literary pantheon.[16] The secularist disaffection with Avison's religious poetry may remain a minority opinion in the midst of continuing affirmation, but it does reflect a genuine problem that a number of critics have experienced in dealing with one of our major poets, and it needs to be acknowledged and, to some degree at least, addressed.

In 1977, Francis Mansbridge noted that Avison's "poetic importance is out of all proportion to the amount of her published work."[17] Indeed, her importance is also out of all proportion to the amount of academic commentary that has been written on her poetry. In the world of self-regarding literary criticism, where it sometimes seems as if literary theory has displaced literature as the centre of attention, a contemporary Christian poet appears to be a contradiction in terms, a kind of hopeless anachronism. As Lionel Adey has so cogently and charitably remarked of a similar situation in Hopkins criticism, "It may be that some non-Christian scholars can only read with comfort Christian poetry of earlier ages than the late-Victorian."[18] Avison's increasingly devotional poetry, the feeling of discomfort some commentators experience with a living and assertive religious faith, and a general unwillingness to recognize the subtle rigours and complexities of a Christian poetic, all help to explain the rather restricted body of sympathetic criticism hitherto devoted to her poetry. There have, of course, been several excellent essays scattered through various journals during the 1970s and early 1980s, in addition to Ernest Redekop's pioneering monograph of 1970, but there nevertheless remains a discernible reluctance to encounter Avison on her own Christian terms.[19]

That a Christian poet inevitably faces certain barriers in reaching even a general readership has been acknowledged by Avison herself. We no longer live, she has said, in a "coherent society"; "more people know more about karma than the Ten Commandments." She realizes that when she speaks about her faith to another, "some things are not heard"; "people on the other side say 'What gives?'" She has discussed some of these frustrating difficulties in a short article published in 1969, "Who listens and how come?":

> The professing Christian and the declared agnostic seem to be talking about the same thing. But there is an absolute, inevitable intolerance, on each side, of the other. Both seem to listen and to meet what is said, but each misconstrues what is heard, and speaks to a different issue.[20]

And yet the Christian poet can neither compromise her integrity nor avoid her mission of witness and testimony. This posture and its result have been appreciated by Denise Levertov:

> The public of a poet such as Margaret Avison, whose content and allusions are frequently unequivocally Christian, is certainly smaller than it would be if that were not the case. But a self-respecting poet does not court the audience but does what must be done to serve the art; so that is not a matter of concern.[21]

In turn, of course, the critic should serve the artist. Critics of Avison need to recognize and acknowledge her fundamental religious commitment and begin to assess her work within the context and tradition of the devotional poet's role. Denise Levertov's poem for Margaret Avison reminds us that this tradition extends back to the seventh century, to Caedmon, the first Christian poet to write in English. The critic must also realize that, as Elizabeth Jennings has observed, "in many ways, Christian poetry is no different from any other kind of verse; if it is good and lasting, this is not because it is Christian poetry but because it is fine poetry."[22] Nevertheless, the tradition of Christian poetry does seem to have certain distinguishing characteristics that mark its composition as a special discipline. Criticism of the seventeenth-century religious poets, for example, has increasingly disclosed that devotional poetry, rather than having a narrow, constricted range, embraces a wide variety of modes and postures: the celebrative, confessional, petitionary, prayerful, testimonial, homiletic, and so on. The matters of morality, role, and audience are of special concern to the Christian poet, as is the problematic relationship between the poet's language and the authoritative word of scripture; all these elements help to guarantee that Christian faith (far from simplifying) only complicates the art of verse immensely.[23] When Avison was asked by A. J. M. Smith in 1943 who her favourite poet was, she answered George Herbert, and this influence can be seen in poems from the early "Intra-Political" (*WS*, 55–57) to the recent "Oughtiness Ousted," (*s*, 64) with its metaphysical wit and word play. She has also acknowledged the profound impact two other major religious poets, John Donne and T. S. Eliot, exerted on her poetry after she had encountered them as a university student. And, of course, there is the stylistic precedent of Gerard Manley Hopkins (see "Song of the Flaming Sword," published by

Contemporary Verse in 1951), as well as his celebration of the vitality of creation. In addition to these discernible debts to the tradition, we are fortunate to have Avison's own comments on the writing of Christian poetry. In an article published in 1968 and reprinted below, "Muse of Danger," she describes her understanding of what the poet who is also a Christian must be about; it is a refreshingly undogmatic view, and one that may help to dispel some of the preconceptions critics bring to her religious poetry.

The essays in this collection do not balk or demur in the face of Avison's Christianity; they begin by accepting it. Together, the critics deal with interrelated and evolving issues in Avison's poetic: the matter of her difficult style, the aesthetic and ideological implications of her religious conversion, and the intricate achievement of her Christian lyricism. Style, conversion, and Christian poetry: each is a facet of the same central mystery this group of essays tries to illuminate. Jon Kertzer's comprehensive essay spans all of Avison's career and treats aspects of "her developing aesthetic"; in particular, he focuses on "how she regards words." He shows that, for the Christian, using language must manifest an attitude of simple faith as well as a sense of God's unfathomable mystery. Larry Mathews and David Jeffrey are also concerned with Avison's development from (to borrow Jeffrey's polarity) *poeta nascitur* to *poeta fit*. Mathews assesses this growth from the perspective of Avison's dramatically altered understanding of the creative imagination. By highlighting her changing response to the heritage of Romanticism, he opens up some intriguing vistas on her relationship to both Wordsworth and Stevens. Jeffrey's essay handles broader antitheses than Christian and Romantic. In particular, he explores the impact her conversion has had on her "philosophical and spiritual progress," and he reveals how 'conversion' has meant 'inversion' of premises in the transformation of her poetic. While Avison's conversion remains the pivotal point in her career, the essays by Robert James Merrett and Ernest Redekop directly address aspects of her achievement as a Christian poet. Merrett's intriguing investigation of syntactical patterns in Avison's verse discloses elements of her art as yet unobserved by readers. Merrett discovers a "theological strategy" in her grammar, especially in the exploitation of participle forms. Redekop's examination of Avison's evolving use of the Bible (inevitably the major pretext for the Christian poet) posits that her mature poetic language is characterized by its kerygmatic or proclamative nature. In providing a valuable appendix recording biblical allusions in her poems,

Redekop demonstrates how often her words are now responses to the Word, and he thereby reveals the complex intertextuality possible in the best religious poetry.

Margaret Avison is regarded by critics and poets alike with profound respect. For Cid Corman, respect rises into love. And for George Bowering, she is "the founder of excellence," "the best poet we have had." Little more need be added here except to repeat Bowering's gracious statement of gratitude — "Thank you for sending her."

NOTES

[1] See, for example, Tom Marshall, "Major Canadian Poets IV: Margaret Avison," *The Canadian Forum*, March 1979, p. 23: "an extraordinary poet from the beginning, Avison has become ever more extraordinary and significant over the years. With Al Purdy, she is probably our most important English-Canadian poet."

[2] The proof sheets of *Winter Sun* (at the Lilly Library, Indiana University) appear to indicate that Routledge and Kegan Paul were the initial publishers. However, after a brief search, the only response to the book in Britain I could locate was a three-sentence notice in *British Book News: Index to Books Reviewed* (1961), p. 217; yet even here it is recorded as having been published by the Canadian co-publisher, University of Toronto Press.

[3] This book is among the books and papers Avison gave to York University in 1984.

[4] See "To a Pioneer in Canadian Studies; And to all in Such Pedantry" (*s*, 83).

[5] This was a principle she adopted early in her career; see Margaret Avison, rev. of *The Task* by Robert Bhain Campbell, *The Canadian Forum*, Dec. 1945, p. 223.

[6] Francis Mansbridge's "Margaret Avison: An Annotated Bibliography" has been published in volume six of *The Annotated Bibliography of Canada's Major Authors*, ed. Robert Lecker and Jack David (Toronto: ECW, 1985), 13–66. The bibliography has been updated for this volume, but it is published here without its annotations.

[7] Margaret Avison, "Muse of Danger," *His*, 28, No. 6 (March 1968), 35. This article and the one in n. 20 below are among the most important new items found among Avison's books and papers at York University. I am very

grateful to Margaret Avison for permission to reprint "Muse of Danger" in this collection. Further biographical details about Avison can be found in my essay on her in the series *Canadian Writers and Their Works* (ECW). See also my " List of Books and Periodicals Given to York University by Margaret Avison (1984)." Available from the Archives, Scott Library, York University.

[8] Richard Tillinghast, "Seven Poets," *Poetry* [Chicago], 110 (July 1967), 266; Margaret Avison, "Poets in Canada," *Poetry* [Chicago], 94 (June 1959), 182.

[9] Margaret Avison, "Back Pew," *Acta Victoriana*, 61, No. 3 (Dec. 1936), 9. The poem is reprinted with the author's permission.

[10] Undocumented quotations are from a conversation I had with Margaret Avison in May, 1984.

[11] Margaret Avison, rev. of *New Poems*, by Dylan Thomas, *The Canadian Forum*, Sept. 1943, p. 143.

[12] A. J. M. Smith, "Margaret Avison," *Contemporary Poets of the English Language*, ed. Rosalie Murphy (Chicago: St. James, 1970), p. 44. See also his "Margaret Avison's New Book," *The Canadian Forum*, Sept. 1966, p. 133; and "Critical Improvisations on Margaret Avison's *Winter Sun*," *The Tamarack Review*, No. 18 (Winter 1961), pp. 81–86.

[13] Milton Wilson, "The Poetry of Margaret Avison," *Canadian Literature*, No. 2 (Autumn 1959), p. 47; Milton Wilson, "Letters in Canada: 1960. Poetry," *University of Toronto Quarterly*, 30 (July 1961), 380.

[14] Keith Harrison, "Poetry Chronicle," *The Tamarack Review*, No. 42 (Winter 1967), pp. 76, 77.

[15] Rod Willmot, "Winning Spirit," *Canadian Literature*, No. 87 (Winter 1980), pp. 115, 116.

[16] Stephen Scobie, rev. of *sunblue*, by Margaret Avison, *Queen's Quarterly*, 87 (Spring 1980), 158–60; Sandra Djwa, "Letters in Canada: 1979. Poetry," *University of Toronto Quarterly*, 49 (Summer 1980), 349.

[17] Francis Mansbridge, "Margaret Avison: A Checklist," *Canadian Library Journal*, 34, No. 6 (Dec. 1977), 431.

[18] Lionel Adey, "The Inscapes of Insomnia in Hopkins, Thomson and Lowell," in *Vital Candle: Victorian and Modern Bearings in Gerard Manley Hopkins*, ed. John S. North and Michael D. Moore (Waterloo, Ont.: Univ. of Waterloo Press, 1984), p. 79.

[19] Valuable essays on Avison include, among a few others, the following: Daniel W. Doerksen, "Search and Discovery: Margaret Avison's Poetry," *Canadian Literature*, No. 60 (Spring 1974), pp. 7–20; J. M. Zezulka, "Refusing the Sweet Surrender: Margaret Avison's 'Dispersed Titles,'" *Canadian Poetry*, No. 1 (Fall/Winter 1977), pp. 44–53; J. M. Kertzer,

"Margaret Avison: Power, Knowledge and the Language of Poetry," *Canadian Poetry*, No. 4 (Spring/Summer, 1979), pp. 29–44; and Ernest Redekop, "sun/Son light/Light: Avison's elemental *Sunblue*," *Canadian Poetry*, No. 7 (Fall/Winter 1980), pp. 21–37.

[20] Margaret Avison, "Who Listens and How Come?" *crux*, 6, No. 2 (Feb. 1969), 4.

[21] Denise Levertov, "A Poet's View," *Religion & Intellectual Life*, 1, No. 4 (Summer 1984), 50.

[22] Elizabeth Jennings, *Christian Poetry* (New York: Hawthorn, 1965), Vol. 118 of the *Twentieth Century Encyclopedia of Catholicism*, Section XI, p. 8.

[23] See Nathan A. Scott, ed., *The New Orpheus: Essays toward a Christian Poetic* (New York: Sheed and Ward, 1964), and the more recent Michael Edwards, *Towards a Christian Poetic* (London: Macmillan, 1984). An excellent study exploring the generical models behind seventeenth-century religious poetry is Barbara Kiefer Lewalski, *Protestant Poetics and the Seventeenth-Caaaaay Religious Lyric* (Princeton, N.J.: Princeton Univ. Press, 1979).

Caedmon

DENISE LEVERTOV

All others talked as if
talk were a dance.
Clodhopper I, with clumsy feet
would break the gliding ring.
Early I learned to
hunch myself
close by the door:
then when the talk began
I'd wipe my
mouth and wend
unnoticed back to the barn
to be with the warm beasts,
dumb among body sounds
of the simple ones.
I'd see by a twist
of lit rush the motes
of gold moving
from shadow to shadow
slow in the wake
of deep untroubled sighs.
The cows
munched or stirred or were still. I
was at home and lonely,

both in good measure. Until
the sudden angel affrighted me — light effacing
my feeble beam,
a forest of torches, feathers of flame, sparks upflying:
but the cows as before
were calm, and nothing was burning,
                    nothing but I, as that hand of fire
touched my lips and scorched my tongue
and pulled my voice
                        into the ring of the dance.

Dear Margaret

CID CORMAN

THERE ARE LETTERS and they would provide the precisions – but let me just jot down some recollected impressions.

We met at her very modest room near the University of Toronto campus (she may have had two small rooms – but we sat – Ray Souster and I – in a room that held her cot-like bed; it was almost military in its simplicity).

I had hitch-hiked that summer of '53 (my first visit to Canada) – July – to Toronto and was staying with Ray and Lee at their place (a very modest dwelling too – but their own). I was looking for "interesting" writers and though Ray had had only slight contact with her (she seemed averse to being involved in any literary scenes) – he did regard her highly/respected her and thought I too might enjoy meeting her. She was older than I was – as was Ray. (I was 29.)

ORIGIN had had 9 issues already. Olson, Creeley, Bronk, Duncan, Levertov, Blackburn, Enslin, Eigner, and myself for the first time were visible. I doubt if she was much aware of the magazine yet then and perhaps he had cued her in. For whatever reason she was quite willing to meet us now and we talked – I suppose about poetry – for an hour or two. With me I had brought some copies of ORIGIN as well as my copy of POETRY:NY with Olson's PROJECTIVE VERSE essay.

She glanced at the Olson and asked if she might hold onto the piece for a while: she'd mail it back to me (which she did in due time). Chances are that I read at least half of it aloud and I may even have read some of his poetry and Creeley's and Bronk's – for I was proselytizing openly. What struck me most was her candour and down-to-earth nature *and* the enthusiasm – the first I encountered in Canada for Olson. (Ray was invariably open – as he still is – to anything new – unusual.) She spoke with a quiet intelligence and feeling. She was utterly unpretentious.

She impressed me deeply. I liked her. When I returned to Boston quite naturally I wrote and asked her to send me work (I knew she was very shy about sending out her work). In fact – I more likely solicited work before I left her in Toronto. Anyhow – she did send me a batch of poems.

I rejected the poems – though I was attracted by them. There was a kind of artificial tightness to them that put me off – but I wrote very frankly – clearly – and *warmly* and said that I hoped she would not be put out and send me other work – that I felt certain that there would be work I would want. The upshot was one of two "lessons" I learned from Margaret. This first one was (and I have never gone back on this piece of learning as an editor – or the other for that matter): Never reject work that has been *solicited*. Or at least accept some of what has been received. After all – the poetry was of a standard that I could live with and if it was worth the criticism I offered – it was worth the encouragement of publishing.

It was another two years virtually before she wrote me again and said that – though what I had said in criticism was reasonably fair and accurate – she couldn't "accept" it at the time. She apologized for the fact – as I did for having behaved so foolishly in the face of someone to whom the poem was very much living flesh. I had torn her. (I wrote a number of letters – of course – to have elicited finally such a response and THE AGNES CLEVES PAPERS – which was printed before the 1st series was completed.)

In the second series – in January 1962 – she was finally featured in ORIGIN with poetry I had no trouble in feeling "at home" with – part of her enduring oeuvre. But this time I made another boo-boo – certainly again with anything but malice in mind. I published one of her letters to me verbatim. My point was to reveal the kind of feeling and thought that was being brought into play – hoping to draw the readers more sympathetically into the work – through a very warm and human letter – the revelation of a very real and distinctive person. In short — I published it out of a sense of affection for her. What happened — however — was a very hurt reply. Why hadn't I asked her permission? She was embarrassed — even more than surprised — by what she clearly regarded tactless on my part and thoughtless — revealing what she regarded as "private."

Yet — if I may — and I have never again printed a letter from any writer without permission — though different writers react in different ways to the same issue — let me quote again (the cat long since out of the bag) some of that very fine letter (enough of it to suggest that her letters may one day be an essential part of her life's work):

(The letter indicates in passing that I must've been back in Boston at the time: winter of 1961 — just before heading back to San Francisco — in fact. And the last time I saw her was probably earlier that season — again in Toronto.)

". . . Your letter made me wish more than ever for a leisurely conversation — yet maybe what I long for is the guide and teacher one cannot look for, past a certain stage. What I mean is — maybe this winter was not the right time for a talk with you, for maybe some work of learning, inly, must be done by me first, in order that I become ready for talk with you.

"What you say of 'pretty' 'poetical' phrasings I *am* by now ready to hear in this sense. I can even spot 'em once poems grow remote from the seizure of writing, and occasionally abort them while working. To date, though, I still need the eye of a good editor — or about 3 yrs' perspective — to weed out the poems that go luscious this way. Still, on this point it's now O.K. — recognizing it means separating from it, as fast as I can make that recognition a truly inner *knowing*.

"But the 'protective coloration' problem — how aware your listening is to have pin-pointed that! — I am still out in the woods with it. There is some corner I have to turn yet, some confronting I have to do — as you would instantly agree, I think, it must come about at the deepest levels in order to find free singing voice. Part of it is a trouble in my aesthetics: that it divorces one from the will to be 'against' any 'group'. Poetry over against the world — if such could exist, I'd stay on the world's side. This is too vague a statement. Aaron Copland says: 'When I speak of the gifted listener I am thinking of the nonmusician primarily, of the listener who intends to retain his amateur status. *It is the thought of just such a listener that excites the composer in me*. I know, or think I know, how the professional musician will react to music. But with the amateur it is different . . . no treatise or chart or guide can ever sufficiently pull together the various strands of a complex piece of music – only the inrushing floodlight of one's own imagination can do that.'

"In order to find harmony between the 'inrushing floodlight of imagination' as writer, with the reader's, I suspect one must listen painfully and long to the experience of living – albeit today an *anti*-poetic one – as amateur listeners know it. Somewhere, in this effort, a wrong self-effacement has taken place in me. I can *feel* the blindfold, the strait jacket – but cannot so far discover where the knots and hooks are to undo them. Maybe this discovery is what I must do in order to come to that conversation with you . . ."

At the close of one of her hard earned poems she says:

"a nowhere to exchange
among us few
carefully."

A nowhere – and a no one – Margaret – but it doesn't stop us from loving one another. It doesn't stop me from loving you – dear Margaret.

Kyoto: 15 April 1983

Margaret Avison and the Place of Meaning

JON KERTZER

SURVEYING THE LITERARY SCENE in 1959, Margaret Avison wrote: "Any Canadian writer, for example, is aware of a scuffle to find his own words, his own idiom . . . . In trying to find his language-level, then, a Canadian poet is trying to assert both an identity and an aesthetic."[1] It is tempting to apply these remarks to her own work: to praise a gradual refinement of style that permits her to assert a distinctive poetic personality in a native idiom. In this view, the early poetry of alienation relieved by imaginative insight (the "optic heart" in *WS*, 27) would yield first to religious doubt (the "blindfold" poems in *D*, 131 ff), and then to a radiant vision of God and His redemption (in *sunblue*). Her scuffle with words would find peace in the divine Word: "God is, in flesh. / Now the skies soar / with song. Heaven utters" (*D*, 160). Although this is an account of her career that I intend in part to endorse, it gives a misleading impression of her developing aesthetic.

A glance through her work reveals that the poems of *Winter Sun* (1960) and of her earlier periodical publications display great authority and assurance. Instead of tussling with words, they offer a composed, sometimes impassive style marked by confident phrases such as "I know you think you want to slam along / At fifty per"; "The autumn wind in midsummer / Is as it will be"; "It is not pity about me for all that."[2] Even passing comments such as "there is no question" and "It's all one" (*WS*, 11, 25) provide strong authorial direction. The early poems are full of challenges, rebukes, assurances, advice, and instructions that show how the poet has the reader at a disadvantage. She is in control; he must be guided, however cryptically:

> Jubilance means shouting.
>
> A man can know angels, but he brooks the
> silence of their music.
> There are oceans.[3]
>
> Yet I declare, your seeing is diseased
> That cripples space.[4]
>
> But if you do, I have a hunch
> You've missed a portent.
>
> (*WS*, 46)

The same commanding tone appears in her condensed surveys of culture: "Geometaphysics," "The Iconoclasts," "Neverness or the One Ship Beached on One Far Distant Shore," "Dispersed Titles." These poetic lectures in history, philosophy, and perception cast the reader in the role of naïve pupil being educated in the workings of his own mind. Finally, Avison's polished style appears in a different tone in the eloquent endings which give several poems a Keatsian resonance. The final lines are gorgeous: "borne in the breathy brown frost-foaming air"; "The singing or its far-borne, aching echoes"; "and a vision / Of diamond majesty, or pilgrim rags / In inaccessible, thin, Himalayan places."[5]

Avison soon mistrusted poems "that go luscious this way"[6] and tightened her style. More important, her religious experience of January 4, 1963, changed her life and challenged her identity and her aesthetic. Her sense of authority shifted ground. If her previous work seemed to encourage a religion of the imagination in which the epiphany is purely aesthetic, her subsequent poetry rejected the proud, creative self-sufficiency of the artist. Her letter to Cid Corman, in 1961, shows that she already mistrusted the isolation and moral disorientation of aestheticism: "Part of it is a trouble in my aesthetics: that it divorces one from the will to be 'against' any 'group.' Poetry over against the world – if such could exist, I'd stay on the world's side."[7] After 1963, her allegiance was clear because it extended beyond the world, and her judgement was more severe: "I see how grievously I cut off His way by honoring the artist: the sovereignty of God was the real issue for a long time, for me."[8] This reassessment affected her "language level," but not necessarily by raising it. In *The Dumbfounding* (1966) and *sunblue* (1978), although faith is assured and often joyously proclaimed, the style is less confident. The poet assumes the role previously assigned to the reader. She receives rather than gives instruction, or appeals to biblical authority. No longer a guide or teacher, she prays for guidance. *The Dumbfounding* tells of blindness, darkness, and silence. Both volumes are scattered with hesitations, reservations, questions, asides, and withdrawals, often suggested by a turn of phrase: "Maybe not any longer" (*D*, 111); "I refuse, fearing; in hope" (*D*, 179); "(Go with us, then?)" (*D*, 115); "I fumble in our fault" (*s*, 34); "No. I do not understand" (*s*, 50); "hope stirs, / not surges" (*s*, 70). As these examples show, assertions are replaced by questions. Words are protected by italics, quotation marks, and question marks to suggest they are offered rather than declared: "There is a direction? And it's / *on*?" (*s*, 36); "And yet, one 'stuck' to / who could 'desire'?" (*s*, 39). Even the titles suggest diffidence: "The Evader's Meditation," "Neighbours?" and "Backing into Being" (apparently a perverse version of Wordsworth's "Immortality Ode").

Another way in which Avison voices uncertainty within her poems is by making the simplest words seem obscure. After *Winter Sun*, she admitted in an interview,[9] she wanted to make her style easier and more immediate, and it is true that her writing becomes less luscious, less pedantic, and more conversational. But obscurities remain even when the words are familiar. In a few cases she even succeeds in making prepositions seem charged with complexity. Since these are the basic words that establish logical, spatial, and temporal relations, they are the hinges of significance, and Avison uses them to question the relations between things, between ideas, or between the speaker and the world. Through a parade of prepositions (over-inward-on-to-under-up-in-forth), "Highway in April" (*s*, 27) quickly sketches a scene and examines the links between its features. The cluttered picture has features that are natural, human, artificial, visible, illusory, and invisible ("a whole underground sea"), all with "dark inwardnesses" or essences that remain disparate until they are unified and animated by the April sun.

Sheer up, the sun
stands whole: the warmth
soaks in, till all
alive come forth.

"*On?*" (*s*, 36) finds remarkable ambiguity in its elementary title. Every time the word appears it shifts its meaning and so suggests a confused human fate involving direction, position, purpose, determination, solitude, helplessness, and need, all caught up in the onward rush of time. Lost and afraid in a "thickety wild place," the speaker yearns for transcendence or simply an end to things, depending on how we read the compensating preposition: "*On* would've been OVER I tell you." At the end, she is left with only the tenacity to hang on.

This brief survey of Avison's idiom suggests that her scuffle with words increases through her career. Her diction grows more rather than less problematic until, in the last example, she (or her speaker) falls victim to the simplest of terms and is left clinging to an untrustworthy preposition. At issue, therefore, is how she regards words: how they assert, convey, conduct, contain, create, direct, or reveal meaning. The verb chosen, and the metaphor on which it is based, will presuppose a theory of language in general, and of poetic diction in particular. It will establish her identity — her poetic presence amid words — and her aesthetic. In poetry, how do words disclose truth, express feeling, and permit understanding? I wish to consider this large and daunting topic by posing a more specific, "geometaphysical" question: where do words locate or find their meanings? As David Kent notes,[10] Avison's conversion marks a shift for her in the "pivot for significance" (*WS*, 82). Before, she looks inward for the place of meaning as well as outward at the world, coordinating the two by means of the "inrushing floodlight of imagination."[11] After, she continues to rely on the imagination, but directs it upward, subordinating it to the revelation of "the flower-light of Beyond" (*s*, 95).

All Avison's critics observe that she is very sensitive to words. She has a good ear and a sharp mind; she delights in word play, riddles, and nonsense. In her M.A. thesis on Lord Byron, she discusses skillfully topics such as aesthetic and social uses of language, "tone and overtone," "class accent," the variations in stress that convey a voice and a personality. More important, she considers the power of words to alter meaning as well as reveal it, to generate or distort facts, to deceive as well as to seek truth.[12] She illustrates the coercive power of words in her introduction to *The Research Compendium*. The style adopted by social workers creates an illusion of accuracy and impartiality that conceals, even from the authors, the subtle ways in which words mislead, bury their implications, or beg the questions they pretend to answer:

> "When there is a 'large turnover' who turned over?" I found myself rephrasing one student's title. These "data" – by whom are they given, to whom, and in what context? If a person is a "delinquent," who delinquished him, or what did he delinquish? And when an alcoholic is not "healed" or "improved" but "rehabilitated," for what is he re-hable?[13]

These playful examples suggest that researchers are often the victims rather than the masters of their writing, because the meaning they seek already lies hidden within their words. They illustrate how Avison looks inside words for their tricks and secrets.

One possible view of language, then, is that there is an "inside" to words. In addition to their referential function (referring to the world) they have an inner history. They are a storehouse of meaning, enriched by tradition and etymology. The poet probes language and discloses the treasure within it. Or words are considered seeds or kernels that can, if properly sown and cultivated, release a significance they already contain potentially. T. S. Eliot praised the style of Lancelot Andrewes by proposing yet another image: "Andrewes takes a word and derives the world from it; squeezing and squeezing the word until it yields a full juice of meaning which we should never have supposed any word to possess."[14] Meaning is intrinsic to individual words, and understanding is a matter of discovering what is already there by reaching back through literature and philology to the source. According to Owen Barfield, we can return to "the genesis of meaning" by digging down to the figurative roots of literal, logical, and abstract terms. Barfield is the most eloquent spokesman for this theory: he pictures "metaphor bending over the cradle of meaning." The literal sense is not primary, but is something man has slowly achieved by forgetting the original, figurative nature of language. Fortunately, words contain their past. They have a "soul," which is dormant, but which the poet can revive: "Like sleeping beauties, they lie there prone and rigid in the walls of Castle Logic, waiting only for the kiss of Metaphor to awaken them to fresh life." Strictly speaking, therefore, the poet is a "recreator of meaning," not the source of it. Although he can extend the metaphoric process to form new meanings by bringing words in contact with each other, the locus of significance remains the individual word: "[The poetic] can only manifest itself as *fresh meaning*; it operates essentially *within* the individual term, which it creates and recreates by the magic of new combinations."[15]

Some of Avison's poems might suggest that she too regards language according to this model, and seeks to release what is already potent in words by returning to their source and unlocking "Adam's lexicon" (*WS*, 29). She frequently marks words by italics, brackets, spacing, and spelling (pink-cheekt, seaborde, singeing-day) as if to encourage the reader to look into them further. She tests synonyms in a poem like "Immobility / Rest / . . . ," whose title suggests limitless alternatives until "stills" is chosen as the richest, most appropriate term.[16] Other poems conclude with a word or quotation that immediately evokes its past: '"He does not resist you'" (*D*, 139); '"take, eat — / live'" (*D*, 159); "John, and the wings, and healing" (*D*, 173); "*spiritus*" (*D*, 175). Sometimes merely capitalizing a word (Love, Life, Morning Star) sends us back to its religious basis. In each case, however, the cradle of meaning is the Bible, which justifies and fulfills the quotation. Words refer, not to themselves, but to another text, which, despite its holiness, is not an absolute source of meaning but an elaborate religious context. Other allusions to William Shakespeare, John Milton, John Bunyan, W. B. Yeats, W. H. Auden, George Herbert, and Archibald Lampman invoke an elaborate literary context. Therefore the individual term cannot be the locus of meaning because it is not self-sufficient. Instead of pointing to a unique inner source, it draws us into something more diffuse. Although meaning may seem concentrated in a single image or quotation, words really act as "dispersed titles," expanding in significance. For example, the word "*spiritus*" sends us back to John 4:24: "God is spirit, and those who worship him must worship in spirit and truth." With this text we then return to the poem "Canadian / Inverted," and reinterpret lines such as "Nailed earth to sky" (the inversion or crucifixion that indicates our spirituality) and "proving" (the experience or argument that leads to truthful worship). The meaning of the single word "*spiritus*" depends on a transaction between two texts.

Avison marks other individual words for special attention, but they are not quotations; they owe their expansive meaning to the context of the poem. Barfield regards the interaction and juxtaposition of words as valuable, but subservient to the spirit of individual terms.[17] Avison shows, however, that words cannot remain solitary, even when they appear to be detached. "Old . . . Young. . . ." (*D*, 101), which describes an orchard at sunset, stresses its final word by isolating it in quotation marks. It serves as the focal point for reviewing the poem by unifying and embellishing its contrasting old and new features. The urge to organize the scene is also encouraged by setting the one logical connective in italics:

> *because* cobwebs are forked away
> and the wind rises
> and from the new pastures long after longstemmed sunset,
> even this springtime, the last
>   light is mahogany-rich,
>   a "furnishing."

Similarly in " A Child: Marginalia on an Epigraph" (*D*, 125), the final word, "fullness," is nourished by earlier references to food, hunger, fulfillment, feasts, and joy. In a clever variation on this technique, "SKETCH: CNR London to Toronto (II)" (*s*, 16) ends with the italicized word "*invisibility*," and prompts us to look back in the poem for what we failed to see. In a few poems, meaning is solely contextual because Avison manages to invent words that have no internal, metaphorical, or allusive significance. These poems are playfully nonsensical, and seem to be about the deviousness of language. They present meaning flirting with nonsense. "Sliverlick"[18] celebrates a word game to the rhythm of a high-school cheer:

> *Sliverlick* .
>
>   *Norgul* .
>
>   *Prabdon* .
>
>   *Frull* .
>
> (The bleachers give the Poet's yell)
>
> *Flandople* .

Porntottie .

Gnishgiddle .

Sprill .

("they" forgot the ball.)

The game ends abruptly. These words are without an "inside," without a past, coined for the occasion and jingling together. A different sport is played in "HIALOG (any number can play),"[19] where any number of meanings can be ascribed to words that all begin with the letter h, but have been twisted beyond recognition. They defy our attempt to translate them. Perhaps that is why the poem ends apologetically: "(Horry, hallus horc / a o)." Finally, in "About a New Anthology Again . . ."[20] Avison subjects Barfield's theory to a mischievous parody by delving into the word "anthology." Within it she finds *thole*, *ant*, *anth(r)o*, *logo*, *art*, and *ho*, terms she uses to explain and mock the job of her anthologist.

Meaning may be conceived as referential (corresponding to reality), internal (in Barfield's sense: lying within words and their history), or differential (arising from a context of differing verbal relations). However, Avison's religious poetry suggests another, more remote place of meaning. If there can be a plenitude of significance, it cannot be established by burrowing back into language, by citing other texts, or even by establishing an intricate poetic context. These are inadequate because thought can exceed language, even if it depends on language. The mind can reach further than the words that conduct it. T. S. Eliot suggested this possibility in a passage that recalls his own poetic aims: "the poet is occupied with frontiers of consciousness beyond which words fail, though meanings still exist."[21] In a 1956 review of a Raymond Souster book, Avison noted the dilemma whereby knowledge relies on words that prove insufficient and untrustworthy: "To *know* what we see or feel involves stating it, at least to ourselves, and often in the process our words — inexact, overcharged with borrowed associations or emotional overtones — end by blurring the experience rather than converting it into knowledge." At this stage in her career, she sought a solution to the problem only in poetry: "Souster's simplicity, in his best poems, conveys the knowledge of what he has seen and felt, and it then registers with the authority of an absolute."[22] Later, she appeals to a higher authority. The religious Avison, like the religious Eliot, is confident where the pivot of significance really lies – at the still point of the turning world.

The problematic relation between experience, knowledge, and language appears as the paradox of the Logos. God is the "silent Glory" (*s*, 55) who remains "out there, inaccessible / to grammar's language" (*s*, 21). Yet as Logos, He is sanction and sanctification for human speech:

> Your voice
> never falters, and yet,
> unsealing day out of a
> darkness none ever knew
> in full but you,
> you spoke that word, closing on it forever:
> "Why has Thou forsaken . . . ?"
>
> (*D*, 150)

Christ speaks, but tells us of our loss and of our distance from truth. This condition suggests in religious terms a problem prevalent in modern poetry and criticism. On one hand is the utter certainty of Avison's faith, secured by the voice of God speaking to her, telling the truth, offering His Gospel: "The breeze wafted / your voice through and through / our hearts" (*D*, 160). In her own life, she found "the Jesus of resurrection power would speak to me very quietly when I was, as I thought, alone."[23] In her poetry, this still, small voice sounds as the "Word of power" (*s*, 94): "the word You utter / in me, because I know / the voice" (*s*, 58). The divine voice assures ease of understanding to the receptive listener. The truth is clear and easy. All one need do is "Let Love's word speak plain" (*D*, 142) because "He makes Love plain" (*s*, 77).

On the other hand is a principle of indeterminacy within faith and essential to it. Faith is certain, but also a challenge, because God is an unfathomable mystery surpassing human faculties of knowledge and speech. He is "something nameless / and ultimate – and touched / with sunlight / forever."[24] He is "I AM" (*D*, 151), being itself without properties, defying our propositions about Him. Avison has always felt that there is an inexhaustible reality that man can only probe in wonder, awe, or delight. In her earlier poetry it is evoked indirectly by her desire for a "jailbreak" outward into the world, and by her strategic vantage point located at what W. H. New calls "the edge of perception":[25] at thresholds, window sills, doors, whirlpools, turning-points. All express an urge to move out into a cosmos without end, "in an everywhere of sunwardness" (*WS*, 53). "The Butterfly" asks: "can't we stab that one angle into the curve of space / that sweeps so unrelenting, far above . . . ?"[26] Agnes Cleves drifts "Pure out of thought" past mist and evening star toward "The wild smell" on "the other side / Of the impenetrable world of stone" (*WS*, 97, 98). In her religious poems, Avison's urge for transcendence is redefined in Christian terms. Now her thoughts, hopes, and prayers are directed towards the "light / shining from beyond farthestness" (*s*, 91). They aspire "towards the / inconceivable elsewhere" (*s*, 70). God dwells at the frontiers of consciousness. "He from elsewhere / speaks" (*s*, 59), and although we can hear His words, we cannot reach their source because He is "unsourced" (*s*, 98). The place of meaning is always elsewhere, "powdering off in a diminishing-past-vanishing point."[27]

Therefore, to describe how Avison regards words, we need a new model of understanding that accounts for both faith and mystery, certainty and indeterminacy. In the quest for meaning, we cannot accept words at face value; we cannot descend within them, nor can we merely traffic between them in a contextual play. Instead, Avison's poetry suggests, we need a metaphor based on the metaphorical process itself, one that asserts truth only through displacement, indirection, and impertinence. It is the rhetorical equivalent of the religious experience, which she calls "the long willful detour into darkness."[28] Only an "evasive" metaphor (*s*, 99) can give voice to "wordlessness / plumed along the Dark's way" (*D*, 141). As noted earlier, Avison acknowledges in her thesis on Byron that language is coercive and deceptive; it compels meaning, but also distorts it. Poetry must work by means of that distortion. In her review of Souster's book, she notes how knowledge depends on the language that blurs it, and in an earlier review of A. M. Klein, after observing that "everybody's speech is defective," she calls on poets to "discipline speech into clarity."[29] She can do so, however, only through a metaphorical detour to truth, like Polonius, who, through indirection, hopes to find directions out; like Browning's Bishop Blougram, who "said true things, but called them by wrong names."

The wilful detour to truth is precisely the model of meaning challenged by post-structuralist critics. They argue that there is no literal or proper language in which the final truth can be stated or to which metaphorical fiction could point. They argue too that there is no secure authority that can escape the deviousness of language in order to sanction that truth. Instead, there is only the perpetual detour of indeterminacy. Jacques Derrida claims it is impossible to complete the detour, which is composed of an infinite play of Polonius' indirections and Blougram's wrong names, or, as Derrida calls them, traces and differences. Any attempt to arrive at a final truth must unwittingly presuppose it as a transcendent, divine principle or "presence": "Only infinite being can reduce the difference in presence. In that sense, the name of God, at least as it is pronounced within classical rationalism, is the name of indifference itself . . . . The logos as the sublimation of the trace is *theological.*" I suspect that Avison might, in her own way, agree with this conclusion. Derrida declares, "The age of the sign is essentially theological"; that is, our ordinary use of language presumes a presiding deity (logos), which serves as the source of meaning.[30] Avison, following the example of her parents, calls Christ "the basis of meaningfulness."[31] And Michel Foucault asks us to conceive of God as "not so much a region beyond knowledge as something prior to the sentences we speak; and if Western man is inseparable from him, it is not because of some invincible propensity to go beyond the frontiers of experience, but because his language ceaselessly foments him in the shadow of his laws."[32] For Avison, however, God is both prior to and beyond human knowledge. He is both the basis of meaningfulness and the truth towards which understanding aspires:

> I wish I had known that although thinking, comprehending, understanding, probing are good – faculties God gave to us human beings – yet these faculties are given so that we can come to some notion of his unapproachably beautiful thinking, comprehending, understanding, and probing, even of me . . . . [33]

Derrida and Foucault examine what happens to language, meaning, and the comprehending subject when their metaphysical sanction is lost. Following Nietzsche, they joyfully accept the death of God and picture language, now displaced, turning on itself, exploring its own ceaseless activity, challenging its own limits. Derrida speaks of the resulting free play, risk, danger, and monstrosity. Foucault speaks of transgression as the problematic insight language achieves when "it is no longer a question of the One

Good, but of the absence of God and the epidermic play of perversity. A dead God and sodomy are the thresholds of the new metaphysical ellipse."[34] Avison's attitude is somewhat different. She is well aware of the deviousness of language, and delights in its playfulness. She knows that communication moves through speech from one mystery to another: from "heart-warmed lungs" to the "de-/ciphering heart" (*D*, 117). She also knows how language aims at an ideal purity, which it can express only in its own image as the Word. In this sense she is willingly – in Derrida's term – "logocentric." Unlike Derrida and Foucault, however, she has faith in the divinity of the Word, and confidence that the Word was made flesh in order to make Himself accessible to man. When he renounces God, Foucault is brought back to the flesh as the site of transgression; hence his fascination with writers like Sade and Artaud. Avison still trusts in transcendence; hence her fascination with the Incarnation, the Christian mystery to which she devotes most attention. She often simply expresses awe at such intimate contact between the divine and the human ("A Story," "The Circuit," "Intercession," "Hope"). She displays her wonder that God's love was so great that He chose death in order to reveal "the Truth with the / bite of final cold, and marvelling in it / of bleeding, and waiting, and joy" (*D*, 119). The Incarnation is the touch of God. "Your touch would prove all" (*D*, 142), that is, it would test, demonstrate, approve, and confirm the truth:

> you could
> come back, in flesh, living, and
> open out the shaft and sweep
> of clarity and scope,
> flooding us with your risen radiance.
>
> (*D*, 159)

The "all-enabling Infant" provides the place of meaning that is the ultimate ground for human knowledge and identity:

> indomitably coming:
> the flint-set-faced
> ready-for-gallows One,
> on, on, into glory, and His
> place of my being to be
> His as will every

place
be.

(*S*, 93)

Every place will finally be illuminated, but until then man must not remain passive, waiting for the touch of revelation. God's grace, which is prior to the sentences we speak and which reaches down, "sounding" us, is matched by the human effort, "searching" out God. Our faculties are given to us so that we may approach his unapproachably beautiful thinking. Accordingly, several poems trace the trajectory of hope as it "stirs" (*S*, 70), rises from within (*S*, 73), and then fearfully and dangerously (*S*, 71) reaches towards a mystery it can hardly express: "In hope I say: it is a / listening into a / voice-sound, a voice making with silence" (*D*, 178). Avison often resorts to paradoxes like this to describe the detour through hope to truth. The vocabulary of mysticism is full of such paradoxes, some of which she uses: language baffles itself to express the inexpressible, unspeakable, ineffable, and dumbfounding; knowledge arises from ignorance, light from darkness, wisdom from "unnoticing" (*S*, 63). However, she is not a mystic, despite the intensity of her hope and faith. She remains concerned with ordinary perception, everyday experience, and the sensuous details of a world that is fallen but beautiful. When she announces, "In the mathematics of God / there are percentages beyond one hundred" (*D*, 145), she offers a witty calculation; as she does in the convoluted syntax of ". . . Person OR A Hymn on and to the Holy Ghost" (*D*, 147), where she prays for a revelation within reality ("I may show him visible") rather than a mystical ascent or union with God. She remains aware of her distance from the self-effacing source of meaning, and uses that distance to explain her own place. Ants Reigo argues that "Avison was a mystic before she became a missionary," but the experiences he cites as metaphysical, transcendental, and even physiological are not, strictly speaking, mystical. "The orientation of 'Snow'" – his chief example – "is not toward the possibility or promise of an encounter with ultimate reality, but rather toward the question of accommodating it to ordinary life, toward the problem of the alienation of the visionary from society."[35] Using the vocabulary of existential theology, Robert Merrett confirms that Avison remains attentive to the physical, secular world in order to establish "the sacramental nature of reality."[36]

In her religious poems, therefore, Avison's aesthetic depends on the intricate duality of the ordinary and the visionary, the human word and the divine Word, the devious indeterminacy of speech and the glorious plenitude of meaning, the boundlessness of hope and the security of faith. In practice this means she uses a pattern of evasive metaphors to express her divided condition. I have already mentioned the paradoxes of language and silence, wisdom and ignorance, and of the Incarnation by which we are "wounded, and healed" (*s*, 69). Francis Zichy discusses imagery of confinement and liberation,[37] a dialectic he sees as a tragic trap, but which the religious poetry presents as the necessary condition of transcendence. "Person" (*D*, 146) tells a parable of existence, meaning, and language; of being, knowing, and saying – all summed up in the assertion, "'I AM.'" It is the imperfect human word, unconsciously echoing the Word of God, achieving full significance only through the Incarnation. The self is entombed until liberated by Christ's love, again registered by an amazing preposition: "In all his heaviness, he passes *through*" the stone walls and is drawn up towards the Morning Star. For mankind, however, deliverance must retain the qualities of both confinement and freedom, of blindness and insight. We are "folded close, and free / to feed," while He is "shining, unseen." This dilemma, which is the place of man divorced from the fullness of meaning, is heightened in "On Goodbye" (*s*, 68). In this poem, the poet's position is not clarified by biblical echo or assurance, and the poem is about separation and parting. The self is not sealed within itself, as in "Person"; rather "this distance seals / both parties to outwardness." The distances we suffer involve time and space, youth and age, memory and forgetfulness ("the blank hourlessness"), as well as personal relations ("walls of you and me"). Combined, they suggest an absolute separation from the "failed place" of "not-being." She is not "drenched with Being," as in "Person," because she does not pass through the walls of isolation and is not inspired by religious example. Her title is the word of parting, not transcendence. However, she does recognize that only through metaphorical analogy could she give meaning and substance to the absence she senses because it excludes her:

> Distance, through this time I listen to
> you, learning not-being, looking through for
> an analogous point in vacancy,

with walls of you and me,
as boundaries, set, that that which is not may be.

Avison wants to look through the indirections of language so that which is not may be. Her subject need not be explicitly religious, in which case it is usually associated with nature. The distance or invisible place of meaning appears — or, more accurately, fails to appear — in several poems, and consequently must be evoked by its absence. She tries to imagine a point in vacancy by picturing it as wind, breath, seed, and angel. It is "the Christmas presence" (*s*, 94), "the implicit touch" (*s*, 24), and "a clarity beyond the mist" (*s*, 30). It is the self-effacing Holy Ghost, which is "unseen, unguessed, liable / to grievous hurt" (*D*, 147), the last phrase indicating it is accessible through Christ, whom the poet calls on as an intermediary. It is the robust but transparent spirit of life that "informs" several natural scenes and urges on the rebirth of spring even in the midst of winter: "under-mantle Life whanged on a tree-root" (*D*, 175). "Hid Life" (*s*, 23) asks:

Botanist, does the seed
so long up held
still somehow inform
petal and apple-spring-perfume
for sure, from so far?

A sequence of poems in *sunblue* celebrates this theme by using spring (*s*, 23–27) or Christmas (*s*, 91–96) as the moment when the imminence of rebirth is so urgent that, although it remains absent, it feels palpably present:

The extraordinary beyond the hill
breathes   and is   imperturbable.

(*s*, 24)

breathing the
crocus-fresh   breadwarm
Being —
easy as breathing.

(*s*, 25)

yes, and now in glory
quickening love and longing,

till the angel of His presence
becomes our Christmas incense.

(*s*, 92)

Sometimes the unseen subject can only be inferred through its absence or vacancy. Sometimes it can be felt vigorously, preciously, or ominously. Sometimes it is actually glimpsed, like the comet Kahoutek, whose "weird-brightness" is visible briefly when it issues cryptically "from far unlanguaged precincts" (*s*, 90). Lurking somewhere in the midst of the scene described in "SKETCH: CNR London to Toronto (II)" (*s*, 16), "they listen under banks / badger foreheads sleek." The wording makes us wonder whether "they" really are badgers; while the final word, "*invisibility*," gives strange force to their equivocal presence. Similarly in "Thirst" (*s*, 31), the deer stand "beyond the rim of here"; they have not yet drunk; their thirst is not yet quenched; the stream clears "pure, onflowing." This remarkable poem evokes a shy, evasive purity that is "not yet known" because it is a perfection always about to be accomplished, but never completely realized. As in the spring poems, the stillness signals the imminence of something about to be revealed. On the other hand, in "SKETCH: End of a day: OR, I as a blurry" (*s*, 19), a play on words reverses the perspective. It empties the crisp autumn scene of its immediacy when the poet, now playing the role of badger or "blurry groundhog," retreats downward and indoors:

Indoors promises
such creatureliness as disinhabits
a cold layered beauty
flowing out there.

In these poems Avison has two competing tasks: she must enforce the remoteness of her subject even as she displays her desire to draw close to it. The strange inaccessibility of her goal confers its value, but this value is something with which mankind can, at special moments of insight or revelation, become familiar. "To hear far off the unseen / can make a here of there" (*s*, 85), can make the absent seem present. But "there," the place of meaning, is never fully present. Like the Holy Spirit, the deer and the badgers, it is elusive.

Therefore it must be pursued indirectly through metaphor and paradox, like the mountain in "Let Be" (*s*, 28), which can be perceived only as "the unseen mountain's / no-sounding soundness."

One final image Avison uses to express the mystery of meaning is light. The sun shines (or is obscured) in all her poetry, and like Kahoutek, its brilliance comes "from somewhere else," from the depth of the cosmos, infinity, God, or the Son. Light illuminates and makes vision possible, but is not itself visible. Rather, it is the condition of seeing, as Wallace Stevens said of the imagination:

> The acute intelligence of the imagination, the illimitable resources of its memory, its power to possess the moment it perceives — if we were speaking of light itself, and thinking of the relationship between objects and light, no further demonstration would be necessary. Like light, it adds nothing, except itself.[38]

For Avison, too, "Light, the discovering light, is a beginning / where many stillnesses / yearn" (*WS*, 20). It is the beginning and possibility of human discovery. It is the light of the imagination and of God's "sunward love" (*D*, 118). It adds nothing except itself, yet paradoxically it also withholds itself. Christ's "Being-in-Light" (*s*, 55) is the dazzling, sometimes blinding source of revelation. He is, she says in an earlier version of "Christmas from Summertime Seen" ("Midsummer Christmas," *s*, 95), the darkened Epiphany:

> Don't come here Jesus.
> No.
> What you must know, here
> who *here* can know, unless by obliterating
> the flower light of beyond which is
> has been . . . must remain . . . . all
> source, all safe hope.[39]

The necessary tension between here and there, ignorance and knowledge, hope and faith appears in the three poems entitled "Light" (*s*, 59–61) as the drama of a brilliance that creates shadows, which in turn long for their pure source. The "eye of day" (*s*, 59) animates lumpish matter with a fierce, inquisitive vitality that rises from its "self-shadow" (*s*, 60) and sends "the constructed power / of speculation" reaching upward to its origin: "The light has looked on Light." God's grace inspires man's hope, and the three poems end with an affirmation of presence ("now," *s*, 60), permanence ("ineradicably," *s*, 61), and proximity:

> He from elsewhere
> speaks; he breathes impasse-
> crumpled hope even
> in us:
> that near.
>
> (*s*, 59)

NOTES

[1] "Poets in Canada," *Poetry* [Chicago], 94 (June 1959), 182.

[2] "The Road," *Contemporary Verse*, No. 26 (Fall 1948), p. 4; "Omen," *Here and Now*, No. 1 (Jan. 1949), p. 68; "The Typographer's Ornate Symbol at the End of a Chapter or Story," *Origin*, No. 4 (Jan. 1962), p. 15.

[3] "Chestnut Tree — Three Storeys Up," *Poetry 62*, ed. Eli Mandel and Jean-Guy Pilon (Toronto: Ryerson, 1961), p. 10.

[4] "Perspective," *The Book of Canadian Poetry*, ed. A. J. M. Smith (Toronto: Gage, 1943), p. 475.

[5] "Mutable Hearts," *The Canadian Forum*, Oct. 1943, p. 155; "Another Christmas," *Contemporary Verse*, No. 26 (Fall 1948), p. 5; "Song of the Flaming Sword," *Contemporary Verse*, No. 35 (Summer 1951), p. 16.

[6] Letter to Cid Corman, *Origin*, No. 4 (Jan. 1962), p. 10.

[7] Letter to Corman, p. 10.

[8] "Angela Martin," "I wish I had known that . . . I couldn't have my cake and eat it," *I Wish I Had Known* . . . (Grand Rapids, Mich.: Zondervan Publishing House, 1968), p. 92. I am indebted to David Kent for providing me with a copy of this essay.

[9] "Conversation with Margaret Avison," University of Toronto Library, videocassette 001085.

[10] David Kent, "Margaret Avison," *Canadian Poetry, Volume One*, ed. Jack David and Robert Lecker (Toronto and Downsview, Ont.: General and ECW, 1982), pp. 319–20.

[11] Letter to Corman, p. 11.

[12] "The Style of Byron's *Don Juan* in Relation to the Newspapers of His Day," M.A. Thesis Toronto 1964.

[13] *The Research Compendium: Review and Abstracts of Graduate Research 1942–1962* (Toronto: Univ. of Toronto Press, 1964), p. 5.

[14] *Selected Prose of T. S. Eliot*, ed. Frank Kermode (London: Faber and Faber, 1975), p. 184.

[15] Owen Barfield, *Poetic Diction* (London: Faber and Faber, 1928), pp. 132, 88, 115, 112, 131; "The Meaning of 'Literal,'" *The Rediscovery of Meaning, and Other Essays* (Middletown, Conn.: Wesleyan Univ. Press, 1977).

[16] *Impulse,* 1, No. 1 (1971), 16.

[17] Barfield is aware of the distinction between referential and contextual meaning, but he criticizes the latter as an aspect of analytic thinking, which he rejects for figurative or mythological thinking: ". . . I am aware that there is a sense of the word 'meaning' in which an individual word outside a sentence has no meaning. But this limiting sense of the term 'meaning' is really based on the premise that all meaningful language is discursive and therefore that the only meaningful symbols are the discursive symbols of logic" ("The Meaning of 'Literal,'" pp. 34–35).

[18] *The Cosmic Chef Glee & Perloo Memorial Society under the direction of Captain Poetry presents an evening of concrete*, ed. bpNichol (Ottawa: Oberon, 1970), p. 74.

[19] *Ganglia,* 1, No. 1 (1964), n. pag.

[20] *The Poets of Canada*, ed. John Robert Colombo (Edmonton: Hurtig, 1978), p. 154.

[21] *Selected Prose of T. S. Eliot*, p. 111.

[22] "Poetry Chronicle," *The Tamarack Review*, No. 1 (Autumn 1956), p. 80.

[23] *I Wish I Had Known*, p. 91.

[24] From "A Continuing Tribute to Karl Polanyi," *The Canadian Forum*, June 1964, p. 52.

[25] W. H. New, *Articulating West* (Toronto: new, 1972), p. 237.

[26] *The Book of Canadian Poetry* (1943), p. 429.

[27] *I Wish I Had Known*, p. 89.

[28] *I Wish I Had Known*, p. 93.

[29] *The Canadian Forum*, Nov. 1948, p. 191.

[30] Jacques Derrida, *Of Grammatology*, trans. Gayatri Chakravorty Spivak (Baltimore: Johns Hopkins Univ. Press, 1974), pp. 71, 14. Spivak discusses the "detour to truth" in her introduction, p. lxxiv.

[31] *I Wish I Had Known*, p. 90.

[32] Michel Foucault, *The Order of Things* (New York: Vintage, 1973), p. 298.

[33] *I Wish I Had Known*, p. 91.

[34] Michel Foucault, *Language, Counter-Memory, Practice*, trans. Donald F. Bouchard and Sherry Simon (Ithaca: Cornell Univ.

Press, 1977), p. 171. See also the essay "Preface to Transgression" in this volume.

[35] Ants Reigo, "Margaret Avison and the Gospel of Vision," *CV/II*, 3 (Summer 1977), 18, 16.

[36] Robert James Merrett, "'The Ominous Centre': The Theological Impulse in Margaret Avison's Poetry," *White Pelican*, 5, No. 2 (1976), 14. I do not, however, support Merrett's claim that Avison rejects all transcendental and "figural thinking," or that she "does not speak beyond the actual to the ineffable." The essay does not consider the *sunblue* poems. In his review of *sunblue*, Ernest Redekop confirms that for Avison "the poetic process is less a mystical insight than an unceasing wrestling with whatever angel she encounters." "sun/Son light/Light: Avison's elemental *Sunblue*," *Canadian Poetry*, No. 7 (Fall/Winter 1980), p. 36.

[37] Francis Zichy, "'Each in his Prison / Thinking of the Key,': Images of Confinement and Liberation in Margaret Avison," *Studies in Canadian Literature*, 3 (Summer 1978), 232–43.

[38] Wallace Stevens, *The Necessary Angel* (New York: Vintage, 1942), p. 61.

[39] *Exile*, 1, No. 2 (1972), 105.

Neverness

MARGARET AVISON

Old Adam, with his fist-full of plump earth,
His sunbright gaze on his eternal hill
Is not historical:
His tale is never done
For us who know a world no longer bathed
In the harsh splendour of economy.
We millions hold old Adam in our thoughts
A pivot for the future-past, a core
Of the one dream that never goads to action
But stains our entrails with nostalgia
And wrings the sweat of death in ancient eyes.

The one-celled plant is not historical.
Leeuwenhoek peered through his magic window
And in a puddle glimpsed the tiny grain
Of firmament that was before the Adam.

I'd like to pull that squinting Dutchman's sleeve
And ask what were his thoughts, lying at night,
And smelling the sad spring, and thinking out
Across the fullness of night air, smelling
The dark canal, and dusty oat-bag, cheese,
And wet straw-splintered wood, and rust-seamed leather

And pearly grass and silent deeps of sky
Honey-combed with its million years' of light
And prune-sweet earth
Honey-combed with the silent worms of dark.
Old Leeuwenhoek must have had ribby thoughts
To hoop the hollow pounding of his heart
Those nights of spring in 1600-odd.
It would be done if he could tell it us.

The tissue of our metaphysic cells
No magic window yet has dared reveal.
Our bleared world welters on
Far past the one-cell Instant. Points are spread
And privacy is unadmitted prison.

Why, now I know the lust of omnipresence!
You thousands merging lost,
I call to you
Down the stone corridors that wall me in.

I am inside these days, snug in a job
In one of many varnished offices
Bleak with the wash of daylight
And us, the human pencils wearing blunt.
Soon I'll be out with you,
Another in the lonely unshut world
Where sun blinks hard on yellow brick and glazed,
On ads in sticky posterpaint
   And fuzzy
         At midday intersections.
The milk is washed down corded throats at noon
Along a thousand counters, and the hands
That count the nickel from a greasy palm
Have never felt an udder.
   The windy dark
That thrums high among towers and nightspun branches
Whirs through our temples with a dry confusion.
We sprawl abandoned into disbelief
And feel the pivot-picture of old Adam
On the first hill that ever was, alone,

And see the hard earth seeded with sharp snow
And dream that history is done.

* * * *

And if that be the dream that whortles out
Into unending night
Then must the pivot Adam be denied
And the whole cycle ravelled and flung loose.
Is this the Epoch when the age-old Serpent
Must writhe and loosen, slacking out
To a new pool of Time's eternal sun?
O Adam, will your single outline blur
At this long last when slow mist wells
Fuming from all the valleys of the earth?
Or will our unfixed vision rather blind
Through agony to the last gelid stare
And none be left to witness the blank mist?

On first looking into Avison's Neverness

AL PURDY

Inside this squiggly universe
thinking: it's a gloss on eternity
but does eternity go forward or backward
or is it an ambience?
One does run into such characters
tho: lonesome Adam and no Eve
Leeuwenhoek puttering around
absentmindedly with a dog penis
searching for one-celled organisms
— the "squinting Dutchman" peering
all night into his crude microscope
yawning beside a fish-smelling canal
with green moss at the margins
rubbing his eyes and his feet
stumbling over a thought in his head
that his one-celled Alpha
precedes Adam — precedes — dare
he think it maybe — God?
And Omega a many-celled
mutation after the last Bomb?
And I — like Avison
— "know the lust of omnipresence"
and "thousands merging lost"

live on in these brain tissues?
But my non-plussed Adam
blurs and becomes anyone
becomes one-celled organism
speeding outward past the traffic
light at far Centaurus
looking for his lost leader
whom he never knew
                                        anyway
a man needs something to believe in
Her Adam brightens
— beyond the settlements of God
with Leeuwenhoek in a spare bedroom
puttering around in an attempt
to examine sin under his new
model guaranteed for life
microscope but can't
find a specimen
in sinless heaven thinking
                                                anyway
a man has just got to keep busy

with love from Al Purdy

Poetry and Honey Dew: My First Meetings with Margaret Avison

GWENDOLYN MACEWEN

IN 1960 I OPENED a copy of *Winter Sun* and read a line which gave me such a start that I felt I had just missed being hit by a car by about half an inch. *Saturday I ran to Mitilene.* That single stark naked line grabbed me in a stranglehold and has never since quite let me go. I was 19, and just beginning to give shape to my own wordy, precocious, and largely incoherent poetry. I thought: Can you do this? Can you plunk a line like that down at the very beginning of a poem and get away with it? How daring, and how glorious!

With the horrible audacity which I now know all 19 year old poets possess, I sent Margaret Avison a copy of my first privately printed and hand bound (with needle and thread) chapbook. It is a work I cannot look at now without wincing, yet she responded with warmth and generous comments. Then we met on a few occasions at the Honey Dew Restaurant which was on Bloor Street near Bedford Road, and talked about poetry and people and I don't know what else, because I was so enchanted to be in the company of this superb poet and wonderful human being that I didn't retain much of our conversation. What I now remember most is the golden orange drink that gave the restaurant its name, a drink which cannot be found anywhere else on earth, a drink whose ingredients are known only to the Honey Dew people themselves, a drink which tasted like summer in the middle of that long dark Canadian winter.

The Vancouver Poetry Festival, 1963

ROBERT CREELEY

ONE'S FIRST INFORMATION of Canadian poetry came from the association with Irving Layton, Louis Dudek, and Raymond Souster in the early fifties, particularly from the magazine *Contact* and from the anthology which Contact published during the same period. I recall being much impressed by the nervous exactness of P. K. Page's poems, for example, the interesting shifts she was able to make on familiar Audenesque patterns. But much otherwise seemed flaccid and run-of-the-mill, at least to myself, given my commitment to the authority of Pound and Williams.

Then, in 1962, I moved with my family to Vancouver to take a teaching position, truly the most lowly of the low, at UBC, and found in my company the exceptional contemporary Phyllis Webb, who many mornings saved me from absolute despair by the delights of her ironic and most accurate wit. She, of course, has long since proved the solid capabilities of her wry genius. But it was nonetheless a drear time, as colleagues like Warren Tallman can well remember. It was he, in fact, who almost single-handedly devised the Vancouver Poetry Festival of the summer of 1963, and though I served on that confused committee with him, I can't say I did much more than stand in awe at how adroitly he managed all persons and terms, to make the most significant company of poets I've ever had the pleasure of sharing.

Margaret Avison was the one Canadian. The others were Allen

Ginsberg, Denise Levertov, Charles Olson, Robert Duncan and myself – with Philip Whalen, and many, *many* active younger poets, from both Canada and the States, filling up our numbers. Margaret was by no means a token choice. I can think of a number of others, decorous and conforming, who would have served that possibility far better. We wanted altogether the opposite, that is, a Canadian who could be as particularly rooted as Olson, say, yet share also in that range of technical authority or habit which might characterize Marianne Moore or Elizabeth Bishop. Neither did we want simply a token "woman," as our company with Denise had long since made very clear. In fact, both Margaret and the rest of us well knew what such consorting with the Americans might cost her. The sad echoes of such argument have hurt a good number of the younger poets of that time, and the fact that she *was* there, and *chose* to be, has been often all they had as retrospective defense.

It was a lovely summer, as is usual in Vancouver. There seemed an absolute physical permission to it all. So good nature was solid and resourceful. Margaret Avison herself I remember as alert to the discussions, a bit preoccupied by matters at home in Toronto, shy but firmly specific. There was a loner quality to her that was endearing, a steady, clear way of looking at things. It must have been a displacing group to walk into, and I would suppose that Olson's clear interest in her must have been reassuring. He was certainly our leader, no matter we chafed or simply didn't follow. I think he liked her style very much, her independence – and the strength of her ability to keep a quiet hold on things. He was very moved by her I know.

Reading her work, listening to it, I much liked the formal particularity, the movement to an intellectually defining "thinking," call it, but never absent from feeling's impulse or direction. That was what we were all working to accomplish, and she had made her own determinations in the same respect. One might offer a range of inevitably glib parallels: Emily Dickinson, in the shifting, the quickness of intellectual movement; or, again, Marianne Moore, in the pace, though less dense, more reflective and "thinking as it goes"; or Denise, in the feeling, though less directly offered, more ambient. But as with all comparisons, the associations finally distract one from the actual writing.

At one point we were on a panel together? Something of that kind, with rostrum, so that some sat while one stood, back of it, talking. She was sitting just to my right, it must have been, so that I was aware of her doodling on a piece of paper, as I tried to avoid the audience in my own nervousness, as it was now my turn to lecture, propose whatever it was that I've now these years later utterly forgotten. That doodling attracted me, must have piqued me also. I do remember myself saying, at one point, something about the fact that one *ought* to do this or that, whatever, something crucial in the conduct of the artist no doubt, simply one *ought* to, etc. So talking, I looked to see Margaret's doodles now changing to words, which said: "Why *ought*?" All time stopped, like they say, though my lagging voice went on and on.

In any case, the existential implications of that moment have stayed in mind all the years since, and the question is as solid as ever. Truly, one doesn't need further persuasion!

Stevens, Wordsworth, Jesus: Avison and the Romantic Imagination

LAWRENCE MATHEWS

I

Nobody stuffs the world in at your eyes.
The optic heart must venture: a jail-break
And re-creation.

(*WS*, 27)

THE OPENING LINES of "Snow" are the best-known in Margaret Avison's *Winter Sun*; they leave no doubt that she is indebted to English Romantic tradition. The speaker's account of the optic heart's venturing is consistent with Coleridge's famous definition of the secondary imagination, which "dissolves, diffuses, dissipates, in order to re-create" and is "essentially *vital*, even as all objects (*as* objects) are essentially fixed and dead."[1] So in the octave of "Snow" we have the mobile "Sedges and wild rice," the quaking cinders, and the trundling "candy-bright disks," which have already borne the weight of too much commentary for me to wish to add to it. And Coleridge's notion of Fancy, which "has no other counters to play with but fixities and definites,"[2] seems to hover behind Avison's image of the "desolate / Toys," which these things become "if the soul's gates seal." The activity of the optic heart is apparently identical to that of the Romantic imagination.[3] If "Snow"'s octave were typical of *Winter Sun*, that volume would be filled with exuberant declarations of the imagination's triumphant jail-breaking and re-creating. And if it were typical of her work in general, one could do nothing but conclude that Avison is a twentieth-century evangelist for the old-time religion of Wordsworth and Coleridge. But neither *Winter Sun* nor *The Dumbfounding* nor *sunblue* is a paean to the Romantic imagination.

Like any twentieth-century poet of sophistication, the Avison of *Winter Sun* is self-consciously "modern." Of the many familiar descriptions of the relation of modern to Romantic, J. V. Cunningham's is particularly useful for my purposes. Cunningham observes that for both Wallace Stevens and for Wordsworth, "the problem of traditional religion and modern life, of imagination and reality" is central:

> The problem is the relationship of a man and his environment, and the reconciliation of these two in poetry and thus in life. The two terms of this relationship are really Wordsworth's two terms: the one, what the eye and ear half create; the other, what they perceive. The reconciliation in Wordsworth is in a religious type of experience . . . . The reconciliation in Stevens is sought in poetry . . . . For poetry is the supreme fiction of which religion is a manifestation.[4]

The ideas here are of course close to public domain, but the juxtaposition of Wordsworth and Stevens is conveniently apposite to a discussion of Avison and the Romantics. In *Winter Sun* Avison is drawn, powerfully, to Stevens' position as Cunningham describes it. Yet there is also a nostalgia for the traditional Romantic epiphany that Wordsworth celebrates and Stevens urbanely dismisses, a desire — however tempered by irony — for the "reconciliation" to occur "in experience" as well as "in poetry."

Anyone familiar with the course of Avison's poetic development will expect the post-conversion work of *The Dumbfounding* to bear witness to a true reconciliation "in experience." But the *kind* of religious experience described in that volume is neither Wordsworthian nor Romantic in any broader sense. Jesus does not enter Avison's poetry like some Santa Claus with a sackful of Romantic epiphanies. Nor is he, as one critic has argued, an exemplar of Keats's negative capability.[5] In certain of these poems, the possibility of making some traditional Romantic affirmation is raised in order to be repudiated. And the influence of Stevens disappears as well. The world of *The Dumbfounding* and *sunblue* is neither Romantic nor conventionally post-Romantic – a world in which the optic heart continues to venture, but the nature of its venturing has been transformed.

II

Given the prominence accorded to the octave of "Snow," it is perhaps surprising to find that *Winter Sun* is on the whole closer in spirit to Stevens than to any traditional Romantic poet. Even the sestet of "Snow" itself – which may be a response to Stevens' "The Snow Man" – hints at this affinity. The "sad listener" may correspond to "the listener, who listens in the snow" of the Stevens poem.[6] The speaker's assertion about the triumphant venturing of the optic heart sounds like an affirmation of the imagination's power to reconcile us to our environment "in experience," against the view espoused by Stevens, that whatever power the imagination has, the fictive nature of its achievement must be acknowledged. But Avison's "sad listener," under the delusive spell of "snow's legend," cannot enjoy the vision of a world transformed by the optic heart – except, presumably, by listening to the hearsay evidence of the octave of "Snow," reconciling himself to his environment (if at all) "in poetry" but not (and hence his sadness) "in experience."

That there should be a connection between "Snow" and "The Snow Man" may seem somewhat far-fetched. But elsewhere in *Winter Sun* there is significant evidence of the influence of the early work of Stevens. Sometimes this influence reveals itself in the form of a phrase or image that seems to have been inspired directly by Stevens. For example, the miraculous "ointment of mortality" that touches the face of the astonished clerk in "The Apex Animal" (*WS*, 11) seems analogous to the "golden ointment" sprinkled on the beard of Stevens' speaker in "Tea at the Palaz of Hoon,"[7] and the "periwinkle eyes / of seaborde men" in "Dispersed Titles" (*WS*, 15) remind us of the conjunction of "periwinkles" and "an old sailor" in consecutive lines of "Disillusionment of Ten O'Clock."[8] More frequently, certain of *Winter Sun*'s lines and passages that have no specific source in Stevens nevertheless bear the unmistakable signs of his rhetoric. Compare Avison's archness in such lines as "Such men are left possessed / Of ready access to no further incident" (*WS*, 82) with Stevens' in "The Comedian as the Letter C," or consider the ways in which a passage such as the following evokes Stevens:

> But as the weeks pass I become accustomed
> To failing more and more
> In credence of reality as others
> Must know it, in a context, with a coming
> And going marshalled among porticos,
> And peacock-parks for hours of morning leisure.
>
> ("Chronic," *WS*, 18)

The phrase "credence of reality" suggests Stevens' "Credences of Summer," but more generally the exoticism and playful alliteration of "porticos, / And peacock-parks," the philosophical tone established by words like "reality" and "context" and then undercut by the gorgeousness of the last lines, the epistemological theme – all this makes it hard to believe that Avison's reading of Stevens did not influence the composition of "Chronic." Similarly, "The Fallen, Fallen World" (*WS*, 33–34), despite its Blakean title, has a section called "The Learned" that echoes the language of "Sunday Morning," and the poem's closing lines seem a pastiche of early Stevens:

> Yet where the junco flits the sun comes still
> Remote and chilly, but as gold,
> And all the mutinous in their dungeons stir,
> And sense the tropics, and unwitting wait.
> Since Lucifer, waiting is all
> A rebel can. And slow the south returns.
>
> (*WS*, 34)

It should not be puzzling, then, to find Avison expressing Stevens' characteristic attitude to the problem of "imagination and reality." In *Winter Sun*, the "reconciliation" that Cunningham speaks of occurs with some frequency "in poetry" but rarely – and fleetingly – in the characteristically Wordsworthian manner "in experience." In order to demonstrate this point, I will examine two groups of poems: those whose settings are clearly symbolic, as far removed from "reality" as we ordinarily perceive it as Stevens' Palaz of Hoon; and those set in a world that we can recognize as ours, the world in which Wordsworth visits the valley of the Wye, climbs Mount Snowdon, walks across Westminster Bridge. This distinction is, of course, too crude to cover every case, but my intention is only to point out a significant general tendency in *Winter Sun*, namely that the unqualified triumph of the optic heart is celebrated in poems almost all of which belong to the first group, while those in the second record its failure or very limited success.

Poems of the first group include "Meeting Together of Poles and Latitudes (In Prospect)" (*WS*, 31–32), in which the apocalyptic coming together of "Those who fling off" and "those who are flung off" is described in terms that can have reality only "in poetry":

> runways shudder with little planes
> practising folk-dance steps or
> playing hornet . . .

and so on. Similarly, in "Apocalyptic?" (*WS*, 60), the speaker experiences this vision of a world transformed:

> Old scores for hautboy
> Sing from forgotten winters. The faint cry
> Where the wheel verges upwards peals
> A splendour in our hearts. An amnesty
> No prince declared yet shines. The old man reels.
> Love in absurdity rocks even just men down
> And doom is luminous today.

The language of both passages stimulates emotions appropriate to "jailbreak / And re-creation," but the absurdity of the first and the carefully controlled vagueness of the second warn us away from asking how, exactly, their content is supposed to be related to our ordinary lives. It is as if Avison wanted to write poems affirming the power of imagination to impose meaning upon experience (or to discover it there) but without committing herself to anything else — in the way of personal testimony or advocacy of any system of value or belief — that would tell us, for example, how we can recognize the "amnesty / No prince declared" or how "doom" can be "luminous." Similar questions might be raised about the "heaven" of "R.I.P." (*WS*, 74) and the "news . . . / That all, rejoicing, could go down to dark" of "Birth Day" (*WS*, 83). Elsewhere Avison herself substitutes questions and prayers for assertions. The speaker of "Intra-Political" asks "might there not be an immense answering /

of human skies?" if we were to "unbox ourselves" by "putting aside mudcakes" and "daring to gambol" (*WS*, 57). She does not answer her question, contenting herself with her report of George Herbert's affirmation. And the speaker of "Rigor Viris" (*WS*, 71) prays for the "Opening" of "peacock vistas that can no man entomb."

The poems discussed in the preceding paragraph are typical of those in *Winter Sun* in which the optic heart is celebrated; its triumphs occur in heaven, in Mitilene, "at the node, the / curious encounter" (*WS*, 32), in hypothetical futures – in short, they occur "in poetry," not "in experience." But this is not the only kind of poem in *Winter Sun*. Elsewhere, Avison's affinity with Wordsworth rather than Stevens makes itself evident, as she writes poems with very specific settings in the world of ordinary experience. But here the optic heart does not fare so well.

In "Apocalyptics" (*WS*, 61–64), for example, sketches of urban banality are juxtaposed in the first two sections of the poem with brief descriptions of creatures detached from the human scene, referred to as "The mongrel of God" and "The bird of God," although the poem never makes clear in what sense they are "of God." The point seems to be that there is no connection between them and the human beings. In the third section, the speaker laments the fact that

> Each broods in his own world
> But half believes
> Doctrines that promise to,
> After some few suppressions here and there,
> Orchestrate *for* all worlds . . .
>
> (*WS*, 64)

and concludes with a tentative prayer that an old piano "In Bowles Lunch, in the passage to / the washrooms and the alley exit" might be the medium of a truer orchestration than that promised by the half-believed doctrines:

> Don't you suppose
> Anything could start it?
> Music and all?
> Some time?
>
> (*WS*, 64)

The wistfulness of these lines contrasts with the passionate desire expressed earlier in the poem that the alienation characteristic of modern life be transcended. The speaker makes no claim to have the means to effect such a transformation; that she has had an inkling of its possibility is perhaps a minor consolation.

In "New Year's Poem" (*WS*, 39), the speaker prizes "This unchill, habitable interior" which has been "won from space," the inhospitable winter landscape outside. In "Unfinished After-Portrait or Stages of Mourning," the speaker celebrates a mysterious "human, human presence" in the midst of "the insurance company's mica-glinting sidewalks" (*WS*, 48). But in neither poem does the human presence humanize the scene. There are no astonished cinders quaking with rhizomes; the imagination holds its own against the forces that are inimical to it, and that is the most the poet can say.

In other poems, the speaker is granted a momentary vision of a humanized world, but the vision disappears almost as soon as it is perceived. The city-dwellers of "All Fools' Eve" (*WS*, 12) are able to imagine pastoral settings they associate with home and childhood, but soon the reality principle asserts itself as "Doors slam. Lights snap, restore / The night's right prose." Although lovers are apparently able to retain some of the "magic," the poem's rhetorical emphasis is on disillusionment. In "The World Still Needs" (*WS*, 37), there is a moment "When the piano in the concert-hall / Finds texture absolute" and brings the audience together in "a single solitude." But the potential for real community revealed by this moment is never realized; instead, it is parodied: "From this communal cramp of understanding / Springs up suburbia . . . ." In "Watershed" (*WS*, 58), the speaker begins by referring to "The general, and rewarding, illusion" that prevents the world from crumbling apart. In the poem's central stanza, the illusion is punctured when the speaker experiences a vision of a "buck" that emerges from a "painted grove, hung stiffly with cold wax / And fading pigments," a metaphor for the power of art. But by the end of the poem, the general illusion has again taken control, as "the sour / Rain pastes the leather-black streets with large pale leaves," and urban desolation again prevails. If all three of these poems can be said in some sense to describe "jail-breaks," it seems an important part of their meanings that, in each case, the fugitive is recaptured almost immediately.

It is true that in a small minority of poems in this group — "Prelude" (*WS*, 19–21), "Easter" (*WS*, 53), "Far Off from University"

(*WS*, 86) – the optic heart is more successful. In "Prelude," the speaker watches "A woman with her hair / fixed like a corpse's"; speaker and woman are both transformed by a "cryptic change," a movement out of the crypt of death-in-life into "the moment of held breath" in which "the light takes shape."[9] But these are exceptions. In general, there is a striking contrast between the exuberance of Avison's claims for the imagination in the poems written in the manner of Stevens and the timidity of her claims in the more "Wordsworthian" poems.[10] There is, for example, a poignancy about a poem like "To Professor X, Year Y" (*WS*, 45), whose speaker describes in meticulous detail an inexplicable gathering of a "few thousand" people in a civic square during a November rush hour. The speaker tells the historian in the future that "cause-and-effect" is not adequate to analyze people's behaviour, that "all suburbia / Suffers, uneasily," that the event is "a portent." The underlying theme is the human need for transcendence of the mundane; the few thousand are refusing to behave like automatons, making a gesture that is hilariously useless. Like Vladimir and Estragon, they have kept their appointment. But nothing actually happens. Neither the speaker nor the people whom she describes perceive anything resembling the sort of vision promised in the octave of "Snow."

III

A post-conversion rewriting of "Snow" might begin with "Nobody stuffs Jesus in at your eyes," for the world, in *The Dumbfounding* and *sunblue*, is pre-eminently the world redeemed and made new by the action of Jesus Christ. The imagination is still central to Avison's poetic, but her understanding of its significance has changed. The goal is no longer to make traditional Romantic affirmations; the longing and timidity characteristic of the "Wordsworthian" poems in *Winter Sun* have disappeared. So, too, has the influence of Stevens. Jesus is the figure who *can* start the piano in "Apocalyptics," and he is present not merely "in poetry" but in Avison's experience.

The dismissal of Stevens can be seen most clearly in a poem like "In Truth" (*D*, 143–44). The Palaz of Hoon has its Christian counterparts, but Avison's rejection of them could hardly be more emphatic:

("Gemmed Palace? Marble Island?
Cathedral under the Sea?
These are the dark blood's dream.
My being would listen
to Him.")

Imagery of exotic otherness is no longer valid. To "listen / to Him" is to acknowledge that quotidian reality has been transformed, that reconciliation in experience has replaced reconciliation in poetry.

The poem that most clearly illustrates Avison's new understanding of the traditional problem of "reality and imagination" is "Person" (*D*, 146), which begins:

Sheepfold and hill lie
under open sky.

The door that is "I AM"
seemed to seal my tomb
my ceilinged cell
(not enclosed earth, or hill)

The "ceilinged cell" of the self is the prison, not an indifferent external world of "earth, or hill." The "door that is 'I AM'" suggests the speaker's perception of the unapproachable God of Exodus 3:14, a God remote from her experience, a God whose absence seals the self's tomb, as the soul's gates are said to seal in "Snow" when the optic heart fails to venture. The rest of the poem describes two attempts at "jail-break / And re-creation," the first one unsuccessful:

there was no knob, or hinge.
A skied stonehenge
unroofed the prison?
and lo its walls uprising,
very stone drawing breath?

They closed again. Beneath
steel tiers, all walled, I lay
barred, every way.

The phrase "skied stonehenge" suggests the imposing of some human form upon nature, or at least human interaction with nature to perceive the form that is there, and the phrase "very stone drawing breath" suggests the dynamic universe depicted in the octave of "Snow," a world transformed by the power of the individual imagination. The reader of *Winter Sun* should not find it surprising that "They closed again." But the next attempt is successful:

> "I am." The door
> was flesh; was there.
>
> No hinges swing, no latch
> lifts. Nothing moves. But such
> is love, the captive may
> in blindness find the way:
>
> In all his heaviness, he passes *through*.

In the encounter with Jesus, the "captive," not the world, changes. The walls do not levitate or come alive; they are simply no longer a barrier. It is not a matter of clear vision; the captive is "in blindness." But she has been granted this key perception: "The door / was flesh; was there." Jesus is a person and is real. This is the knowledge that brings the power to escape from the self's prison. After the jail-break, the re-creation:

> So drenched with Being and created new
> the flock is folded close, and free
> to feed — His cropping clay, His earth —
> and to the woolly, willing bunt-head, forth
> shining, unseen, draws near
> the Morning Star.

The divine imagination, not the human, is responsible for the new creation; the "Morning Star" draws near to the "bunt-head," who is "willing" but has no other qualification. But the willingness has been enough. Avison's notion of the proper function of the imagination has changed radically from what it was in *Winter Sun*.

We can see this most clearly, I believe, in "Searching and

Sounding" (*D*, 154–56), a poem in which Avison acknowledges her Romantic ancestry while at the same time in a sense declaring its irrelevance. Specifically, the poem in many ways echoes and responds to Wordsworth's "Tintern Abbey,"[11] at whose centre is the poet's struggle to convince himself that "Nature never did betray / The heart that loved her," that what he has lost in terms of intensity of sensory response to the "beauteous forms" of the valley of the Wye has been compensated for by his knowledge of "The still, and music of humanity" and of " motion and a spirit" that "rolls through all things." In "Searching and Sounding," Avison writes of a Jesus who, in a sense, *does* betray the heart that loves him, since he does not lead us "From joy to joy" as Wordsworth asserts that Nature does, but leads instead to places of desolation, into deeper knowledge of sorrow rather than multiplication of happiness, leads unpredictably "To what strange fruits in / the ocean's orchards?" But Avison receives her own "Abundant recompense" for this vulnerability, namely that no experience or perception need be shunned or feared, since Jesus is equally present in all situations. There is no question of fearing or mourning Jesus' absence in the same way that Wordsworth pretends not to mourn for the time when "nature . . . / To me was all in all" or pretends not to fear that Dorothy will one day lose her own faith in Nature.

Avison's poem, like Wordsworth's, is set in July, but where Wordsworth describes the setting and connects landscape and sky, Avison writes of a sky that is already also a landscape, the connection having been made by some agency apparently external to the speaker:

> In July this early sky is
> a slope-field, a tangled
> shining — blue-green, moist, in
> heaped up pea-vines, in milk-hidden
> tendrils, in light so strong
> it seems a shadow of
> further light . . .

In general, things that are in essence separate or brought into tenuous relation by the speaker in Wordsworth's poem are united or identified in Avison's. Thus Jesus is "here":

in the sour air
of a morning-after rooming-house hall-bedroom;
not in Gethsemane's grass, perfumed with prayer,
but here . . .

while the "beauteous forms" of the Wye are present in Wordsworth's "lonely rooms" only because his memory has imported them there. But Jesus is immediately present to Avison's speaker, is himself (not merely some memory of him) alive in the speaker's consciousness. Jesus' failure to minister to the man of "scalding self-loathing heart" is partly the speaker's, but she is apparently unable or unwilling to confront the situation:

I run from you to
the blinding blue of the
loveliness of this wasting
morning . . .

Superficially, the speaker's flight resembles that of the young Wordsworth whose first visit to the Wye found him

more like a man
Flying from something that he dreads than one
Who sought the thing he loved.

But Avison's speaker is both "flying" and seeking. Jesus, she thinks, is to be looked for in the light; it is a shock to find him in the sour air of the rooming-house. But the blue is ironically "blinding," and the speaker knows

it is only with you
I can find the fields of brilliance
to burn out the sockets of the eyes that want no
weeping . . .

The unexpected violence of this image recalls the well-known lines from Book I of *The Excursion*: "And they whose hearts are dry as summer dust / Burn to the socket."[12] Eyes that wish to remain dry, that want no weeping for the distress of another, seek to burn out in contemplation of "the fields of brilliance," the distraction of the pure light obliterating consciousness of human suffering. But Jesus is Lord of both the brilliance and the rooming-house. Wordsworth can escape from the city to "nature," but there is no escape from Jesus in the world of "Searching and Sounding."

And Jesus has his own version of the still, sad music of humanity:

> But you have come and sounded
> a music around me, newly,
>
> as though you can clear
> all tears from our eyes only
> if we sound the wells of weeping with
> another's heart, and hear
> another's music only.

For Wordsworth, "humanity" is, in "Tintern Abbey," an abstraction. The person he loves is Dorothy, his sister and "dearest Friend," all the dearer for her being a version of his earlier self. For Avison, instead of "humanity," there are individuals: the man in the rooming-house, or "a babbling boy / aged twenty, mentally distracted" (ironically resembling the young Wordsworth of "aching joys" and "dizzy raptures"). The speaker's own tears are cleared as she participates in their suffering.

But the poem does not end there, with catharsis and convenient moral. In the last third of "Searching and Sounding," corresponding to the section of "Tintern Abbey" in which Wordsworth preaches to Dorothy about Nature's faithfulness and loving care, Avison describes a journey away from safety:

> From the pearl and grey of daybreak
> you have brought me to
> sandstone, baldness, the place
> of jackals, the sparrow's skull . . .

as the speaker re-enacts the kenosis of Jesus on a desolate beach "where your Descent began." Wordsworth's poem ends with his wish that Dorothy remember the "warmer love" for Nature he now espouses, and an assertion that the "steep woods and lofty cliffs" are now more dear to him than they have ever been. Avison, on the other hand, has a vision of a "ravening shore," with "gull-blanched cliffs"; viewing this landscape causes her to "shiver."

The Jesus who "put off" his "fullness" in this landscape wants us to be like him, to follow him, to know ourselves as fragments, as emptiness – and not to despair. Compare Wordsworth's anxiety that Nature protect Dorothy from "solitude, or fear, or pain, or grief" by allowing her to remember him with Avison's knowledge that the ocean itself is paradoxically an orchard, that any suffering we experience has already been given value by Jesus' suffering, that the desolation she experiences towards the end of "Searching and Sounding" is also the occasion for the revelation of his "Light that is perfect," and that we may pray for "the / all-swallowing moment" of direct knowledge of his presence.

In this respect, then, Avison's notion of the imagination differs from the traditional Romantic one: all experience is equally useful in revealing the action of Jesus, and therefore the poet has no need to exalt certain kinds of experience, nor to hope that certain kinds of experience will keep happening (while fearing that they will not). "Searching and Sounding" dramatizes the speaker's atavistic Romantic impulse to flee from a Jesus who is no respecter of "beauteous forms"; but the point is that the speaker learns that she is wrong.

The poet is now free to confront evil without anxiety. There can be no question of Romantic dejection, no need to lament the failure of one's "genial spirits" as Coleridge does in "Dejection: An Ode."[13] Whatever desolation the poet may be led into, Jesus has already been there and has prevailed. Again and again Avison is inspired to proclaim the paradoxical triumph of the Crucifixion:

> unsealing day out of a
> darkness none ever knew
> in full but you,
> you spoke that word, closing on it forever:
> "Why hast Thou forsaken . . . ?"
>
> ("The Word," *D*, 150)

> . . . the outcast's outcast, you
> sound dark's uttermost, strangely light-brimming . . .
>
> ("The Dumbfounding," *D*, 153)

> . . . you could wholly
> swallow our death, take on our
> lumpish wingless being, darkened out
> to cold and night . . .
>
> ("For Dr. and Mrs. Dresser," *D*, 158)

Avison can include in *The Dumbfounding* her translation of Gyula Illyes' "Of Tyranny, in One Breath" (*D*, 162–67), in which tyranny is ubiquitous and omnipotent, a parody of the Holy Spirit. It is unlikely that Avison would herself write such a relentlessly pessimistic poem, but there is no need for her reader to flinch at its presence; light seeps through from the adjoining pages. No one who has himself seen this light need ever fear "dark's uttermost."

IV

Avison's post-conversion poetry is thus also "post-Romantic" in a very specific way. Jesus is the perfect Romantic artist whose poem is the world – coherent, intense, beautiful – redeemed from meaninglessness by his heroic suffering and creativity. (From Avison's Christian perspective, of course, it makes more sense to put the issue the other way around: the Romantics were striving, in a pathetically inadequate way, to be like Jesus, god-hero-artist in one identity.) Either way, the position of the poet who would celebrate Jesus is not analogous to the Romantic poet's, but rather to that of the scholarly commentator whose task is to point to what is significant in the artist's life-work.

That is to say, the Christian poet is creative insofar as he uses his imagination to read the poem Jesus has written. As the true jailbreak is to let Jesus in, so the true "re-creation" is to see with your own eyes what he has made. To attempt to live the life or create the art of Romantic subjectivity is to miss what is really significant. "Riding and Waves" (*D*, 111) is a parable on this theme:

Maybe not any longer
should the meek lover
at slack rein amble through the afternoon
snow-whinged, or sunflower-randy
with a black heart of seeds to take
mumbling home at the
cellardoor of day
past fading rooster-crates, past
CEMENT suddenly.

(why not cement?)

Specific associations with Romantic poems – Wordsworth's "Strange Fits of Passion Have I Known" with its riding lover, "Blake's "Ah Sun-Flower" with its theme of unfulfilled desire – may or may not be immediately relevant. But the last lines certainly remind us of the "sweet cement" that George Herbert writes about in "The Church-floore," the cement that "is *Love* / And *Charity.*"[14] The self-absorbed "meek lover" is apparently in the habit of ambling "past / CEMENT." If he were to stop – is "CEMENT" a sign on a building? – he would ("Maybe") apprehend a manifestation of the divine power binding the world together. Perhaps this would transform his lonely and alienated (and quixotic?) existence. (Why not anything else?) See-what-is-meant. Then inherit the earth.

But the "objectivity" implied here should not be overstressed, either. George Bowering has attempted to identify Avison's poetic stance with a form of Romantic objectivity, Keats's doctrine of negative capability. This approach may lead to some useful insights into some of the poems in *Winter Sun*, those in which the optic heart sallies forth with something of the polymorphous perversity of Keats's "camelion poet." But negative capability does not provide a viable framework for understanding Avison's post-conversion poetic practice. Bowering misleads when, writing of Avison's interpretation of the Crucifixion, he says, "Christ gave himself up to Keats' negative capability, and thus lost all perspective, being no further from any one person than another, through all time and space"; and then adds, "There is the Christ that the artist should try to imitate."[15]

For Keats, Shakespeare is the exemplar of "*Negative Capability*, that is when man is capable of being in uncertainties, Mysteries, doubts, without any irritable reaching after fact & reason." For such a poet, Keats writes, "the sense of Beauty overcomes every other consideration, or rather obliterates all consideration."[16] However accurate this may be with respect to Shakespeare, it has little to do with Margaret Avison's interpretation of Jesus.

The problem with Bowering's theory is that he cannot take Avison's Christology seriously, except as a premise for her poetry. Thus he sees the Crucifixion as an act of perception appropriate to an artist, the act that "opened [Christ's] divine heart to a sharing of all men's condition."[17] If this were indeed the meaning of the Crucifixion, Bowering would be right to invoke the doctrine of negative capability. But for the orthodox Christian, the Crucifixion is the act by which Jesus – who has shared "men's condition" fully from the moment of Incarnation – acts in order to *change* that condition. To pursue the analogy with Shakespeare: Jesus could no doubt delight in identifying himself with a person who has given himself entirely to evil because Jesus both loves everyone unconditionally and also possesses the redemptive power to convert anyone *from* evil. But for Shakespeare, neither love nor conversion would be an issue; we can well imagine his experiencing aesthetic joy in the process of writing a play about an evil person who does not change, the sense of beauty obliterating all consideration. Jesus' artistic task would be to change such a person. In this sense, he must retain a "perspective" that Keats's Shakespeare can afford to abandon.

Similarly, the Christian poet cannot imitate Bowering's version of Jesus-the-artist. If Avison were to "lose perspective," poems like Illyes' "Of Tyranny, in One Breath" would be as common in her work as those like "Riding and Waves": both, after all, describe a power that holds the world together. But to point to this "similarity" is to draw attention to its self-evident irrelevance. Avison does not have the indifference towards the spiritual or moral value of her material that the poet of negative capability must have.

A poem from *sunblue*, "On Goodbye," (*s*, 68) provides a particularly clear example of the way in which Avison's later work contradicts the principles of negative capability:

> The radiant distance, not transparent, remarks
> calm trees in evening water,
> on remote childhood fields, window-seats, quilts,
> on the blank hourlessness the old
> stare at and so bless;
> this distance seals
> both parties to outwardness; it is
> itself the poignancy it would leave
> to that failed place
> where no one is.

If the poem ended here, it would indeed be consistent with Keats's doctrine. Reminiscent of Robert Frost's "Desert Places," with its "stars where no human race is,"[18] these lines capture a certain psychological state with economy and precision, and are therefore "beautiful." That this state is characterized mainly by sadness is, to anyone espousing an aesthetics of negative capability, an irrelevance. But the poem does not end there. Avison adds five lines whose function is to present a "perspective":

Distance, through this time I listen to
you, learning not-being, looking through for
an analogous point in vacancy,
with walls of you and me,
as boundaries, set, that that which is not may be.

Avison must keep reading the world for a sign of CEMENT. The Christ the artist must imitate is the one who transmutes "not-being" into being. What he did (and, for Avison, does) in action, she does in words — and in words intended not to celebrate her own creativity but to reflect his glory.

NOTES

[1] Chapter 13, *Biographia Literaria* in *The Collected Works of Samuel Taylor Coleridge*, ed. James Engell and W. Jackson Bate (Princeton, N.J.: Princeton Univ. Press, 1983), VII, 304.

[2] Coleridge, p. 305.

[3] For a detailed discussion of Avison's notion of the imagination in "Snow," see Robert Lecker, "Exegetical Blizzard," *Studies in Canadian Literature*, 4 (Winter 1979), 180–84. For an excellent discussion of this topic in Avison's work generally, see J. M. Kertzer, "Margaret Avison: Power, Knowledge and the Language of Poetry," *Canadian Poetry*, No. 4 (Spring/Summer 1979), pp. 29–44, especially pp. 34–37.

[4] J. V. Cunningham, *Tradition and Poetic Structure* (Denver: Alan Swallow, 1960), pp. 115–16.

[5] George Bowering, "Avison's Imitation of Christ the Artist," *Canadian Literature*, No. 54 (Autumn 1972), pp. 56–69; rpt. in George Bowering, *A Way With Words* (Ottawa: Oberon, 1982), pp. 5–23.

[6] Wallace Stevens, *The Palm at the End of the Mind: Selected Poems and a Play*, ed. Holly Stevens (New York: Vintage, 1972), p. 54.

[7] Stevens, p. 54.

[8] Stevens, p. 11.

[9] Ernest Redekop has commented at some length on this poem, concluding that it shows that the optic heart "can see unity in diversity and changeless life under the mutability of existence." See *Margaret Avison* (Toronto: Copp Clark, 1970), p. 36. Redekop's pioneering study is immensely valuable for anyone seriously interested in Avison's work, and

his first chapter, "The Optic Heart," draws attention to a centrally important feature of Avison's method. But while this chapter discusses poems from both *Winter Sun* and *The Dumbfounding*, the most compelling evidence in support of his thesis ("Margaret Avison insists on the power and privacy of the poetic imagination," p. 4) is drawn from the latter volume. When applied specifically to *Winter Sun*, the statement needs some modification.

[10] Redekop notes a number of possible echoes of Wordsworth and other Romantics in some poems of both groups: Wordsworth's "Immortality Ode" in Avison's "Rigor Viris" (Redekop, p. 45) and "All Fools' Eve" (Redekop, pp. 76–77); Coleridge's "Kubla Khan" in "Meeting Together . . ." (Redekop, pp. 24, 41); and Blake's "London" in "Prelude" (Redekop, p. 34).

[11] "Lines Composed a Few Miles Above Tintern Abbey" in *William Wordsworth: The Poems*, ed. John O. Hayden (New Haven: Yale Univ. Press, 1981), I, 357–62.

[12] *William Wordsworth: The Poems*, II, 54, ll. 501–02.

[13] *Coleridge: Poetical Works*, ed. Ernest Hartley Coleridge (1912; rpt. London: Oxford Univ. Press, 1967), pp. 362–68.

[14] *The Works of George Herbert*, ed. F. E. Hutchinson (London: Oxford Univ. Press, 1941), p. 67.

[15] *A Way With Words*, p. 10.

[16] Letter to George and Tom Keats, 21, 27 (?) Dec. 1817, in *The Letters of John Keats 1814–1821*, ed. Hyder Edward Rollins (Cambridge, Mass.: Harvard Univ. Press, 1972), I, 193–94.

[17] *A Way With Words*, pp. 9–10.

[18] *The Poetry of Robert Frost*, ed. Edward Connery Lathem (London: Jonathan Cape, 1971), p. 296.

Dancing in the Dark

GAIL FOX

Poetry is a way of finding out
the truth. There are other ways.
Some people eat. And some starve.
And then there is the bedangled-
with-miracles Christ.

According to Simone Weil, "Christ
likes us to prefer truth to him,
because before being Christ he
was Truth."

"I believe because it is absurd,"
said the 8th century heretic. My
position too. For who would attempt
to fly with the tiny wings of a sparrow?
Music is meaningless if you are deaf.

And only God knows the true function
of the Cross.

And so I turn to poetry. Dancing
in the dark. Hoping for an alchemical
thunderbolt to dispel all my doubt.

So that I, like Christ, can love
heroically.

It is not belief I talk about. For
even devils believe, and tremble. It
is truth. The thing I go after when
I write.

For when I write, I worship Christ.
And risk heresy and an imagination which
is not happy without a question mark.

Is this poem true or not? Dare I
trust a poem to find the truth? My life
is all I have. Attached by fervent
prayer to Christ's.

Well? What news? You have me upside
down and inside out. You have this poem.

A kind of poetic Absolute.

✷

I have known Margaret Avison about 3 years and our friendship has centered around phone calls which I make to her office. We have talked about many things aside from poetry, but it is the poetry I want to focus on.

✷

Avison absolutely hates therapeutic writing and has greatly curbed my tendency to write confessional poetry and poetry that is a cry from the heart. Characteristic of her response to such is an exchange I had with her recently which wasn't about poetry: "Well, I've given up smoking." "Yes, and the rain on the street is *violet*."

✷

Avison's influence on me has been considerable although I must admit that I have only read *The Dumbfounding* and *Winter Sun* twice and skimmed *sunblue* in a bookstore. (I have just spoken to her to let her know that my remarks would not be personal, and she answered: "I'm 5′6″, goodbye.") Our styles are totally different although our Christian concerns often converge.

✷

I share most of my work with Avison — I read it to her over the phone and her response is as quick as a reflex. Often I find myself in awe of her comments. She *hears* so accurately. After I wrote "Dancing in the Dark," I waited for several hours before I dared call her. Her response was positive and she asked me for a copy. Avison's approval of my work means a great deal to me and I always take her comments seriously. She allows me no self-pity for which I'm grateful. Her most frequent comment to me is: "Forget the I's."

February, 1984

Light, Stillness, and the Shaping Word: Conversion and the Poetic of Margaret Avison

DAVID LYLE JEFFREY

> Otter-smooth boulder
> lies under rolling
> black river-water
> stilled among frozen
> hills and the still unbreathed
> blizzards aloft;
> silently, icily, is probed
> stone's secret.
>
> (*S*, 21)

CRITICISM of a finely balanced poetry, especially, perhaps, *explication de texte*, tends too easily to make of the critic a voluptuary. Remembering her caution, "That Eureka of Archimedes out of his bath / Is the kind of story that kills what it conveys" ("Voluptuaries and Others," *WS*, 73), the critic of Margaret Avison ought probably to be drawn, in apprehension, through a slow measuring of words to quietness. Indeed, if it could remain articulate, this would be of all responses the most just, since it would faithfully mirror the transformation of her own perception, through language, towards the quiet understanding that is her strength. Yet she merits also our attempt at responsible acknowledgement, however exacting a self-critical prospect that may entail.

Margaret Avison is distinctive among our poets for many

reasons. Not the least among these is her spiritual wisdom. Despite the centrality of her religious vision, she seems less a mystic than a sage, and her poetry less lyric than gnomic. Her work as a whole rests securely as testimony to a philosophical and spiritual progress: it is a *chef d'oeuvre* on our slim national shelf of true "wisdom literature." One thing about the tone of her work seems safe to declare; that over its opened pages there descends almost immediately in the reading a perceptible and peculiar stillness, a composition of tranquility and tension in which one's head tilts forward and the ear strains to listen. And as we are drawn into her own sense of presence,

> Moving into sky
> or stilled under it
> we are in the becoming
> moved: let wisdom learn
> unnoticing in this.
>
> ("The Effortless Point," *s*, 63)

To try to talk about conversion in Avison's poetry, and to do so without reduction or offense, seems in this context hardly less difficult than probing the stone's secret before its time; who knows what is in a heartbeat? Yet conversion of purpose, transformation of perspective, and the metamorphosis of object and light to inner light is near to the heart of all Avison's poetry, and in what she tells us of her life, there and elsewhere, the objective correlative for that movement in her poetry is the subjective experience of a spiritual awakening and reconstitution thereby of an intrinsically religious imagination.[1] It seems inescapable, then, that with due respect to the inevitable shortcoming of whatever distance and self-consciousness we have as readers, we nonetheless should take her at her word and try to consider what it means for her that

> The evasive "maker"-metaphor,
> thank God, under the power
> of our real common lot
> leads stumbling back to what it promised to evade.
>
> ("Creative Hour," *s*, 99)

To consider responsibly we must begin, I think, by asking about her earliest expressions of her poetic vision, the poetic it implies,

and the nature of the experience with which it seems to correlate. Only when we can have some minimal satisfaction concerning these things will we be able to ask the first pertinent question of her post-conversion poetry: what is it that has been transformed?

The reading of *Winter Sun*, even when focused on that book's non-religious aspects, leads most readers to the conclusion that Avison's poetry from the very beginning is implicitly religious in character.[2] The issue of change in her poetry following her experience of conversion is thus not one we may expect to be defined in terms of a sudden shift in basic human concerns or ostensible subject matter. The track between "Identity" (*WS*, 70) and "The Two Selves" (*D*, 102), for example, or "A Conversation" (*WS*, 79–80) and "The Earth That Falls Away" (*D*, 131–39) is a nearly unremarkable continuum. As David Kent has aptly observed, "the pre-conversion poetry is deeply moral, and it is committed to 'recreation' of the self and to responsibilities that were engrained in Avison during her Christian childhood."[3] Whether focused on the self or upon society, her reflections on nature and human nature probe through the flesh to a desired transcendence, through object to meaning. Overwhelmingly involved in the acquisition of perspective, she is driven to reflect again and again on the imagination of ultimate perspective, of "One, in a patch of altitude / . . . Who sees, the ultimate Recipient / of what happens, the One Who is aware" ("The Apex Animal," *WS*, 11), and though some of her reflection concerns the achievement of perspective as a kind of mastery ("Dispersed Titles," *WS*, 13–17), there is also a persistent theme of seeking and yearning after transformation of habit-locked subjectivity ("Prelude," *WS*, 19–21). It is here, in "Prelude," that we can see a little of what, in *Winter Sun*, she hopes for, and for the most part what sort of transformation she imagines may be possible; the aspiration — and its attendant uncertainty — is cryptic in her rubric:

> *The passive comes to flower, perhaps*
> *a first annunciation for the spirit*
> *launched on its seasons.*

This poem is representative of her early work in its keen dissociation of darkness and light, and transvaluation of the latter. "The turning-point is morning," the light diurnal light, and it creates such meaning as the world affords in history and in memory; its shadowed delineation is shaping the meaning in each recollected image and, by extension, "rooting the word." Yet this demarcation is evidently both an opening and a closing:

> The honeycoming sun
> opened and sealed us in
> chambers and courts and crooked butteries,
> cities of sense.

Already in this poem we see Avison's profound sense of an incompleteness of understanding in what light shows: objects, like the poetic language in which they are reflected, both clarify and obscure:

> . . . Sparrows in the curbs
> and ditch-litter at the
> service-station crossroads
> alike instruct, distract.

As if by the same token, repositories of collected human wisdom offer uncertain reclamations of light's values, "palaces of sense . . . / patchy after years of hopeless upkeep." It is as though light, when so "locked in" by the pursuit of enlightenment, can hardly touch the ordinary world. Avison expresses in this poem her valuation for a simple experience of light that transforms the ordinary. In the probing eyes of the poet, even unreflecting consciousness and the objects of institutional art ("The stone lip of a flower") "suffer the cryptic change" when the rising sun sweeps away shadow and

> The turning-point of morning, and the
> unmerging child,
> like the sadness of the summer trees,
> assert their changelessness
> out of this day-change.

What is revealed in the transformation wrought by light is, if not as radical a renewal as the "sea-change" sung by Shakespeare's Ariel, at the very least a prospect:

> Light, the discovering light, is a beginning
> where many stillnesses

yearn, those we had long thought long dead
or our mere selves.

Not in the Shakespearean, but certainly in the Wordsworthian sense, "Prelude" is a 'romantic' reflection – and an affirmation of transvaluing perception. It recognizes the troubling limits of subjective vision, but holds out for a somehow-transcendent valorization of the personal, where "In each at least light finds / one of its forms / and is." This is the theme that rises to its high point of confidence in "Snow," (*WS*, 27) with its call for the venturing optic heart. But in "Snow" also is added the attendant doubt, reflected in Avison's paradoxical challenge to the reader, in which we are warned that within the burgeoning of life that light reveals are also shadows of death: "The rest" (what follows, and our inevitable repose) may signal another less splendid transformation.

All of Margaret Avison's poetry is marked by a persistence in self-questioning, by a desire for honesty that goes beyond the merely intellectual, but which is profoundly intellectual in character. This alone would set her apart from many of her contemporaries. From the point of view of her poetic, in which "Prelude" is the central early document, this means that she is continuously subjecting to scrutiny not only history and the world but also the virtues of language, metaphor, the conventional forms of poetry, even her very vocation as a poet. "Butterfly Bones" (*WS*, 29) is in this sense more than a principled questioning of the high traditional artifice of the sonnet, but a disturbing query concerning the value to perception of trophied language – even, perhaps, of any language. Avison is not primarily concerned here with the atrophy of poetic idiom, I take it, but rather with the failure of language as an instrument, and so expresses her consistent worry that poetry, like criticism, might become "the kind of story that kills what it conveys." This line ought to be read in the context of Avison's growing concern, from the early poetry on, to see poetry as means and not as an end. Just as light for her is the means whereby the world is known, so poetry, as an experience of light, is to be valued in proportion as it illumines. The final question of this sonnet:

Might sheened and rigid trophies strike men blind
Like Adam's lexicon locked in the mind?

is thus a question of profound concern not only for her poetic but for poetic language as well.

Avison's central image in this poem is, of course, far from insignificant. The butterfly, symbol of the psyche since the ancients, is also a central symbol for psyche's transformation, or as Ovid suggested, for the concept of metamorphosis itself. For Avison, as for Ovid, poetry is about metamorphosis. The concern is with transformation – not only of the poet's perspective, but of all life. Avison cannot detach her romantic aspiration for transformed personal vision from her conviction – equally romantic even as it is morally "Christian" – that this transformation of vision ought to be able to change something in the world. In this sense too she appears almost Wordsworthian. If poetry is a means, and light exists to enlighten, to light up "the terrain" (*WS*, 73), then what is effected by light – and by poetry – is to be asked about carefully. Avison asks, and sometimes comes to disturbing and unflattering answers. In "Grammarian on a Lakefront Park Bench" (*WS*, 35) she expresses her frustration in passionate language reminiscent of Donne:

> Skewer my heart and I am less transfixed
> than with this gill that sloughs and slumps
> in a spent sea. Flyspecked and dim
> my lighthouse signals when no ships could grind.

How can she signal meaningfully to a world not in tempest but in stagnation? Rejecting for herself the role of a midway prophet, she is overwhelmed by colour washes from an unknowing world and disturbed by her inability to place upon that reality a satisfactory light or perspective.

Here, then, is a poet whose concern is with what in general terms we regard as religious values, who has a romantic poet's celebration of personal vision and subjective light, and yet who paradoxically feels increasingly frustrated and in doubt that the encoding of personal vision can demonstrate that light, language, or the world have communicable interpersonal value (see "Extra-Political" [*WS*, 54] and "Intra-Political" [*WS*, 55–57]). How should the poet face this – perhaps the inevitable dilemma when a romantic subjectivity is coupled with a persistent desire for truth in the "outer" world? "The Swimmer's Moment" (*WS*, 47) is one instance in Avison's early work of an almost Kierkegaardean intensity to these questions. But in *Winter Sun*, there is not any dramatic existentialist resolution, no plunge into the Devil's Hole or the swimmer's abyss.

Rather, there is at last a resignation, a concession to isolation, to alienation and silence. Whereas early in the volume Avison's verse is brilliant with definition, it later expresses in shadowed translucence a deepening skepticism. In "Identity,"

> Half-sleeping, unbewildered, one accepts
> The countless footsteps, the unsounding thud,
> Not even asking in what company
> One seeks the charnel houses of the blood.
>
> (*WS*, 70)

Here, even her identity as a person is in question: "The presence here is single, worse than soul," though finally her cynicism will attach itself more firmly, if reflexively, to persona and vocation:

> So pressed, aloft, the errant angel sings.
> Should any listen, he would stop his breath.

This returns us, reflecting on *Winter Sun*, to one of Avison's plainest-speaking poems, "Voluptuaries and Others" (*WS*, 73). Because it so succinctly summarizes her evaluation of the poet's enterprise at this point in her career, I quote the entire first stanza:

> That Eureka of Archimedes out of his bath
> Is the kind of story that kills what it conveys;
> Yet the banality is right for that story, since it is not
> a communicable one
> But just a particular instance of
> The kind of lighting up of the terrain
> That leaves aside the whole terrain, really.
> But signalizes, and compels, an advance in it.
> Such an advance through a be-it-what-it-may but
> take-it-not-quite-as-given locale:
> Probably that is the core of being alive.
> The speculation is not a concession
> To limited imaginations. Neither is it
> A constrained voiding of the quality of immanent death.
> Such near values cannot be measured in values
> Just because the measuring
> Consists in that other kind of lighting up

That shows the terrain comprehended, as also its containing
space,
And wipes out adjectives, and all shadows
(or, perhaps, all but shadows).

"Lighting up of the terrain" is here not at all a high-flown advertisement for the triumphs of poetry, but rather a kind of down-grading barely compensated for by that last tentative saving of the appearances: general recognition, at least, is communicable, and "that story about Archimedes does get into public school textbooks." (Avison had prepared such a text for Ontario public schools at the time this poem was written.[4]) Here, the romantic poet's self-refulgent "Eureka" is certainly gone, the poem intensely self-ironic. The quest for Light and the poetic drive to climb up out of the Plato's cave of conventional representations into the Light have been severely disappointed. "The floor of heaven is really / Diamond congoleum," she writes ("R.I.P.," *WS*, 74), and though "All of us, flung in one / Murky parabola, / Seek out some pivot for significance" ("The Mirrored Man," *WS*, 81–82), in fact, "the long years' march deadens ardour, a little," until finally "no sun comes / Beyond the yellow stoneway . . ." ("The Agnes Cleves Papers," *WS*, 96, 97). The day-change no longer seems to illumine, "The wild smell is the other side / Of the impenetrable world of stone" (*WS*, 98) and Avison, superbly accomplished as a poet, sets her hand to the last pages of this remarkable first volume as one disappointed in poetry. Already she seems to have suspected that the inefficacy for real transformation in the romanticism she had espoused was somehow inherent in it from the beginning, locked in its very premises.

It is evident that Avison's poetry after *Winter Sun* undergoes a profound transformation, a conversion both of sense and sensibility. Nonetheless we may recognize as incorporated into this conversion a finely spun thread of persistent inquiry. In her poetry she moves from delight in the thing seen to ambivalence concerning the possibility of precision in capturing it, always subtended by careful meditation on the medium by which she sees (and by which, as she later affirms, the objective world lives at all) — Light.

In her early work, light and poetry are nearly synonymous. The emphasis on seeing is an emphasis on the poet, on poetic vision. Avison's poetic has been implicitly a version of the romantic *poeta nascitur.* After her religious experience, which she dates precisely to

January 4, 1963, the development of this poetic takes a dramatic turn. Light does not at all disappear as a value, but rather is clarified. Light is now the Apex; poetry is reflective understanding. The transformation is rendered explicit in *The Dumbfounding*, but it is helpful to contextualize it with her own perspective on her conversion experience.

Avison's cryptic and pseudonymous spiritual autobiography discusses an early desire to "have her cake and eat it too," to revel in gifts of "music, libraries, and winter mornings burning with cold beauty" as if they were intrinsic to her own personality, and without admitting to herself their otherness, and "that these things fade if not acknowledged."[5] What she talks about in this almost innocuous little essay reflects on many of the "re-evaluations" in her second volume of poems. The problem she sees in her earlier intellectual and spiritual life is a subversive lack of any transpersonal reference for ultimate meaning – implicitly a tendency to solipsize, a subjectivism which localizes all reference in the self while imagining otherwise. Of this phase she writes:

> I wish I had known that although thinking, comprehending, understanding, probing, are good – faculties God gave to us human beings – yet these faculties are given so that we can come to some notion of His unapproachably beautiful thinking, comprehending, understanding, and probing, even of me, my feelings and contacts and plans and responses to situations and openings from moment to moment in history (a history which, too, He comprehends).[6]

She goes on to consider her opacity to the Light she finally came to recognize. In their informality, these words make all the more plain, perhaps, that Avison's religious reassessment and her reassessment of her place as a poet are not really separable:

> I see how grievously I cut off His way by honoring the artist: the sovereignty of God was the real issue for a long time, for me. Of course I rue the years when I confused conscience with adapting to what certain approved people expected of me. I wanted to be liked, and on the basis of "genuine merit" too! In the arts I had my touchstone for scope and vividness – and poetry seemed to promise aliveness too. But this orientation allowed me to neglect or distance some real elements of

> humanness as alien to my own sense of what mattered. In questions of behaviour, too, my priorities were confused. A social gaffe could make me burn with shame upon every remembrance. Yet on ethical issues, I tended to generalize.[7]

Her observations bear fairly on the poetry of *Winter Sun*. Despite her desire for uniqueness of vision, she says, she felt overwhelmed by pressures to conformity in the world of her peers. In her remembrance one finds easily enough a correlative to the pervasive spirit of many of the later poems in that first volume – a lack of conviction, scepticism, a self-protective drawing down of the blinds.

> One had to try to serve the general interest – stuffing envelopes in some chilly committee room on into the evening, or working up copy for leaflets and mimeographed magazines. Gradually, a malaise, a false peace, settled in. Persons, events, and my own responses grew more and more indeterminate, lost the bite of uniqueness. I was going down into living death.[8]

Then, the dramatic change. While reading the fourteenth chapter of John's Gospel, she was suddenly and decisively moved to a self-abandoned reordering of priorities for her whole life. In the following two months she wrote compulsively, drafting most of the poems which make up *The Dumbfounding*.[9] *Winter Sun*, elegant testimony to the modern *poeta nascitur* that it is, had taken by contrast more than fifteen years to assemble.

> Word has arrived that
> peace will brim up, will come
> "like a river and the
> glory . . . like a flowing stream."
> So.
> Some of all people will
> wondering wait
> until this very stone
> utters.
>
> ("Stone's Secret," *S*, 21–22)

What was being transformed? The poems in their own best way make this clear. Hanging over *Winter Sun* from the outset there had been a sense of the poet's isolation, her alienation from any enduring community of like or unlike mind and prospect. The poems are solitary, their voice a single voice. In *The Dumbfounding*, as in *sunblue*, the heretofore impossible "many" of human otherness enters almost immediately into possible dialogue. Even as the dominant array of winter images yields to the fragrance of spring and summer's colour, so the "newspaper house" ("Chronic," *WS*, 18) gives way to a deepening "heart's room" ("Many As Two," *D*, 115): a community takes shape. Dialogue springs up on the pages, living conversation enters into poem after poem. For Avison there is beauty in the irony that it should be an "outcast's outcast" ("The Dumbfounding," *D*, 153) who makes relationship possible, even as he is bringing stillness to a clatter of words that are forever asimtotic, always falling short of their imagined relational effect.

There is in *Winter Sun*, especially in the last poems, a sense of oldness and of growing old, of unconsummated life and withering leaf as the twilight fades. Such tranquillity as is felt is like composure before death, a resignation to the lengthening shadows. In *The Dumbfounding* there is, by contrast, a kind of recovery of childhood, a trustful openness, a simple desire to be whole that makes healing possible. In " A Child: Marginalia on an Epigraph" (*D*, 125–27) the epigraphs on which Avison's poem is a commentary are the often misunderstood scriptures linking an experience of the soul's elected peace to child-like lack of defensive self-consciousness. In the first of these, Matthew 18:3, the effect of conversion is a passing from world-weary perspective into child-likeness of heart; indeed, such a conversion is made to be a condition of communion and community: "Except ye be converted, and become as little children, ye shall not enter into the kingdom of heaven." This movement, from old to new, bookends *The Dumbfounding* ("Old . . . Young. . . . [*D*, 101]; "Unspeakable" [*D*, 188]) and is a recurrent theme there and in *sunblue*. It is consistent with the richness of vernal imagery in these volumes, and with the passage from city to garden, from sterility to fecundity, and from ice to flowing water ("SKETCH: Thaws," *s*, 9; [cf. "Thaw," *WS*, 50]; "Released Flow," *s*, 24; "Stone's Secret," *s*, 21–22, and so on.)

In *Winter Sun*, as we have seen, Avison had begun in a fascination with light and with poetry as a kind of light, its choicest words as amiable sunbeams. She then began to lose confidence in language, and to drift towards shadow and silence. Now, confronted by Light in a way she had not imagined, the "Light that blinded

Saul" ("Branches," *D*, 140), she finds herself reduced to silence in a different way, speechless and "dumbfounded." The new posture is neither one of scepticism nor of defeat; it is one of humility, and perhaps its most concise and beautiful realization comes in the graceful poem ". . . Person or A Hymn on and to the Holy Ghost" (*D*, 147): "How should I find speech / to you, the self effacing . . ." she asks, "to you whose self-knowing / is perfect . . . ." To the Holy Spirit, the "unseen," she prays:

> to lead *my* self, effaced
> in the known Light,
> to be in him released
> from facelessness.

What she asks for is not, as we might casually expect, for Light to see by and words better to write about it, but rather to be herself led into the Light so that, listening to Light 'articulating,' she may come to know herself as one who is seen; instead of imagining herself to be doing all the interpreting, she herself asks to be read out and interpreted. It is a courageous prayer. What she longs for, then, is to be able to "show him visible" – not at a comfortable aesthetic distance, but in life, in the difficult places where He ("unseen, unguessed, liable / to grievous hurt) would go." Avison has spent most of her subsequent life in inner-city social work and modestly paid labours as secretary in the Toronto office of a Southeast Asia mission. The personal evasion of ethical issues with which she charged herself before her conversion came quickly to be redressed in personal action as well as in the articulate social criticism in her poetry ("Of Tyranny, in One Breath," *D*, 162–67; "July Man," *D*, 116; "Needy," *s*, 78, and so on).

In all of this change we see that her fascination for Light continues, but that her sense of what Light can do is radically transformed. From the beginning she had resisted the notion that light experienced passively – even as enlightenment ("Prelude") – could be sufficient light. Now she had come much further, to say that the experience of light worth having is the one that cannot be achieved by mastery or merit, because it shines beyond (and in spite of) poetic inspiration or boot-strap ambitions for a self-induced epiphany. Avison, in her early poetry, had always been a seeker after truth in the legitimate sense: the obsession with light was not merely an absorption in poetry, but also represented a desire to see and to know. In her troubled days after the last of *Winter Sun*, she took refuge in the "heart's room" spoken of in John 14, and it led her to an encounter with God not as abstract idea or, as she says in "Strong Yellow, for Reading Aloud" (*s*, 40–41), nor mere "Possibility," but as Person. "Let not your heart be troubled," says Jesus in the opening verse of John 14, "ye believe in God, believe also in me." He goes on to offer not only comfort but the Comforter: "Even the Spirit of truth: whom the world cannot receive, because it seeth him not, neither knoweth him" (v. 17). Avison seems to have always been the sort of person who could identify comfort with the truth. Here, at the turning point in her life, she reached for the Comfort and found it Light.

It is apparent to a reader of her poetry that this is Light strikingly mediated by language; indeed at its own highest reach of biblical metaphor, it is explicitly juxtaposed with the Word. From the point of view of her poetic, Avison's transformed understanding of Light from natural to spiritual aesthetic has immediate roots in the gospel she was reading at the time of her conversion. That gospel begins, of course, with a statement about creation, one in which the medium reveals its message unqualifiably: neither invented nor inventable, it is Itself all-Creating. The Word creates life, and it is this life which then becomes Light to the world:

> In the beginning was the Word, and the Word was with God, and the Word was God.
>
> The same was in the beginning with God. All things were made by him; and without him was not anything made that was made.
>
> In him was life; and the life was the light of men. And the light shineth in darkness; and the darkness comprehended it not.
>
> (John 1:1–5)

This image of creating Light, central to John's Gospel (and Epistles), is developed there in a way that parallels the relationship of Light to Word in Avison's imagination. She further reflects the spirit of John's prologue in dissociating the prophet (or poet) from the Light itself (v. 8), and seeing prophetic (or poetic) words as a witness to a Word they cannot contain, a "Word made flesh" (v. 14). By analogy, the poet's words do not create. The Word that creates life — or more properly, is life — is before and beyond poetry, and thus not finally utterable. Rather, it is, as for John of the Cross, a word known in silence — not a silence of despair, but a stillness of waiting.[10]

This relationship of Light to Word well underscores the poetic which is expressed in Avison's three-poem sequence in *sunblue*, "Light I; II; III" (*s*, 59–61). The first poem begins with a statement that dramatically undermines a traditional romantic perspective:

> The stuff of flesh and bone
> is given, *datum*. Down
> the stick-men, plastiscene-
> people, clay-lump children, are strewn,
> each casting shadow in the eye of day.
>
> Then — listen! — I see
> breath of delighting rise from
> those stones the sun touches
> and hear a snarl of breath
> as a mouth sucks air. And with
> shivery sighings — see: they stir
> and turn and move, and power
> to build, to undermine, is theirs,
> is ours.
>
> The stuff, the breath, the power to move even thumbs
> and with them, things: *data*. What is
> the harpsweep on the heart for?
> What does the constructed power
> of speculation reach for?
> Each of us casts a shadow in the bewildering day,
> an own-shaped shadow only.
>
> The light has looked on Light.
>
> He from elsewhere
> speaks; he breathes impasse-
> crumpled hope even
> in us:
> that near.

The poet does not invent the world, nor reinvent. She sees it now as a given: Light makes her listen. In each of us who move in the light, she says, there is the power to speculate or to hide; the wonder of creation is our freedom to will. Self-shaped shadow fables, seeking an invented, not a created world. Light needs to look on Light before Light speaks. "Any shadow," she says, is "self, upon / self" ("Light [II]"). To overcome that self-clouding, she adds, one needs to "look to the sunblue." In "Light (III)," the whole cosmos is transformed in this knowledge; the whole sky has become Light. Under it one accepts that seeing leads to hearing, and hearing to self-knowledge. The poet's role is not at all that clichéd Blakean proclamation of unique vision and special revelation: far from it. It is a view of the poet still seeking after truth, now in petition, listening, for wisdom:

> Because I know
> the voice of the Word
> is to be heard
> I know I do not know
> even my own cast burden,
> or oh, the costly load
> of knowing undisturbed.
> There is a sword
> enters with hearing. Lord
> who chose being born to die
> and died to bring alive
> and live to judge
> though all in mercy, hear
> the word You utter
> in me, because I know
> the voice.

("Listening," *s*, 58)

Avison is no longer *poeta nascitur*, nor, as we might fear, some television evangelist's "Eureka" version of *poeta re-nascit*, but astonishingly simply *poeta fit*, the poet who harkens, who makes and is made.

To be sure, Avison's *poeta fit* ought not be construed in narrowly neo-classical terms; she means something more. Yet her poetic now is far more akin to neo-classical than to her erstwhile romantic premises. There is a new openness to a community of understanding for self-knowledge, to the past as relevant authority for the present, and to the time-honoured classical conviction that it is not just we who interpret or "create" but we who are being interpreted by the light we walk in and the texts we read. This poem intends a commentary on the Epistle to the Hebrews 4:12; her sword that "enters with hearing" is that same two-edged sword that "is a discerner of the thoughts and intents of the heart" (cf. her use of this Epistle in "For Tinkers Who Travel on Foot," *D*, 130). But it also bears reading in the light of Psalm 19 (upon which text she has also composed a superb reflection). The plea that the Lord who is the Word may "hear / the word You utter / in me" parallels the plea of the psalmist at the conclusion of his meditation, which is also that the Word may interpret him, so to speak, rather than the other way around: "Let the words of my mouth, and the meditation of my heart, be acceptable in thy sight, O Lord, my strength, and my redeemer" (v. 14). As an emphasis on visionary light is normative to the *poeta nascitur*, so is the wisdom of the word inspiration to the *poeta fit*.

Avison in *sunblue* is a craftsman keenly aware of herself also as a creature. She makes because she is first made in the image of a Maker. Creation and creativity are indissolubly linked; the poet who strives for truth is no Faustian inventor of unbidden worlds. Rather, she is herself a reader, ferreting truth and artistic form out of a world already charged with meaning: "The word read by the living Word / sculptured its shaper's form. / What happens, means" ("The Bible to be Believed," *s*, 56–57). "Creative Hour" (*s*, 99), even in its opening image of the child with colouring book, satisfactorily encodes her statement about a converted poetic. For her, finally,

> The evasive "maker"-metaphor,
> thank God, under the power
> of our real common lot
> leads stumbling back to what it promised to evade.
>
> There is no one reviewed, no viewer,
> no one of us not creature;
> we're apparently at work. But nothing is made
> except by the only unpretentious, Jesus Christ, the Lord.

Here, the statement of faith is a rejection of conventional romanticism and, however atypically, a modern critique of post-romantic aesthetics. In the shift from sight to hearing, we are drawn from the conventions of prophetic vision to a poetry of meditation.

In the *Winter Sun* phase of Avison's reflections on the art of poetry we recognize her exuberance in the light of nature, her careful reification of moments of acute perception in precisely chosen words that acknowledge even as they celebrate the subjectivity of her perception – what later she calls "self-shadow" (*s*, 60). By the end of that volume we can anticipate in her growing scepticism and the character of her habitual restraint a movement towards silence. By the end of *The Dumbfounding* and all through *sunblue* we not only anticipate but experience an entirely different kind of silence. It is not a mere hesitancy to speak. What Avison calls "dumbfounding" and "silencing" (*s*, 57) involves a death to the insistent self that, like the passage of seed into earth, becomes a passage to new life ("A Story," *D*, 120–23). This new silence is really a stillness, a stillness that allows hearing, and that, as in the case of Bunyan ("For Tinkers Who Travel on Foot"), nourishes creativity. However it has suffered "deaf and dumb months," the imagination may be brought to life once it has consented to Life.

The quietness we find in Avison's early work is thus profoundly transformed, transmuted to a stillness that is expectant, listening for the voice of the Creator. The poetry such stillness breathes is deep, clear, and tranquil, almost anomalous in the insistent, self-glorifying hullabaloo of our time, in which even poetry is often mere talkativeness. Perhaps one of the most valuable aspects of Avison's total contribution is to remind us that, as Kierkegaard once put it, "Only some one who knows how to remain essentially silent can really talk – and act essentially."[11]

Three slim volumes are what Margaret Avison has given us to date. She is no more on paper than in person one who could be described as 'talkative.' But such a witness resides in her quietness, and in her stillness such a refuge for our badgered senses, that she has earned a respectful hearing from fellow poets and readers alike – even from those who cannot yet share with her the still centre of her vision, or can at best lay claim to viewing it only from afar. Avison's succinct poetry remains as witness to a remarkable transformation of inner life, and the talk it offers is an exquisitely lucid distillation, a bequest of whispered gold.

No fair assessment will dismiss Avison as a mere votary, let alone a voluptuary of her calling. In her later poems the same patient inquiry after truth persists; in fact, in some respects it becomes more strong than ever.[12] The dialogue poems allow her to air her doubts, to debate with her fellows or with Scripture or with God himself in pursuit of resolution to her questions. In some of her early Christian poems she resents the intrusions of responsibility or the persistence of her singleness openly — running away from comfort even as she is seeking comfort. But what had perhaps been evasion, and fear of "that turned-to-marble chase" ("Research," *s*, 100) is, in the later poems, reconciled by an irony that is pivotal to her "Searching and Sounding" (*D*, 154–56), a joyous reversal in which self-knowledge deepens:

> And as I run I cry
> "But I need something human,
> somebody now, here, with me."
> Running from you.
> The sunlight is sundered by cloud-mass.

The Daphne images echo Thomas Carew's response to the same transfix of wood and wilfulness converted (ironically and passionately) in acceptance:

> Daphne hath broke her bark, and that swift foot
> Which the angry Gods had fast'ned with a root
> To the fix'd earth, doth now unfettered run
> To meet the embraces of the youthful Sun.[13]

Nescis, temeraria, nescis, / quem fugias:[14] running — to embrace the Sun from whom she had originally fled. In a seventeenth-century poet's image, perhaps, is the meaning of Avison's conversion, the metamorphosis of her poetic, and the transformation of her psyche.

We can hardly appreciate the impact of Avison's conversion upon her work without recognizing that she has by now become a significant poet in the English meditative tradition. Quite naturally she joins ranks with Herbert and Hopkins (whom she had always admired), remaining closer to them than to Eliot (about whom she always had deep reservations).[15] This is not to say that she is not as "modern" as Eliot, but that her poetry is much more a species of prayer, dialogue with God. Some of the prayer, too, is even a kind of "Intercession." In her poem of that title she offers commendation of one not identified, who prays and waits:

The old saint, because of her
long hours not spent afield
therefore with searching force
waits it out, for us:
wounded, and healed.

(*s*, 69)

Reading, one is moved to wonder whether such words might not be applied to Avison herself. In her poetry, she offers herself to us as one who waits hopefully, and listens, by her craft interceding between our rumbling darkness and the Light for which she would have us listen, too. It takes, of course, an unusual stillness for that, and faith. Yet in the conversion of Margaret Avison's imagination, even the secret locked in stone is one day to shine forth in purest speech. Against that day, in the incarnation of transformed imagination that is her work, she enacts a generous commitment to our attunement, a graceful preparation of her reader's hearing.

NOTES

[1] See the especially valuable discussion by George Bowering, "Avison's Imitation of Christ the Artist," in *Canadian Literature*, No. 54 (Autumn 1972), pp. 56–69.

[2] See here Daniel W. Doerksen, "Search and Discovery: Margaret Avison's Poetry," in *Canadian Literature*, No. 60 (Spring 1974), pp. 7–20.

[3] David A. Kent, from a forthcoming essay on Margaret Avison in *Canadian Writers and Their Works*, Vol. VI (Poetry Series).

[4] *History of Ontario* (Toronto: Gage, 1951).

[5] Angela Martin (pseudonym), "I wish I had known that . . . I couldn't have my cake and eat it," in *I Wish I Had Known . . .* (Grand Rapids, Mich.: Zondervan Publishing House, 1968), p. 90.

[6] Martin, p. 91.

[7] Martin, pp. 92–93.

[8] Martin, p. 93.

[9] Harry der Nederlanden, "Margaret Avison: The Dumbfounding," in *Calvinist Contact*, Oct. 19, 1979, p. 1; also Merle Shain, "Some of Our

Best Poets Are . . . Women," in *Chatelaine*, Oct. 1972, p. 104.

[10] The signal lines are: "The Father utters one Word and that Word is his Son, / and he utters him forever in everlasting silence / and in silence the soul has to hear him."

[11] Søren Kierkegaard, *The Present Age*, trans. Alexander Dru (New York: Harper and Row, 1962), p. 69. The passage in context is: "What is *talkativeness*? It is the result of doing away with the vital distinction between talking and keeping silent. Only some one who knows how to remain essentially silent can really talk — and act essentially. Silence is the essence of inwardness, of the inner life."

[12] Bowering, pp. 60–61; cf. Doerksen, pp. 15–17.

[13] "Rapture," in *The Poems of Thomas Carew*, ed. Rhodes Dunlop (Oxford: Clarendon, 1949; 1964), p. 52.

[14] Ovid, *Metamorphosis*, I, 514–15.

[15] I am agreeing here with Lawrence M. Jones, "A Core of Brilliance: Margaret Avison's Achievement," in *Canadian Literature*, No. 38 (Autumn 1968), pp. 50–57, and Doerksen, who makes the connection with Herbert in an especially attractive way. The fullest treatment of the matter, and best contextualized, is still Ernest Redekop's seminal monograph, *Margaret Avison* (Toronto: Copp Clark, 1970).

Margaret, A Vision

GEORGE BOWERING

a.

WHEN A PERSON WAS YOUNG he was interested in poetry, of course, but he never thought of the idea of a famous Canadian poet. Well, himself, yes, but that was a matter for the future, and then it wasn't Canadian. He didn't think of that. For the present, then, he never even thought of thinking of a Canadian poet any more than he thought of a Canadian astronaut.

If there was any Canadian poetry it was amateur stuff, stanzas made of convoluted attempts at imitating the debased English coinage, inverted syntax and gentlemanly rhymes, descriptions of landscapes that never existed in the New World. He was not sure there was such stuff but if there was any it would be such. Later he would find that he was right. In the first half of the twentieth century the Canadian poets followed the lead not of the Imagists but of the Georgians, those British gentlemen who chose to ignore the sound of pneumatic drills and pretend that Nature was still peacefully at hand and ready to enter the insides of any tender heart. Of course the images were not nearby, so one had to borrow their faint images from an earlier time, when Nature was an amazing discovery.

b.

So he got along with American poetry, in which the setting was not familiar to him, but at least it gave evidence of being familiar to the writer of the poems. That was until a friend brought some thin books back from Montreal and Toronto; there contact was made. Now he could believe that there were Canadian poets, real people writing in plain language, even though it was the language of Jewish and Polish and UEL eastern city-dwellers. What a pleasure to read a poem naming the streets of the city in which the recognized Habitants walked.

But once those poems were known, and imitated, their plainness seemed not enough. Yes, one could understand that the men who wrote them were making a point, and his own point, against the artificial formulas of sylvan glades and anapests propagated by their predecessors; but the plain language, fresh as it was, nourishing as it was, was transparent. It offered a picture of a world back there on the streets, and it offered a voice he wanted to hear. But it did not rime.

He was not looking for the old abab, or worse, the old abba. He was listening for the kind of musical self-absorption and release he could always hear in, say, Lester Young or H. D. The voice that belonged to the poem itself, it seemed, the sounds that felt around for spirit rather than earth and concrete. The concrete should be there, and the nouns in the poems should be "concrete," but they should delight more than your hands and feet.

He and his friends talked a lot about the senses, about poetry as a business of the senses rather than the discursive mind. But he had been a serious personal Christian a few years back, and had turned his Christianity into Poetry. He wanted to hear rime, even rhyme if it came to that. He knew that rime, as long as it was not plunked down doggedly at the end of eight syllables, spoke of mind delighted by spirit. For the poets who had stayed with his seriousness after their job was done on the survey courses he had sat through in college, rime had meant the enjoyment of God.

John Donne. William Blake. Gerard Manley Hopkins. William Butler Yeats. Emily Dickinson. Robert Duncan.

Thank you, he said to those eastern Canadian city poets. Do you have a poet who is in love with language because it is not just the poet saying it?

c.

They sent Margaret Avison.

Or rather it was not they who sent her; she came by way of the conventional literary apparatus, the University of Toronto, a few academic poet editors. But there she was. Her poems were filled with the streets and street habitués to be found in the plain poets:

> The rushing river of cars
> makes you a stillness, a pivot, a heart-stopping
> blurt, in the sorrow
> of the last rubbydub swig, the searing, and
> stone-jar solitude lost, and yet,
> and still – wonder (for good now) and
> trembling:

But (no, not but; rather and) the lines of her poems, often such portraits, sounded in his own mouth as he read, so that the city rubbydub was not only there but also here, significant not because of what the poem was saying about him, picked out from among the many, but because the music is intense, because it is filled with delight.

It is not too hard to sound filled with delight on patronizing a pretty flower or a lofty tree. If a bum on a street bench is part of the delight of a sequence of words, the reader knows that he is in the presence of spirit. He is not a point proven. He is a vision.

d.

When that first person got older and had been published a lot, and had landed some teaching jobs because of that, he was heard to say over and over that Margaret Avison is the best poet we have had. Whether he was asked or not, he said it everywhere.

She does not like to hear people say that.

Nowadays there are more and more poets in Canada who are very good. This would not have happened if it had not been for those plain poets in the cities back east.

But when it comes to making a canon, and wanting a figure to look to as the founder of excellence and the first name in the canon, the writers with regard for precise language and delight tend to agree. In fiction they tend to agree on Sheila Watson, and in poetry they tend to agree on Margaret Avison.

Sheila Watson and Margaret Avison do not like to hear people say that.

e.

People say why didn't Sheila Watson publish another novel. They say why hasn't Margaret Avison published more poetry.

Margaret Avison has a big pile of poetry that she has not published. Publishers across the country have written to ask her for a manuscript. This has been going on for years and years.

If she will not publish another book of poems, he said to himself and then to others, one will just have to go back and read the books we have. He often said that "Searching and Sounding" and the poem that rimes with it, "The Dumbfounding," are not likely to be bettered by any work that any poet will ever publish.

A poet who wants to learn from someone in his own country, to learn how to make a poem as best he can, will be well advised to turn to those two poems. It is a great pleasure to be able to turn to a Canadian poet for such instruction and delight.

Thank you for sending her.

January, 1984

Faithful Unpredictability: Syntax and Theology in Margaret Avison's Poetry

ROBERT JAMES MERRETT

THE LANGUAGE WE SPEAK in our daily affairs classifies our experience. Unless we are conscious of our speech, we take its classifications for granted. Poetry confronts the mundane with the unexpected; poems employ ordinary language precisely but resist its classifications. In a sense, poetic discourse should violate the rules of daily speech without becoming predictable; it should alert us to how language works so that we may grow in knowledge of the world and ourselves. One way poetry can do this is to use syntax oddly. Transformational grammar, in its exploration of deep surface structures, has shown how the mind interprets identical statements differently, how our speech involves more complicated syntactic processes than we think. By using syntax oddly, poets can exploit the difference between deep and surface structures to prove that what we ordinarily say is more interesting and exciting than we assume. Poets should use syntax oddly, then, not just to renew our daily speech, but also to reveal how language is instrumental to life.[1]

Margaret Avison uses syntax oddly. Her poetic discourse is marvellously unpredictable because she follows important syntactic principles. Her poems reveal her conviction that what makes sentences meaningful is the desire to interpret them, and that the less predictable a sentence is the more meaning it has. She knows the effort to understand language is a precondition of understanding it. She also knows we must struggle to reach meaning before we can resolve alternative parsings, that our determination to arrive at the right interpretation enables us to be creative with unpredictable syntactic structures. Her poems move towards meanings that require alternative grammars, the reason being that she assumes the ultimate cause of grammar is experience of the world. But her world is not limited to the phenomenal. She realizes speech can point to things that do not factually exist: she trusts that language refers to the ineffable and to elements of reality not normally envisaged. Using syntax oddly, Avison offers us a challenge; breaking conventional relations between concept and referent, she invites us to mend these fractures. We respond only if we reconceive the relation of language to creation imaginatively.

If we therefore ask what explains Avison's power as a poet, we are less likely to attribute it to figurative expression than to a fundamental understanding of grammar. Syntax may seem a cold, mechanical subject, perhaps because of the inscrutable parsing exercises of our school days or the unreadability of much recent linguistics. But syntax does reveal how our minds work and how we react to the world. It is largely through her syntax that Avison achieves an unpredictability that obliges us to explore the spiritual nature of reality.

The first poem in *The Dumbfounding* will provide an initial illustration of how syntax endows Avison's poetry with unpredictability.

OLD . . . YOUNG. . . .

The antlers of the ancient
members of the orchard lie
bleaching where the young grass
shines, breathing light;

the candles are carried
to seek out those in the cellars
granular in their lees:

because cobwebs are forked away
and the wind rises
and from the new pastures long after longstemmed sunset,
even this springtime, the last
 light is mahogany-rich,
  a "furnishing."

(*D*, 101)

The poem is unpredictable for various syntactic reasons. First, the minimal grammar of the title clashes with the full grammar that makes of the poem a single, periodic sentence. Second, if we scrutinize the grammar of the text, we see that its formality is deceptive. It is not full: there are no personal nouns or pronouns; one demonstrative pronoun has no antecedent; "candles are carried" and "cobwebs are forked away" are agentless passives. Third, ambiguous qualifications work against personifications to break down the distinction between old and young. If "antlers" is personified by the first prepositional phrase because it contains "members," the second one undoes the personification, for the antlers are rendered phenomenal by "of the orchard." Whereas grass is personified because it is "young" and "breathing," it also shines like a reflective object, and, while "those" seems to refer to bottles that need to be sought out as if they possess human mobility, they are very much sediment-filled containers.

The syntax affects schemes other than personification; it makes problematical the topical structure within and between stanzas. From the title, we do not know whether the relation between the old and young is serial or antithetical. This ambivalence is detectable in the tension between surface and deep grammar. The first stanza seems to oppose the old and young. But the antithesis is unsupported by the deep grammar. If we consider the phonetically balanced but inverted phrases "lie bleaching" and "breathing light," we might conclude they contrast the old and young. But the participle in the first phrase is not just a present continuous tense in the active voice. The bones are less dead than receiving the action of the sun. The participle "bleaching" has a passive aspect in deep grammar: it means "being bleached." If we recall that the participle "breathing" is ambivalent, that it is limited to neither inhaling nor exhaling, we realize that the syntax makes the antithesis between old and young also a comparison.

Now, if we look at the relation between the first two stanzas, we see how complicated the topical patterns are, how unschematic the contrasts between old and young, outer and inner. The first stanza deals with the outdoors, the second with the indoors. Although light is a common topic, its sources are antithetical: the first stanza treats of sunlight, the second of candlelight. Then again, the implicit fusion of old and new in the first stanza is maintained in the second: the bottles, long put down in the cellar, are about to be recovered. Their promise, however, is ambiguous; it is unclear whether they have aged for better or worse.

The third stanza begins defiantly with a subordination, defiantly since the conjunction renders the logic of subordination unclear. There follow three clauses of reason; they are coordinate but not parallel. Active and passive voices differentiate the first two, and the third is delayed by three prepositional phrases ending with a compound adjective complement that is qualified by a gerund in apposition. As the poem progresses, the syntax becomes increasingly complex, blocking any immediately rational or purely aesthetic appreciation of topical pattern.

The third stanza is unpredictable because it reverses topical order by beginning with the indoors. After passing to the outdoors, it merges the topics. Since, however, we do not usually fork cobwebs, the relation between indoors and outdoors is extraordinary from the start: we usually brush cobwebs and fork hay. The logic of comparison and contrast is further defied by the extended sense of the present-tense verbs. They define rather than describe; their definitional sense gives them an imperfect aspect. This extended sense gives special force to the "is" of the final subordinate clause. This clause is topically difficult because the light it defines is neither natural nor man-made, but a light the pastures project into the atmosphere after sunset. This light is both unnatural and earthly.

The ambiguity of the pastures reinforces that of the light. They are new, but not ordinarily so. New because the season is spring and the sun has renewed them, they are also new long after sunset. The participle form describing the sunset, since it is ambiguous, helps explain this newness. The sunset is "longstemmed." Perhaps it cast long shadows or transpired slowly. But "longstemmed," through its association with cellar and lees, relates to the implicit theme of drinking: it is what wine glasses can be. This participle form merges the domestic and natural, the indoors and outdoors. This fusion of topics, which, paradoxically, breaks down logical patterns, reaches a climax in the last two lines. The light produced by earth is, besides the medium of sight, a substance that furnishes mankind. It is mahogany-rich. This elliptical simile shows that the light results from a long organic process: the light is old like mahogany, the hard wood made into furniture. The implicit simile makes the pun in the final participle form richer. Light is a "furnishing," a material fashioned by a maker. Light is to be relied on because it is a physical and spiritual property offering rest in the face of temporal dualities. The syntax of the poem makes light into a new sacrament because its oddness destroys and recreates figures and schemes.

This exegesis suggests how syntax establishes unpredictability, how grammatical ambivalence realizes ideological conflict. Avison's syntax is more than an instrument for displacing facile dualities, more than a tool for sharpening abstract nouns; it bridges material and immaterial reality. From their grammar, Avison's poems acquire theological substance. In the following survey of *The Dumbfounding*, we shall try to justify this by seeing how and why the poet exploits oppositions between transitive and intransitive verbs, personal and impersonal constructions, and present and past participles. We shall concentrate on participles because Avison acutely understands how they shift grammatical rank, how they work in compounding and puns, and how they embed transformations.

Although ten of the sixty poems in *The Dumbfounding* have participles in their titles, this is not odd. As headings, titles require the economy and density of reference provided by participles. However, economy affords syntactic ambiguity, as evident in the poem whose title gives its name to the volume (*D*, 152–53). To dumbfound means to amaze, to cause to be unable to speak. The gerundial title provokes us to think of meanings beneath the surface of the poem. The text illustrates the word negatively, describing the people of Christ's time as far from dumbfounded by him. They reject aloud his authority to tell them anything, trying to dumbfound him. After his death, they say they want the Resurrection but they permanently stop the voices of those who would announce it. To Avison, people still make a din to shut out Christ's attempts to reach them; they still betray a merely physical sense of dumbfounding. By contrast, Christ gives a new and extended meaning to physical presence because he can confront evil and "sound dark's uttermost." The puns on "sound" and "uttermost" show that, in fathoming the depths of evil, Christ puts significant sound into uttering. Christ is not dumbfounded. Rather, he is the dumbfounding because he makes ultimate paradoxes meaningful, founding a spiritually audible silence.[2]

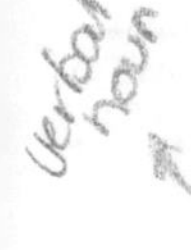

Since this is to anticipate somewhat, let us consider how Avison's unpredictability stems from her participles. Although found in almost every other line, they sometimes occur in clusters. For example, here are the five past-participle forms that begin "The Earth That Falls Away":

Brine-crusted, thread-knobbed,
odd-shaped scrap,
clay-soaked, wadded crooked,
rag.

(*D*, 131)

Similarly compounded, these participles vary in function. We are implicitly invited to determine the head word of each adjectival phrase, to uncover each transformation. The rag has been crusted with brine and soaked with clay. These passive transformations, though parallel, join solid and liquid references in an antithetical way: liquid produces a solid on the rag, a solid liquid. One of the participles is an attributive adjective: the rag has an odd shape. In the phrase that tells us the rag has been wadded crookedly, the second term, despite its form, is adverbal: it functions as manner, not instrument. Lastly, in the phrase saying the threads of rag have become knobbed, the nominal term is subject rather than instrument. Each compound has a unique deep grammar.[3]

Occasionally, Avison clusters present participles. The following thirteen lines from "The Absorbed" contain ten. The poem focuses on a boy playing alone in the winter landscape,

sometimes bumping
down to the Japanese yews, sometimes
scooter-shoving athwart the hill,
then, with a stake,
kneeling,
he paddles, thrusting, speed-wise, then
stabbing, uphill; then
dangling the rope and poring on
slope-sheen, standing, he stashes
the aluminum, upright, in a frost-lumpy shoal
and beside coasting motorcars and parked cars
listens . . . and off again, toque to the eyebrows,
alone still in the engulfing dark.

(*D*, 128–29)

Mostly from verbs of motion and action, the participles convey the child's physical energy. He is also responsive; the pun on "speed-wise" shows as much. It is appositive adjective and adverb: the boy, wise about speed, moves speedily. The participles substantiate his responsiveness; intransitive, even when deriving from transitive verbs, they emphasize his freedom of play. Not limited by winter, he imagines battling nature in other seasons. To him, the elements are not frozen; they are fluid. He concentrates on his environment; he pores upon it, the homophone suggesting he pours himself into it, because it matches words such as "shoal," "paddles," "coasting," and "engulfing." The participles stress the boy's imaginative courage, the mental process that allows him to enter the gulf of being without fear. By contrast, at the end of the poem, the adults are unresponsive. They do not look at nature closely; their fear of being induces illusion. They think they are "pitted" against the "grape-white" stars, their cowardice revealed by the unself-conscious pun on "pit," a pun clashing with the one stressing the boy's elemental concentration. The adults hear only the silence of creation, suffering from pretensions to grasp the cosmos; the boy listens, living simultaneously within different dimensions of reality. The participles inform the puns and establish the surprising thematic opposition.

Usually, rather than clustering participles, Avison mixes them. We see this in "July Man," a poem about a tramp in an urban park (*D*, 116). He has been passive: he is "rain-wrinkled" and "time-soiled." Yet, "weeping" for the flowers and the "hurting" motes of time, he is active in his suffering. Worn by weather and time, he remains open to them. He has reduced his alertness through drink: he is "rotted with rotting grape" and "puzzled for good by fermented potato- / peel." The syntactic oppositions between participles suggest that his alcoholism is organic and genuine. He has not retreated into aesthetics, like the bird-cranks who escape from reality by holding that beauty is "fan-tailed." They admire plumage as a "folding in / from the white fury of day." The opposition between participle adjective and gerund heightens the bird-cranks' contradictoriness; identifying beauty with open tail feathers, they value plumage for concealing itself from daylight. Not an escapist, the tramp is a real presence, a "heart-stopping / blurt." When he takes his last swig, "the searing," and realizes his "stone-jar solitude" has ended, he can "wonder (for good now)" in "trembling." The first "for good" is ambivalent; the second is spiritual rather than temporal. The participle forms, referring simultaneously to physical and mental experience, illustrate how the tramp converts the paradoxes of time and suffering into insight. Alive to the "too much none of us knows," he experiences the substantial and evanescent aspects of nature, the "weight" of "sunlight, falling" on him in time. The opposition of weight and light proves him alert to the solidity within process. Working as gerunds and as adjectival and adverbal transformations, and serving as puns that reinforce other puns, the participle forms show how and why the tramp can enjoy a vision of being and a heightened sense of concept and referent.

The mixed participles in "July Man" are fundamental to the tramp's vision. Though a product of the dehumanizing urban environment and vulnerable to himself, he yet has a means of recovery. The clash of transitive past participle with intransitive present participle in the phrase that has him rotted by the rotting grape implies his alcoholism is a natural, humanizing problem. He is more human than the "buzzing" populace, which is bee-like in its dependence upon the garden. When he takes his last swig, the "searing" leads directly to his "trembling" realization of time. He wonders "for good" because the temporal meaning of that phrase now embraces moral good. This double vision is climaxed in his paradoxical sense that weight exists in the light of the sun. By experiencing time, the tramp knows being; transience gives him a sense of the demanding permanence of creation.

By mixing participles, Avison juxtaposes sense impressions and mental abstractions to derive dynamic opposition from their conjunction.[4] Section eleven of "The Earth That Falls Away" exemplifies this well (*D*, 137). Here Avison records impressions of a snowstorm. Snow falls on snow, the falling flakes appearing as shadows of moths in the street lights, which are "snow-candled." The impressions of the mundane are mixed with whimsical associations; reality seems remote if street lamps are candles made of snow and flakes are the images of moths. Yet, concentrating on this mixture, the poet not only sees light in the night sky but also a needy face mirroring her own: a "shed / pallor" waits for an "uptilt-faced, flying / creature, its eye-curves / soft-lashed, soundlessly wide-eyed, / upsweeping, staring into night." The night's face is both "loving" and "terrifying." The poet begs the face not to blink, not to disappear into "charred snow" where humans cannot go, where they dare not fathom the "enfolding depths."

The participles, referring to fixed and moving stances, to past and present processes, to animate and human features, and to destructive and protective actions, reveal that impressions can mediate abstract desire, that whimsical experiences can show nature to be supportive. Nature, it appears, upholds anthropocentric images. By turning perceptions into occasions for merging human and natural images, the poet moves towards theological truths. The participles manifest the paradoxes of anthropocentric thought, showing it to be creative as well as naïve. In asking the face in the sky not to blink, she prays that it not to allow her to blink and cause it to disappear. The reciprocal images reflect a theological desire to connect man to the cosmos. But for mixed participles, Avison could not fuse impressions and abstractions with such provocative reciprocity.

If mixed participles help to approach theological issues, they also help to confront them. Take, for example, ". . . Person, or A Hymn on and to the Holy Ghost" (*D*, 147). In this poem, participles convey the paradox of identical difference in the Trinity. The Holy Ghost is "the self-effacing" whose other self has alone been "seen" by God. The Holy Spirit possesses perfect "self-knowing," "known" only to God the Father. The Spirit is "unseen"; his role is to be "seeing" only God and "loving / with him." The poet prays to the Spirit to allow the visible one of God, Christ, to intercede for her with him to guide her spirit, which has been "effaced" in "the known Light," and to let it be "released" in Christ from facelessness. Wherever the Spirit goes "unseen" and "unguessed," she wants to manifest Christ "visible" in her life. The participles demonstrate a theological strategy; they fuse performance with description, matching the two prepositions of the title. The involvement of the three persons of the Trinity, their distinct but complementary roles, and the free yet restricted power of the Holy Ghost require circular and riddling terms rather than a dogmatic formulation. Along with difficult pronoun reference and the ambivalence that makes "visible" both an adjectival complement and an adverb, the participles form a prayer to the Holy Ghost that implicitly defies regular syntax to address theological issues.

Her mixing of participles takes Avison beyond traditional concepts of grammatical agency. She does not view past and present or active and passive as irreconcilable opposites; participles help her avoid simple dualities. Take, for example, "Christmas: Anticipation" (*D*, 182–83). The poem begins at a Christmas-tree lot in which the "unlit needles" of the trees "waiting" for buyers whisper "another presence." It then depicts a histrionic young man whose "solitary / pacing" results from being "lost from his love"; he is "flesh-chilled" by a short separation. A "hope of holiness" makes his emotional blindness into an "aching." The poet then alludes to Zacharias, the childless priest of Luke 1, who, having served in the "appointed place," was rendered "dumb with unbelieving" until Elisabeth bore a son, the forerunner of Christ. Zacharias, "flame-touched," saw in the desert the "rustling" of grasshoppers, the "yielding" of honey, and the "starting" of a brook. In the last stanza, the buyers are "waiting" for material things, the young man moves purposelessly in and out of the bright and "fading" light, but an old man, the type of Zacharias who through the centuries has been "dazed," looks out with and towards joy, "rays his / dry-socketed eyes, dimming / still." The whispers in the "lopped" and "waiting" firs are "Down falling."

The buyers are dead to symbolic meaning, but the trees have spiritual intuition, the assonance of "whispers," "stir," and "firs" in the final lines imitating the trees' articulate awareness of Zacharias' presence. The alternating past and present participles allow us to compare the various agents. Buyers and lover are hollow in comparison with trees and old man. The trees, violated by conventional ritual, contact spiritual presence, and the old man embodies Zacharias because of his capacity to be surprised out of religious convention and into an intense desire for faith. There is a bond between the trees and the old man, since they intuit his double desire for belief towards and with joy. He creates seeing out of failing eyes from a trust in spiritual agency, which the double prepositions help convey. The participles reflect Avison's faith in the closeness of the subjective and objective, her wish to break down their duality. The ambiguous phrase "Down falling" is significant in this regard. It yields a physical sense: the whispers of the trees fall down. Yet the inverted adverb of the phrasal verb suggests a transitive meaning, that is, bringing about a downfall. The waiting of the trees, more spiritual than that of the humans, is also more threatening. Victims of commercial insensitivity, the trees symbolize the spiritual violence that befalls the type of Zacharias.

To similar effect, Avison challenges conventional dualities about nature in "And Around" (*D*, 184). In this poem, her alternating participles achieve a unique view of the cycle of the seasons.

> A tree its twigs up-ending
> November had bared:
> drenched in height, brisk with
> constellar seed-sprigs, thrusting

its ancient ranginess towards
the cold, the burning, spared
of leaf, sealed in, unbending.

Is the first clause inverted, or does it contain two ellipses? Has November bared a tree which has up-ending twigs, or is there a tree with up-ending twigs that November has bared? Since the adjectival phrases after the colon have "tree" as headword, the second parsing is more plausible. However, the qualifiers of the headword are in dynamic tension. This tension begins in the first clause: the tree has been stripped by the season, but is not simply passive since its twigs are "up-ending." The twigs point upwards. The tree is also active because of the double meaning of "up-ending." It is transitive as well as intransitive: the twigs can upend. The participle phrases maintain this ambivalence. The tree is passive because it has been drenched, spared, and sealed in; it is active because it is thrusting and unbending. There is tension within as well as between the past and present participles. The tree has been bared and spared: its loss of leaves is reductive and gracious. The tree is thrusting and unbending: it is assertive and resistant. The participles generate oppositions within oppositions: they separate and fuse active and passive meanings for our enlightenment.

The second stanza puts the tree into an ambiguous cosmic perspective by describing the earth "showering like a sparkler" and "shedding its growth." These participles are either parallel, or the second qualifies the noun of the first phrase. The earth, active as well as passive, is both a star and a tree. In this context, the tree's ambiguity is heightened: it is a barb riding tinily towards spring. The adverb "tinily," used oddly, as if size is manner, the pun on growth and weapon, and the metonymy involved in the barb's riding help us see how mixed participles avoid dualistic ideas of action, resist conventional metaphor, and then turn themselves into figures.

We shall end this survey of unpredictable syntax in *The Dumbfounding* by examining poems that show that Avison's participles mix metaphors to resist traditional figurative and schematic meaning. "Pace" (*D*, 105) contains a dialogue about "faintly clicking groves." Not caused by raindrops, the sound could be an effect of the pigeons' conversation, since the paths in the park are "nutmeg powdered and / bird-foot embroidered." With the capacity to make patterns, perhaps the birds cause the clicking. But the squirrels are responsible. These "beechnut-cracking" creatures click because, oblivious to the urban scene, they enjoy their hideaway, which, if "thin-wearing," is also "silk-fringed." The people in the park are "striped stippled sunfloating." Rather than listening, they are "letting the ear experience" the clicking.

The sensuous passivity of humans is stressed by participles that embed and mix metaphors. If we consider "nutmeg-powdered," we see the dust on the paths is both powder and nutmeg. By saying the birds have powdered the paths with nutmeg, the participle joins metaphor to metaphor in a personification. In "birdfoot-embroidered," we have the incongruous double figure of birds embroidering paths with their feet. The personification of the squirrels is also incongruous. Behaving with human complacency as they crack nuts, they regard their trees as a luxurious retreat. The figures de-personifying the humans are mixed. If people have the coloration of fish, they float not in water but in sunlight. Heightening the artificiality of metaphors by compounding them, the participles invite us to see the syntax underlying figurative meaning and to recognize through it unusual aspects of being.

Displacement of schemes by participles is equally exemplified in "The Store Seeds" (*D*, 124).

THE STORE SEEDS

The seeds   sorted in bins
clean   strange   and plain
under sagging tarpaulins
sifted   several   fine

shifting as the scoop tilts
or the bins are sloped
walled off from loams   rain silt
the darkness that corrupts

in grocery shoals here
or in paper parcelled
for water   pot   and fire
or cupboarded   dry bottled:

the seeds that lie   go
down   go under   go in

go on.   However slow
the   encompassing.

In this poem, triplings are upset. Let us consider the syntactic relations of the two sets of adjectives in the first stanza.

The first set of adjectives could refer to seeds or to bins. The apposition is unclear because of the interposing participle "sorted." Although the set of adjectives in the fourth line is remote from its headword, we know it refers to seeds because of the syntactic and semantic force of the participle "sifted." If the first adjectives refer to bins, we have an apposition within an apposition. The appositive lines are parallel in form but not in function, one qualifying a noun in an embedded adjectival clause and the other referring to the headword after being delayed by embedded adjectival and adverbal clauses. The order and simplicity of the stanza is undermined further by collocation. Since there is little cumulative order in each set, we wonder whether any of the adjectives work like adverbs. Does "clean" refer to "sorted" or "bins"? The sets of adjectives, though referring to order, do not form schemes; they are disordered.

Participles also interrupt schemes in the second stanza. A present participle governing two adverb clauses is balanced by a past participle governing three prepositional phrases. Both participle phrases are in apposition to seeds. Disjunction operates in the coordinate adverb clauses; they are unbalanced because one has an active and intransitive verb and the other a passive transitive. Moreover, the phrases governed by the past participle have distinct rather than parallel grammar. In the third stanza, the triplings that describe the packaging of the seeds are not real triplings because the participles, on the surface offering single categories, actually propose compounded ones. The seeds may be in shoals, parcels, and bottles, but the expressions, "grocery shoals," "paper parcelled," and "cupboarded dry bottled" use syntax so that we cannot conceive of seeds and containers as determinate. Besides impeding pattern, the unpredictable grammar heightens metaphorical irony. If the seeds are protected from the soil and moisture that would corrupt them and cause them to grow, they yet behave as if they are shoals. The seeds have an elemental motion that resists the order of humans. Their "encompassing" means they possess a comprehensive, directional capacity ensuring their fertility. Participles break pattern and render imagery ironical because Avison wants to challenge human classification.

In "Branches" (*D*, 140–41), patterns broken by participles lead from human to theological classifications. In the first stanza, "diseased" elms are "lashing" the "hollowing" vaults of air and pale selves stare "echoing" into mirrors. The participles image simultaneous processes and synaesthesia. In complaining to the Light that blinded Saul that the "whistling sunset" has a "disheartened shine," the poet links quality of synaesthesia to spiritual energy: the light makes a human noise but is heartless. This paradoxical image of the sunset – it is personified and de-personified – suggests why contemporary prayer is not real. Praying voices lack wholeheartedness; "craving" adults make the sound of a "squalling" child.

To support the belief that voice is integral to the light of prayer and that prayer sustains the world, Avison contrasts King David, the divine musician whose prayer kept seeds "splitting" and seas "rolling," with her contemporaries, who value darkness as a drug and flowers as funeral incense. Their ritual is morbid; it is a "silenced care." Their silence is different from Christ's; when taunted by the soldiers, he kept quiet from awareness of their spiritual need. Contemporary silence is not spiritual; it is a "blanking," a featureless, negative, obliterating whiteness. The noise of the elms is a wordlessness more positive than blanking. Contemporary people are silent because they do not listen; their words are formulaic because they disregard multiple meaning. Ignoring the storm, they expect to come directly to light: they are "crowding for light." They "make light of" the heart's bitterness, wishing simply to "light on" the Light that blinded Saul. They will not realize Christ died only once and that he hangs the "cherried heart of love" on the "charring bough" of the world, inviting us to see fruit in destruction, light in darkness. Here the participles contain the imagination necessary to prayer; they attack idiomatic formulae.

The participles in "The Word" (*D*, 150–51) also complicate schemes and heighten linguistic awareness for theological purposes. Mindful of Christ's invitation to follow him, "*Forsaking all*," the poet hesitates because she is "fallen in the / ashheaps of my / false-making, burnt-out self and in the / hosed-down rubble" of what her anger destroyed. She knows Christ offers a "skyward Love" that makes the universe throb with "rivering fire"; she knows the elemental, transcendental paradox of the invitation. Her sense of the invitation is acute because Christ's use of "forsaking" derives from his eternal "closing" on the word when he asked the Father why he had forsaken him. Christ's use of the word represented the "unsealing" of day from profoundest darkness; it indicated he is the Word and reflects his "being all-out, and / meaning it." This conjunction of participle and idiom testifies how the Word transforms human idiom. He "put" everything "on the line" humans wanted to draw around him in their desire merely for a superior human. Intent upon making man's need for him a "head over heels / yielding," Christ "crossed" and still "cross[es] out" that line. He traverses and erases the line with the cross; the Logos, he puts reference into idiom and tautology. As the poem progresses, the poet gets closer to accepting the invitation, upholding Christ's unpredictable speech and showing he is the Logos because he remotivates ordinary language. The poet's use of language imitates the Logos, allowing theological meditation to overcome human passion.

"Searching and Sounding" (*D*, 154–56) fittingly ends this survey of syntactic irregularity in *The Dumbfounding*. The pun on sounding in the title is a common motif; it signals the struggle to establish theological reference in ordinary language. Throughout this poem, participles expose dualities. At the beginning, Avison describes the sky in horticultural terms. Its "tangled / shining" is a "slope-field" the colour of "heaped up pea-vines, in milk-hidden / tendrils." The light might also be the shadow of a more distant light, if man could feed on it without glutting himself. The double view of light reveals a split attitude towards figurative language: if metaphors bring the sky to earth, they cannot reach the light behind light. The poet experiences a similar split in looking for Christ; she searches for him because he knows the "melding and the forming" of the heart able to feed on far light. But, inaccessible to traditional contemplation, "Gethsemane's grass, perfumed with prayer," he is found in a slum rooming-house "seeking to cool the grey-stubbled cheek / and the filth-choked throat" and "failing." The opposition of present and past participles evokes Christ's problematic struggle to transform human misery. Wanting to escape the reality Christ enters, the poet runs impulsively to the "blinding blue" of the lovely but "wasting / morning." She knows it is only with Christ that she can reach light and possess eyes free of "weeping." Not unsympathetic to the down-and-out people she visits as a social worker, she is unwilling to sound Christ in them. Ironically, she runs from him, wanting human comfort. Unpredictably, the "sunlight is sundered by cloud-mass." An inversion of the usual notion of sunlight piercing clouds, this expression is also odd because of the phonetic repetition of "sun," which suggests the light behind light is active and accessible after all. Thinking to lose herself in the blinding but wasting natural elements, she finds that they have suffered a surprising change. Yet, if this change prevents her from an easy identification with the natural elements, it helps her to reconsider them.

But she cannot easily overcome perverse self-destructiveness: her "bricked-in ovens smoulder." Disturbed that Christ has sounded a music around her that will banish tears if she sounds the wells of weeping with his music, she is "spent," content to be kept close "into sleeping" by having Christ touch her with the little light she can bear. Because of this confession, the beautiful light of daybreak becomes Golgotha, a place of "tumbled skeletons" of hills "clothed" in forests, a place of "baked stone" and "howling among the tombs." Having learned to see nature doubly, to relate the "budding" of the morning to the place where Christ began his descent on the beach "ground by sea-slimed teeth," she accepts the truth that Christ's "Reaching" with perfect Light needed no signs or emblems. It was all newness and "*all* being"; it needed "no further making." Christ's being resists the "ravening shore." But, on her "gull-blanched cliffs," the poet fearfully prays to have her fragmented being gathered for the "all-swallowing moment."

From regarding the sky as a pictorial retreat to viewing the landscape as the scene of the apocalypse, from seeing herself as spiritual to recognizing in herself an evasive flight from Christ's being in other humans, the poet spans a range of dualities in this poem. She learns, however, to appreciate the problematics of faith, to recognize that the conflict between escapism and absorption must be resolved through prayer. By the end, the participle oppositions suggest she has managed to integrate the local with the absolute, being with nothingness. The participles, dramatizing the fragmentation and coherence Christ represents, reveal the poet with a theological rather than figurative view of the world. Sensing that Christ is beyond imagery, she realizes that figurative meaning should derive from him.

sunblue is an advance over the earlier volume because its grammar is more unpredictable and because the theological effects it wins from syntax are more profound. Syntactic oppositions still provide prominent motifs, but participles collocate more provocatively. As motifs, they more often tie poems together, and the tensions they afford between ellipsis and tautology are better exploited. The poems in *sunblue*, since they tend to be more impersonal than those in *The Dumbfounding*, are less indebted to the traditional modes of confessional poetry. Consequently, a syntactic examination of the later volume shows parsing to be even more essential to the discovery of its theological ideas.

In exploring the syntactic unpredictability of *sunblue*, we shall focus on grammar's cumulative impact on literary and theological figures. But, before beginning, we should point out the volume's three movements. The first one deals with external nature; its poems stress the visual, using impressions to reconceive the boundaries of worldly reality. The second treats biblical topics by questioning traditional interpretive categories. Merging these aims, the last defines the holiness of the world. The final group of poems returns to the visual emphasis of the first movement, but with theological implications that reveal the nature of the sacramental.

In the first poem, "SKETCH: Thaws" (*s*, 9), the collocation "melting bright," which qualifies the compound noun in the clause "snowflow / nearly-April releases," fuses physical and visual effects, besides repeating the idea of flow. Our bearings in the phenomenal world are also disturbed by the third main clause: "Swepth of suncoursing sky / steeps us in / salmon-stream / crop-green / rhubarb-coloured shrub-tips." We do not expect "suncoursing" because it suggests the sky runs through the sun. If we hold on to the common sense position that the sun courses the sky, we must parse the compound participle not as an adjective but as a transformed adverbal clause. The coined headword "swepth," a compound of sweep and depth, together with the ambivalent verb "steeps," supports the unpredictable participle because of their reference to both space and water. The sky soaks us and makes us look up at it steeply. Throughout *sunblue*, Avison prevents us from assuming that air is our element: air and sky are often water and sea. The transposition in the volume title, from sky blue to "sunblue," warns us that our cosmic and elemental sense is to be exercised. Returning to the poem, we notice that the participle phrase "heaped tumbling," referring to the lilacs for which everything, as distinct from everyone, waits, tests our sense of time. The present participle is an adverb qualifying the future reference of the past participle: the lilacs will be tumblingly heaped. Without analyzing the coinage that allows Avison to say "darkdown" rather than sundown and to use "Needles" and "shells" as verbs describing the action of frost, we can say this first poem, while seeming to deal with external, physical reality, uses grammar unpredictably to defy complacency about the world. Its odd syntax challenges us to see that, in understanding its rules, we must understand the world freshly. In its reference to the world, it obliges us to reconceive the rules of grammar.

"SKETCH: Overcast Monday" (*s*, 11) questions the physical world in ways suggested by the pun in the title. Overcast means cloudy, but also thrown over. The poem challenges our sense of natural environment and daily routine. The air is "earth-soakt." The element we breathe is wet with soil. This fusion of three elements, a double metaphor, has a richness that contrasts with "undeathful technicalities," the routine matters that fill our lives and hurt us because they deny our mortality. Strangely, the overcast day, which makes the light seem that of the sea floor, produces an oil for clicking mechanisms. Not only is elemental reality questioned, so is figurative understanding. Can oil be produced and lubricate machines under water, when it floats on the surface? To renew our awareness of reality, the poet questions the figurative sense by which we imagine the world.

The early poems in *sunblue*, besides probing our material and figurative sense, suggest that insight can be simple, that simple actions can appropriate the world. If men divide themselves from one another and from their own impulses in the construction of the urban environment, themes explored in "SKETCH: A work gang on Sherbourne and Queen, across from a free hostel for men" (*s*, 12), the man-made world can be repossessed. Thus in "SKETCH: Cement worker on a hot day" (*s*, 13), the worker wrenches the hydrant open to wash off the "oils of sun." He possesses the hydrant, to the poet's surprise, and makes it flow. The boundaries between the mechanical and human can and must be broken down. That is why Avison continually fuses the natural and the man-made. Hence, pasture is "mattressed" and sunlight "butterfat" (*s*, 14). The participle involves a visual sense of pressed grass, and the noun foreshortens by metonymy: grass looks as if it could be used for a mattress, and sunlight, falling on grass eaten by milch cows, produces butterfat. The expansive function of these ellipses emphasizes the congruence of natural and mechanical reality.

Matching Avison's impulse to knock down the barriers between man and the world is her wish to describe colours and the different properties of light. Grass is "bronze and tassel-tawny," and brush may burn with "orange flame and lilac smoke" (*s*, 15). Springtime leaflessness suggests "violet batik" and air can be "wintergreen" (*s*, 17). Variety of colour evokes the indeterminateness of things. Hence, grass is bronze. Colour words are notorious for incongruous material and metaphorical extensions. Avison relies on this to extend point of view. By so bringing categorical confusion to seeing, she justifies visual speculation and synaesthesia; she can talk about invisible things, such as underground badgers with sleek foreheads (*s*, 16), and stress that unusual visual conditions make hearing more acute (*s*, 17).

Participles are instrumental to these goals. Consider the first stanza of "The Seven Birds (College Street at Bathurst): SKETCH."

> Storm-heaped west, wash-soaked with
> dayspill. Light's combers
> broken, suds-streaming
> darkwards and stormwards:
>
> (*s*, 18)

The first modifying participle phrase employs a natural metaphor; the first qualifying one blends domestic and natural metaphors. The west, heaped up with storm clouds, is soaked with the wash of day spill. The light of dawn is given domestic and liquid associations, whereas the rain-producing west has physical and solid ones. The past participle qualifying the word "combers" brings back a natural metaphor of waves breaking on a beach. But the present participle form qualifying the whole phrase reverts to the domestic, wash-day metaphor. The opposition between modification and qualification and between past and present forms makes the clashing metaphors more provocative; the figurative meaning, inviting us to work out the relation of natural elements and to reconceive the boundaries between natural and mental reality, is dependent upon participle grammar. Participles in "SKETCH: End of a day: OR, I as a blurry" (*s*, 19) effect similar goals through metaphorical conflict. The poet finds "autumn storeyed" when she goes "bundling home" like a groundhog. The outside possesses the structure of a building; the human moves with animal scurrying. The natural house is mysterious. Its "cloud-thatch" is "torn," its roof replaced by the "disappearing clear." Retreating indoors, the poet hopes for creatureliness to disinhabit the "layered beauty / flowing" outside. The paradox of nature's accommodation of man is heightened by the tension between the modifying "layered" and the qualifying "flowing."

In this last poem, participle tensions establish paradoxes. The poet takes on an ironical confessional mode; the tension between natural and domestic metaphors she heightens in order to dramatize spiritual timidity. The clash of participles in "Stone's Secret" (*s*, 21–22) encourages spiritual involvement with the physical realm partly because the poem deals with the relation of grammar to the world. The poet describes an otter-smooth stone under "rolling" water "stilled" among "frozen" hills and "unbreathed" blizzards. The stone lies at the centre of involved processes. Scientists use "dotting signals" to track the paths of stars made of the same cosmic stuff. But stone is "inaccessible / to grammar's language." The Bible has promised peace like a "flowing" river, but there are those who "will / wondering wait" for the stone to speak, since they prefer phenomenological imagery to biblical metaphor, choosing to concentrate on stone rather than river. If participles create the figure of the stone in terms antithetical to biblical metaphor, they also support the concept of wise passivity before the phenomenal world. "Hid Life" (*s*, 23) also employs participles to encourage spiritual interpretation of material reality. This abstract pictorial poem, significantly not entitled "still life," describes "frozen" apples of a "wizzening red" hanging against a "crooked woodenness." Although the fruit is "frost-bruised," its seeds are "up held" in a double sense that allows the poet to consider the weight of the fruit in her heart "a waiting." That the suspended seeds have their viability supported lets the poet give equal physical and immaterial sense to the gerund. Once again, participles afford us opportunity to remotivate abstract words in the face of material reality without resorting to allegory.

Avison's use of participles to go beyond conventional material imagery is also evident in "Released Flow" (*s*, 24). The participle forms in the title and at end of the poem clash with such metaphors as "burning snow," "spiced air," "sunstriped maples," and "honeyed woodsmoke." The contrast between the sensuous richness of these participles and the abstractness of "all lookings-forth" that "Sunblue and bud and shoot wait to unlatch" is startling. The contrast stresses that spring, though a fulfillment, looks ahead into and waits for the future. In having nature employ a mechanical operation to prepare for the abstract future, Avison uses participles to emphasize how close the invisible extraordinary is to ordinary reality. Another instance of participles describing natural processes in complex metaphorical ways before designating non-factual existence occurs in "March Morning" (*s*, 25). Here, snowbanks are "Peaking wafering" and "stroked by the / rosey fingertips of young / tree shadows." The two present participles work against one another as well as against the past participle. We cannot be sure whether they are coordinate or whether one modifies the other: one means coming to a crest, the other becoming a thin layer. Difficult-to-visualise metaphors occur in the participle phrase, too, for the shadow of trees is likened to roses. By contrast, we have the metaphors of the "wondering" kid who is "breathing the / crocus-fresh breadwarm / Being" as "easy as breathing." The natural and domestic metaphors describing being are contained by the literal denotation and idiomatic force of "breathing." Syntactic contrasts in the tautology have figurative force: breathing being is as easy as breathing. Intransitive and transitive functions metaphorically merge into comment about re-imagining figurative ways of seeing the world.

We can appreciate how much Avison obliges us to re-imagine material reality when we consider poems in which water imagery is complicated by puns and irony. In "March" (*s*, 26), for example, the look of the sky "wakes," not just awaking in the springtime, but creating a wake because its look is "deepsea deepwarm." Although water imagery is appropriate to thawing, the season transforms the elements sacramentally: it produces "earth-loaf, sky-wine." Water loses figurative integrity because the ground is "all soaked in sunwash," the air "shampoos" the brook, and in the less gentle thaw of the polar regions the frothing water is "fleece." As an element, water is metaphor for light, is subsumed into the domestic metaphor figuring the wind's energy, and becomes materially transformed as part of the paradox about the thaw. In "Let Be" (*s*, 28), the multivalence of water imagery serves the theme of passivity before nature. An unseen mountain hidden by the mist needs to be balanced in its "no-sounding soundness" with the "ballast" of ordinary human noises. While this ballast makes the mountain a ship, that the mountain shoulders itself forward suggests it is human as well as marine. The water imagery is uncertain too because of the pun in "no-sounding." In "Water and Worship: an open-air service on the Gatineau River" (*s*, 29), the poet expresses two perspectives on water, the distant and the near. From afar, the water is "ripple-faceted" by the sun, and the "boat-braided river is / wind-riffled." The sun makes the water shine artificially like cut glass, and the boats ornament it. Close to, the water is less aesthetic; it is "self-gulping." Correspondingly, there are two views of the humans; one presents them as if the surface of water, the other as if its depths. Thus, the "all-creating stillness" of the "shining Lord" trembles on the unknowing, yearning, yielding lives of the worshippers, while within them are currents as from "released snow, rock- /sluiced, slow welling from / unexpected hidden springs." This interior water is contaminated by the salts of the earth, but divine love with its cut-glass glory shatters all less worthy glass. The water of humans is purified by God because the sound of his crystal breaks human reflection. The water imagery, instead of serving allegory, is complicated by the imagery of light. Far from baptismal ritual, the water imagery gathers sacramental value only through conflict with other imagery.

While Avison displaces traditional natural imagery, she often uses technical imagery unconventionally, as in "Contemplatives: OR, Internal Combustion" (*s*, 38) and "Technology is Spreading" (*s*, 39). In the former, the contemplatives race old cars noisily through deserted communities while everyone is asleep. The contemplatives sleep during the day, preparing to disturb the night. They withdraw from the "busying" world, "waiting out daylight-solitude." With their noise they are "spanging bullets of sound." They are deadly as they speed down "unseen" tracks. By contrast, the workers are split between mechanical regularity and sordid reality. At night, their offices are sealed, air-controlled, and night-hollowed; the place where they sleep is jumbled and unsealed. The windows are cranked half open and the blinds tap. In the latter poem, two men are plodding, one confiding to the other the desirability of sticking to one computer language. His buried and mixed metaphors are remotivated by machine memory, which proves to be witty about human language. With damaged linguistic sense, the two men pass on "unimpaired." They are not united, not a twosome. But mechanical memory is capable of making puns; it knows unsung words are to be noted.

In the last mentioned poems, Avison presents technical images with an amusing whimsy, her participles giving them a provocative ambivalence. She uses modern, technical imagery for more obvious theological aims in the second movement of *sunblue*, often making her participles deliberately idiomatic and anachronistic, as can be evidenced from the four poems (*s*, 45–48) that elaborate Christ's parable about the unjust steward who excused the full indebtedness of his master's debtors so that he would have people to fall back upon when fired. Avison scrutinizes Christ's commendation of the prudent steward. In the first poem, the steward puts his plan in motion when incapable of further "stonewalling" and Christ, understanding business ethics, praises such "feathering" of the nest. The idiomatic and anachronistic participles stress the unconventional, daring aspects of Christ's parable and afford scope for punning elaborations of the parable. Hence, Christ knew that a "closed" world of rascals "closes in" master and servants with what they choose. The second poem questions the steward's view, generalizing about the false confidence people feel in their accounting; almost convinced they have "made it, had it made," they still fiddle the final ledgers so "made friends" will provide for them. The repetition of the past participle undercuts the rationalization. In the third poem, Avison generalizes the fable by saying that, though people are taught and furnished richly, they are indebted because they do not acknowledge in their conduct that they owe anything to anybody: they are "in debt" because they are not "living it out." Rationalizing their debts, people "lower the boom" on those with lesser debts; they "duck the blame," wasting goods in trust. The fourth poem re-defines the trusts: "Brimming hours of days," "the powers / in one physique burning," "brimming life-ful-ness." The steward used his trusts improperly, not wastefully; he employed all he had for those who would be able to provide. By contrast, Christ proved trustworthy; he did not waste a word. "Stripped bare to give, He then / entrusts, awarded all as His possession." These paradoxes could not wield theological force, did not the participles present worldly morality in idiomatic and technical imagery.

In the "Embezzler" poems, Avison emphasizes the gap between the creative morality of Christ's fable and the imperatives he embodies. Christ rendered the fable eternally effective, yet he represents a superior morality. The parable does not prefigure Christ.[5] Avison further questions typology and figure in "For the Murderous: The Beginning of Time" (*s*, 49). After contrasting Cain, who offered grain and grapes to God, with Abel, who sacrificed a lamb from his flock, Avison sees the paschal lamb, before the "slaying," making "new the wine / and broken bread." The odd syntax offsetting the contrast between Cain and Abel suggests Christ's making of the elements of the sacrament is outside time and yet remakes time. Cain does not make bread or wine; he offers the produce. Bread and wine are truly made long after Cain's murder of

Abel, which starts time. But, although his envy at the successful offering of the sacrificial lamb caused Cain to kill Abel, Abel is no type of Christ, no figure for the paschal lamb. Christ made wine and bread new through sacramental acts rather than through sacrifice. Avison uses gaps in reference and transition afforded by participles to question figurative meanings. Just as she employs grammar to assail figures of speech, she subverts the sense of *figure* important to traditional theology.

Avison questions traditional typology from a conviction that figures of speech and the idea of figure itself derive partly from performative aspects of language. Performative utterances, such as oaths and pledges, signal a change in material circumstance. When they are uttered, part of their meaning is that the reality of the world has changed. At the same time, the ritual use of such utterances shows that figurative meaning, while it changes history, perpetually recurs and is not time-bound. It is this linguistic perspective on figurative meaning that is apparent in "All Out; OR, Oblation" (*s*, 50), where she pictures biblical desert dwellers offering "throat-laving / living / water" in a bowl "shining" and "uplifted" to God. Their sacrifice cannot be comprehended. The poet knows she must learn to expect to pour out water in order to know what it means. Ritual performance is discovery. In "Dryness and Scorch of Ahab's Evil Rule" (*s*, 51), she emphasizes that the scavenging raven was God's messenger to Elijah. Only in the context of the lowest of creatures serving God are the "unfailing meal and oil" permanently enduring signs, prefiguring the bread and drink of Christ. Since they are "lit towards" Christ, the figures consecrate a past leading towards Christ's past time, which is also to come. The relation of past, present, and future, embedded in the past-participle phrase, images Avison's syntactic questioning of traditional conceptions about prefiguring.

Avison redefines typology because she is convinced that material reality is sacramental. This conviction explains why, rather than incorporate figures into allegorical stories, she converts the referential density and ambiguity of participles into figures. She employs unpredictable grammar to obstruct straightforward narrative and unmixed metaphor in order to bring about a figurative meaning that is truly spiritual. This is evident in "The Circuit" (*s*, 55). In this poem, Christ's circuit, his journey from heaven to earth and back to heaven again, is also an electric circuit because God is the Father of Lights and because, while Christ does not fall short in glory, his circuit is not and does not short. Syntactic ambiguity and puns obviate steady metaphorical exegesis: Christ's circuit is indistinguishably elemental and theological, inseparably ancient and modern. Thus, instead of effecting pictorial or narrative images, Avison prefers the imagery of participle compounds: Christ is "Being-in-Light." This is also evident in "The Bible to be Believed" (*s*, 56–57). The poem begins with the reciprocity of biblical language and God: "The word read by the living Word / sculptured its shaper's form." "The Word" is not exclusive; He cherishes all. Therefore, the Word goes beyond "old rites or emblem burial." To use figures is to bury meaning. The devil tempted Christ to a "covenanting song," to give in to the texts he meant and embodies. But Christ resisted, because to have become the figure of Himself would have meant surrendering to time. The Word would have entombed Him, had he subjected Himself to the figurative impulse. On the other hand,

> His final silencing endured
> has sealed the living word:
> now therefore He is voiceful, to be heard,
> free, and of all opening-out the Lord.
>
> (*s*, 57)

The final gerund, along with the syntactic oppositions between the other participle forms, shows that, for Avison, language is figurative in itself because sustained by the ultimate figure. For her, "all that means, is real," since it is willed only by One.

Our final paragraphs examine the third movement in *sunblue* to show how Avison joins her sense of material reality to her view of typology in the service of holiness. We will concentrate on endings of poems, for they best evidence figurative participles working to displace traditional metaphor and typology. At the end of "From a Public Library Window" (*s*, 62), "the Unchanging One / is, inexhaustibly, un-done." The negative past participle does not mean ruined, as "inexhaustibly" helps us to see. Rather it means unmade, reminding us that God is uncreated. If he had been created, He could not be unchanging. The present- and past-participle forms are not simply tautologous; in their syntactic opposition, they figure absolute theological truth.

At the end of "The Effortless Point," we also meet a negative gerund:

Moving into sky
or stilled under it
we are in the becoming
moved: let wisdom learn
unnoticing in this.

(*s*, 63)

The alternation of past- and present-participle forms leads to their fusion. Agency and passivity are opposed, then merged. There is profound figurative ambivalence in "moved" and "unnoticing." The former is both passive past participle and adjectival complement: people must move in order to become. But, as they grow, they are changed emotionally. The latter is a gerund, governed by "learn" and qualifier of "wisdom": wisdom must learn not to perceive, for it learns by being caught up in paradox. What the participles figure is a wise passivity that frees itself from the common sense relation of perception and moral imperative. Not surprisingly, then, at the end of "Oughtiness Ousted" (*s*, 64), Avison employs an unusual past-participle gerund to stress the need to ban traditional moral imperatives. She dismisses her "inventeds," this term conveying a morality dead to divine presence.

At the end of "Contest" (*s*, 66), there is an inversion of the biblical expression "then shall I know, even as also I am known" (1 Cor. 13:12): "until as we are known we know." The inverted syntax is a figure for the human tendency to see the second Adam in the first. The inversion attacks the rationalization entailed in traditional typology: it draws a distinction between Christ's morality, his choosing to know humanity but to behave "otherwise," and the human impulse to subordinate divine knowledge to conduct. The syntactic inversion shows that Christ inverts what men do. Adam is not the type of Christ. Rather, Christ upsets Adam and men. By contrast, the syntax in "On Goodbye" (*s*, 68) establishes an abstract typology. The poet listens to temporal distance, "learning not-being" so "that which is not may be." She imitates the "blank hourlessness" of old people who, staring at their past, bless it. By seeing her own past through abstract images, the poet reveals that, if types do not effect faith, negative participles achieve a faithful unpredictability. They are a new form of figure. While in "As Though" (*s*, 70) the last lines embody metaphors in finite verbs, participles still inform the metaphors. The earth is likened both to a seed about to split with "rotting" towards the inconceivable, "knowing no purposing," and to a comber searching for shells, arched against "waveness." These opposing similes are displaced by the abstract paradox that "becomings are then in now," are unbearable unless suffered. This figure underlies the syntax of the metaphorical antithesis that hope stirs rather than surges, is like a seed and not a wave. In "Scar-face" (*s*, 72), the sea imagery, at first allegorical, ends up more abstract because of a participle figure. The scarred man "prows" his life through the "flow and wash" of other people's looks. His face is good because it is a "looking-out-from." The marine imagery is sustained and transformed by the compound gerund that conveys the man's openness to being. This openness is also recommended in "Neighbours?" (*s*, 75). Here Avison warns against traditional contemplation as the "distancing" of self and object. She forthrightly condemns typological interpretation as too judgemental. People must be open to being because not until the apocalypse will typology be significant; the interpretation of a "found identity" is given only to "recovered innocence."

The problems of anthropocentric contemplation are recurrent themes of the final poems of *sunblue*. In "Kahoutek" (*s*, 90), for instance, the poet struggles to regard the comet from the right perspective. After addressing it personally, she recognizes that its origins are distant and inappropriable. Soundlessly hollowing past the world, it comes from "unlanguaged precincts." She teaches herself to see its impersonal otherness. In "Slow Advent" (*s*, 93), Avison resists her figurative impulse; she questions her "anticipating sense" when thinking of Christ not as a babe but as "the flint-set-faced / ready-for-gallows One" whose place is her "being to be / His." The syntactic oppositions in these participles heighten the contrast between the eternal and the temporal, the past and the future. The poem ends impersonally because it stresses that Christ's omnipresence requires people to think of themselves in spatial terms. Christ is everywhere; it is not just that he is in people. In "Then" (*s*, 98), Avison also warns about the theological impossibility of modelling spiritual life on figurative thought, in this case apocalyptic archetypes. She insists on the huge gap between apocalyptic and contemporary realities. Although the "all-things-upgathering bliss" will prevent "acute, prefiguring moments / of our leaf-flickered day" from losing their poignancy, prefiguring moments are ineffective now. Christ is the hope for figurative meaning, and he is a real prophetic baby who must be worshipped as such. He is "all-cherishing, the unsourced, / the never fully celebrated/ well-spring of That

Day." As eternal love, Christ is the source of figure in the apocalypse, but, since He can never be praised too much, men should praise Him rather than treat Him as a figure. For this reason, in "Creative Hour" (*s*, 99), Avison criticizes the "evasive 'maker'-metaphor." Rejecting the analogy of artist and God, she insists that our "real common lot" exposes the evasiveness of the metaphor and leads "stumbling" back to what it promised to evade. The only maker is the unpretentious Christ.[6]

For Avison, poetry that relies on aesthetic and exegetical traditions without discovering theology in material reality and human nature is superficial. In "Bereaved" (*s*, 105), she laments how insensitive people are to ordinary language, how heartless they are when it comes to seeing speech as a spiritual resource. The "barbarous tongue" of children, who embody the truth of the Tower of Babel, is "lost on / that unmirroring, immured, / that thumping thing, / the heavy adult heart." By contrast, the child in "SKETCH: Child in Subway" (*s*, 104), though bombarded by the urban scene, is essentially engaged with material reality. He goes "wherever his day's lifetime may / go in its faithful unpredictability." His spiritual intuition responds to the paradoxes of time. The paradox of the ancient language of children and their suitability to represent and transcend the curse of fragmented natural language are surprising figures of theological significance, which Avison's syntax constantly embeds in her poetry. This odd syntax brings into being the figurative and theological meaning of her poetry; it testifies to her trust that ordinary language can be made to encounter the sacramental holiness of creation, the faithful unpredictability of life.

NOTES

[1] Throughout this essay, I am indebted to Graham Dunstan Martin, *Language Truth And Poetry: Notes towards a Philosophy of Literature* (Edinburgh: Edinburgh Univ. Press, 1975), for a brilliant synthesis of the nature and value of syntax. The following studies, because of their emphasis on grammar and poetry, also proved useful: Winifred Nowottny, *The Language Poets Use* (London: Univ. of London, The Athlone Press, 1965); Geoffrey N. Leech, *A Linguistic Guide to English Poetry* (London: Longmans, Green, and Co., 1969); Victor Erlich, "Roman Jakobson: Grammar of Poetry and Poetry of Grammar," in *Approaches to Poetics*, ed. Seymour Chatman (New York: Columbia Univ. Press, 1973); and

Gerald L. Bruns, *Modern Poetry and the Idea of Language* (New Haven: Yale Univ. Press, 1974). I have relied for syntactic terms on Barbara M. H. Strang, *Modern English Structure* (London: Edward Arnold Publishers Ltd., 1962), and for ideas about the relation of syntax and style on Virginia Tufte, *Grammar as Style* (New York: Holt, Rinehart and Winston, Inc., 1971) and G. W. Turner, *Stylistics* (Harmondsworth, Eng.: Penguin, 1973). David Crystal, *Linguistics, Language and Religion* (New York: Hawthorne Books, 1965), is essential reading for the relation between language and theology.

[2] Lawrence M. Jones, "A Core of Brilliance: Margaret Avison's Achievement," *Canadian Literature*, No. 38 (Autumn 1968), p. 53, makes this point about the person of Christ, though from a different perspective.

[3] For an interesting reading of how this excerpt fits into the whole poem, see Ernest Redekop, *Margaret Avison* (Toronto: Copp Clark, 1970), pp. 133–40.

[4] Milton Wilson, "The Poetry of Margaret Avison," *Canadian Literature*, No. 2 (Autumn 1959), pp. 47–58, gives an excellent account of the poet's concern to move from perception to conception.

[5] In his fine essay, "sun/Son light/Light: Avison's Elemental *Sunblue*," *Canadian Poetry*, No. 7 (Fall/Winter 1980), pp. 21–37, Ernest Redekop suggests that Avison works within traditional typology. My view is different, informed as it is by the works of Nathan A. Scott. See, in particular, *The Wild Prayer of Longing: Poetry and the Sacred* (New Haven: Yale Univ. Press, 1971), chapter one, "The Decline of the Figural Imagination," and chapter two, "The Sacramental Vision" for compelling studies of the concept of *figura*.

[6] See George Bowering, "Avison's Imitation of Christ the Artist," *Canadian Literature*, No. 54 (Autumn 1972), pp. 56–69. This important essay refuses to allow claims for Avison's religion to displace those made for her art. My emphasis on the poet's attack upon figure and typology does not contradict Bowering's main point.

Sketching

bpNICHOL

> The action of the verb *"sketch"*; to draw the outline or prominent features of (a picture, figure, etc.), esp. as preliminary or preparatory to further development; to make a sketch or rough draught of (something); to draw or paint in this matter.

IN ONE OF MANY CONVERSATIONS i had with Margaret Avison circa 1965 when i worked at the U of T Library shelving books and she was working on a thesis project (comparing, as i recall, translations of Homer [Pound's etc.]) she made the remark that she wished, as a writer, to have the kind of freedom to sketch that painters had, i.e., to not always have to make a "complete" composition. There was an implication here too that not everything that is a sketch necessarily becomes a larger composition; and, as i have pointed out elsewhere, it was Margaret who gave me the title for an early sound poem of mine — "NOT WHAT THE SIREN SANG BUT WHAT THE FRAG MENT" — one of those beautiful, witty, and eventually highly influential asides she used to make to me. Now i put those thots together into one sentence in order to make the point that what she was dealing with in part was a theory of knowing, that knowledge is in itself fragmentary, that we are lured onto the rocks *not* by what the siren sang but by what the frag meant, the few scraps that come down to us — Homering pigeons. We can take this further into our relation to the divine, what we know of the metaphysics of it all. And that, of course, is exactly what happens in her work, in the move from *Winter Sun* thru *The Dumbfounding* into *sunblue*.

I want to focus mainly on the pieces in *sunblue* which include the word "SKETCH" in the title (thirteen in all) but it's worth stopping first to look at that movement in Avison's titling because it does relate to what we're already talking about. Considered purely as themselves (i.e., without reference to what they reference or encompass in terms of groups of poems), we see that movement from a white cold light (light but no heat and hence wintery, minus the green and growing world) thru the moment of recognition (the dumbfounding and hence founding but in an absence of words [dumb]) into that lovely pairing "sunblue" (all lowercase [as opposed to the all caps titling of the words "SKETCH" and "OR" [and i want to make a point of that because she is making a point of that – the definite title is presented less definitely than those two words of indefiniteness "SKETCH" and "OR"]]), evoking the child's drawing of the yellow sun in the blue sky (in which, when i used to draw as a kid, there was always an overlap between the sky and the sun creating a green nimbus, a "sunblue"), a return to a changed notion of the light. In the titling we see an imaging of the spiritual rebirth pointed to in many of the poems. And the term that stays and is changed is "sun."

Xsun / y / sunZ*

The sun no longer closes, it opens, is changed in language, moves from isOLation to being part of a larger cosmos/wordworld/field. And this includes a dumb founding, a rebeginning in not knowing,** a changed notion, therefore, of what knowledge is. We can see this clearly in the two poems that end *sunblue*, one titled "SKETCH: Child in Subway" (*s*, 104) and the other titled "Bereaved" (*s*, 105)***: the first, a quick image of a child hurrying

---

* I've chosen "Y" deliberately here because of its religious *and* algebraic connotations.

** If i am "sunblue" i am green i.e. innocent, in a state of not knowing.

*** There is, of course, another set of referents pointed to, but i'm being selective. And what i'm saying isn't negated by them.

down the subway stairs, hands clutched in his parents', rushing towards and into a waiting train, the poem's concluding couplet

> wherever his day's lifetime may
> go in its faithful unpredictability.

– celebrating the child's differing sense of time ("day's lifetime") but indexing as well the faithfulness of flux, the way in which knowing is undercut by the very unpredictability of the world and that that changeableness is always with us; the second in which the children's "red and blue and green" voices are described both as the Ur tongue and –

> . . . a barbarous tongue,   lost on
> that unmirroring, immured,
> that thumping thing,
>   the heavy adult heart.

The children's voices in that second poem are, in fact, as she goes on to say, "the immemorial chorus." We can see here that whole notion that knowledge is always beginning anew, that we exist not in a state of knowing but in a state of not knowing, that we are constantly being born again into the world not knowing (the child in "From Age to Age: Found Poem" (*s*, 102) is described as speaking "as in the morning day / when Adam names the animals." – and the title here, again, points to knowledge as "found," not possessed, part of the world of chance occurrences, the "faithful unpredictability"). Thus the SKETCH poems move from a noting of detail (as we expect in a sketch) – the lush description of "SKETCH: Thaws" (*s*, 9) with its image of imminent revelation ("everything waits for the / lilacs, heaped tumbling – and their warm / licorice perfume"); the precision of "SKETCH: Weekend" (*s*, 10); the invocational power of "SKETCH: Overcast Monday" (*s*, 11); the imagistically evoked parallelism of "SKETCH: A work gang on Sherbourne and Queen, across from a free hostel for men" (*s*, 12: the piece functions structurally like an extended haiku) – to the sudden change of perception in "SKETCH: Cement worker on a hot day" (*s*, 13) where the yellow hydrant which has been "Just a knob /shape" is transformed by the workman, and the poet exclaims:

Yes   yes   a hydrant
was always there but now
it's his, and flows.

The transformation is an interesting one precisely because something which was once perceived as solid and essentially immutable is now perceived as being in a state of flow, a source of, in that sense, flux. It is also important that the worker's activity is seen as a claiming activity ("it's his") yet not the usual kind of claiming activity, i.e., he does not "possess" it, it "flows." This notion, that the activity of claiming is not an activity which fixes, is repeated in "SKETCH: CNR London to Toronto (I)" (*s*, 15) where the described brushheap's eventual destruction is imagined and included in the sketch. Or similarly in "SKETCH: CNR London to Toronto (II)" (*s*, 16) and "SKETCH: From train window (Leamington to Windsor) in March" (*s*, 17) where what is sketched also includes the notion of what is not sketched, "*invisibility*" and "the hidden culvert."

In both titling and the assumptions and direct statements of the texts, a notion of knowing is constantly put forward, that all this (i.e. poetry and what we knowte down) is partial knowledge, rests on a dumb foundation that we cannot, finally, articulate (as noted in the titling of "SKETCH: End of a day: OR, I as a blurry" (*s*, 19: it's important to focus on that title since the first line of the poem makes "I as a blurry" part of a longer descriptive phrase, thus very deliberately altering its meaning, and the too hasty reader might judge the title phrase to be merely a partial quotation, which it is not – "I" is a concept not in focus, or perhaps composed of multiple elements that together blur it, or create a blur in their flickering back and forth, and "day" too is never a casually used word given the obvious meanings that "sun" has in Margaret Avison's work)). It is the very partialness of knowledge that's emphasized by the use of caps on SKETCH. SKETCHING is foregrounded and writing is backgrounded. The writer cannot *know* (and therefore present a *complete* composition); the writer can only sketch and leave the larger composition in other hands.

a sketch ketchs
amo meant

Toronto and Lethbridge
August 6th thru December 3rd 1984

The Word/word in Avison's Poetry

ERNEST REDEKOP

FOR AVISON, the central process in life as well as in art is Creation/ Redemption/Re-Creation, and she thinks of this cycle as an orthodox Christian as well as an imaginative poet. Thus an understanding of the full scope of her poetry arises out of an understanding of the Bible; the two are as inseparable as figure and ground, or, to use Yeats's expression, as dancer and dance. Critics of Avison's poetry have recognized this, at least to some extent; despite the fact that Pauline conversion and explicit religious devotion in poetry have been out of fashion with critics in general, many critics of Avison have dealt in one way or another with her religious belief and with its role in her poetry.[1] The focus has often been on Avison as a Christian poet, however, rather than on her indebtedness to the Bible, a subject still largely unexamined.

If we restrict ourselves, for the sake of brevity, to a consideration of her major work, the three collections of poetry — *Winter Sun* (1960), *The Dumbfounding* (1966), and *sunblue* (1978) — we discover a great number of allusions to, and quotations and themes from, both Old and New Testaments. In all three books, but especially in the last two, Avison devotes complete poems to Biblical texts; in *The Dumbfounding* and *sunblue*, the major events of the Gospels — Incarnation, Crucifixion, and Resurrection — figure prominently in her imagination.[2]

Since I examined Avison's *sunblue* in *Canadian Poetry* a few years ago, Northrop Frye's *The Great Code* has opened new possibilities for readers of her poetry. Some brief references to this book will help to analyze the relation of Avison's poetic language to her use of the Bible. Frye adapts Roman Jakobson's "distinction between the metaphorical and the metonymic," defining three major uses of the word "metonymic": first, as "a species of metaphor"; second, as "a mode of analogical thinking and writing"; and third, as a "descriptive" mode.[3] He distinguishes the "language of transcendence" from descriptive language. In the first phase, the metaphorical, "the unifying element of verbal expression is the 'god,' or personal nature-spirit"; this is not the level at which Avison is using language. In the second phase, "the conception of a transcendent 'God' moves into the center of the order of words," while in the third, "the criterion of reality is the source of sense experience in the order of nature, where 'God' is not to be found, and where 'gods' are no longer believed in," so that "the word 'God' becomes linguistically unfunctional . . ." (Frye, p. 15). Avison obviously belongs, in some way, to the second phase, and certainly not to the third.

The Bible, however, according to Frye, "does not really coincide with any of our three phases of language . . . . It is not metaphorical like poetry, though it is full of metaphor, and is as poetic as it can well be without actually being a work of literature. It does not use the transcendental language of abstraction and analogy, and its use of objective and descriptive language is incidental throughout." He suggests a fourth term, derived from Bultmann, but used somewhat differently: *kerygma*, or "proclamation," the "vehicle of what is traditionally called revelation . . ." (Frye, p. 29), a word especially associated with the Gospels.[4]

Avison's language, if I may use Frye's terms, is both metaphorical and *kerygmatic*, as an examination of her poetry bears out. Instead of surveying the entire canon, I wish to look rather closely at three poems, each expressing a different and characteristic relation between Avison and the Bible: "Not the Sweet Cicely of Gerardes Herball," "Jael's Part," and "The Bible to be Believed" (see Appendix 1). The first portrays an unredeemed world in an enigmatic and metaphorical language; the second gives an ironic view of a world only partly redeemed, an image of redemption seen "through a glass darkly," and an action that is metaphorical but not quite anagogic or *kerygmatic*; the third is both metaphor and *kerygma*, presenting a redeemed world that begins and ends with the *Logos*.

The three poems express three levels of her use of the Bible: the use of allusion in the first; the use of a specific biblical text in the second; and, in the third, commentary on the typological relation between Old and New Testaments and on the mystical relation between word as language and Word as Person.

The subtitle of "Not the Sweet Cicely of Gerardes Herball" – "(i.e., Oriental Myrrh, not English Myrrh)" – tells us in a roundabout way that Avison is writing, not of *myrrhis odorata*, but of *commiphora myrrha*; not about a plant described in a book published in 1597, but about a plant mentioned from time to time in a book not explicitly named, but which, even without reference to "a too-open Scripture" and "rabbinical gloss," we would recognize as the Bible. This negative subtitle is the first of a long series of negations in the poem. Thus the most important allusion in the poem, though not the first, is to the myrrh brought by the Magi to the Christ child, regarded from early Christian times as symbolizing the Passion of Christ. Along with gold, symbolizing royalty, and frankincense, symbolizing divinity, myrrh stands for the central meaning of the Incarnation: the Messianic role of Jesus as the redeemer.

The poem cannot be understood without this knowledge, which acts as the metaphysical ground for Avison's figure of myrrh hedges. As she so often does, Avison creates an apparently external landscape that is really a landscape of the soul, created out of words by an artistic *logos*, which, for her, is a minor and imperfect expression of the Divine *Logos*. This is a landscape of negation, of loss, of un-being, in which the most common words are the prefix *un-*, the suffix *-less*, the negative *no* and the words *cannot*, *bleached out*, *darkness*, *cancelled*, and *without*. The basic landscape is the "gardenless gardens," a paradoxical place almost sterile, without beetles, birds, weeds, or even fennel seeds, in which

> Mild animals with round unsmiling heads
> Cropped unprotested, unprotesting . . . .

Paradoxically, too, the myrrh imitates the shape of a ram's horn; line 5, with its phrase "in rams-horn thickets," has three words that are brought together in only one verse of the Bible, Genesis 22:13, which describes the finding of the ram that Abraham substitutes for his son Isaac, an event significant enough to Avison for it to be recalled in "The Bible to be Believed." The "unscrolling" (l. 7) of the myrrh suggests that it is the central hieroglyphic, the key to understanding, in a scroll whose ultimate message cannot be read:

> Time has bleached out the final characters
> of a too-open Scripture.

As in "Jael's Part," plants become words in a landscape-Scripture; here myrrh, the "rabbinical gloss," with its dark words, may be offering a cogent commentary on an arcane Scripture; it might even, given another context, "rightly divide the word of truth"; but who can read it? In this time, in this place, it serves only to create a hedged labyrinth within a nameless territory. No one but the poet-observer can possibly remember the fragrance of the perfumed women of *Esther* or of the lovers in the *Song of Solomon* or the gift of the Magi, and even memory cannot restore or resurrect a land caught in the mortality of time, a land caught in a past untouched by the force which, for Avison, continuously intersects and redeems time, which gives meaning to events: the Word.

The poem typifies the earlier work of Avison in its combination of detailed description – on one level, absolutely clear and transparent – with a profound dislocation arising out of the images. Where are these gardens? What are they? What is the "house abandoned"? What voyages were cancelled? This nameless territory we, the readers, must inhabit, this "falling," deserted desert somewhere east of Eden, is in the mind itself – the landscape of the *logos* as cabalistic arcanum or as a desolation much like that in Christ's diatribe against Jerusalem (Matt. 23:37–38). It is a landscape with a tomb but without resurrection, a landscape in which myrrh has lost its functions, a landscape without Messiah or Magi, an unredeemed landscape.

Two other poems in *Winter Sun* are commentaries on stories from the Old Testament: "Jael's Part" (*WS*, 76–77) and "Span" (*WS*, 78). These two are related, in that they deal with Israel in bondage, first to the Canaanites under Jabin and Sisera, and secondly to the Philistines in the time of Eli. Although both poems exemplify Avison's ability to make out of a Biblical story a sensuous and immediate reality, I shall here examine only the first.

"Jael's Part" is a complex poem commenting on the last eight verses of the ancient Song of Deborah and Barak. Operating as metaphor rather than as *kerygma*, the poem expresses ironies of an heroic act that for forty years gives peace to Israel. Although there are only two women in the poem itself – Jael and the mother of Sisera – the prophetic and charismatic powers of a third, Deborah, underlie the story and Song in the Book of Judges. Deborah calls for Barak to take ten thousand soldiers to fight against Sisera's and Jabin's army, with its nine hundred chariots of iron. When Barak refuses to go without her, she prophesies that "the journey that thou takest shall not be for thine honour; for the Lord shall sell Sisera into the hand of a woman" (Judges 4:9). In the battle that follows, Barak and his soldiers pursue the army to the river Kishon and destroy it to the last man; Sisera, however, escapes and comes to the tent of Jael, wife of Heber the Kenite, with whom Sisera is at peace. Jael gives him milk and butter and covers him with a rug so that he can go to sleep, agreeing to watch out for his enemies. The prose version of the rest of the story is told in one verse:

> Then Jael Heber's wife took a nail of the tent, and took a hammer in her hand, and went softly unto him, and smote the nail into his temples, and fastened it into the ground: for he was fast asleep and weary. So he died.
>
> (Judges 4:21)

The brutality of this act should be seen in the context of other acts that, in one way or another, save Israel from its enemies: like that of the left-handed Judge Ehud, a predecessor of Deborah's, in killing Eglon the Fat, King of Moab. Strapping a foot-and-a-half-long dagger to his right thigh, under his tunic, Ehud goes to Eglon, telling him that he has "a secret errand," a "message from God." He then thrusts the dagger into the belly of Eglon so deeply that "he could not draw the dagger out of his belly; and the dirt came out" (Judges 3:22). Ehud escapes, gathers his soldiers, and, with the same ruthlessness, cuts down the ten thousand men of Moab – "all lusty," as the writer says – so that not one escapes.

Jael's act is in this tradition of cunning deception and cold vengeance, but aside from describing the act itself, the writer of the story gives us no additional information. There is nothing in the whole story to indicate a motive, which is a device of descriptive, rather than *kerygmatic*, writing, and only the heroic view of her action is possible within Song and story. Had there been a Canaanite song about Sisera's defeat, it would surely have characterized Jael as one of the great betrayers of history. Avison, however, has yet another perspective, one that focuses not so much on the triumph of Jael over

Sisera as on the ironies that emerge as one contemplates the Biblical accounts. To understand these, we must remind ourselves of the original Song, whose tone leaves no room for doubts about the moral implications of Jael's act:

> Blessed above women shall Jael the wife of Heber the Kenite
>   be,
> blessed shall she be above women in the tent.
> He asked water, and she gave him milk;
> she brought forth butter in a lordly dish.
>
> (Judges 5:24–25)

Jael, it seems, improves on the counsel of the writer of Proverbs:

> If thine enemy be hungry, give him bread to eat;
> and if he be thirsty, give him water to drink:
> For thou shalt heap coals of fire upon his head,
> and the Lord shall reward thee.
>
> (Prov. 25:21–22)

But hammering, rather than heaping coals of fire, is more in Jael's line. Here Avison's poem becomes as interesting for what it leaves out as for what it adds to the original Song. Between the milk and butter and the image of a man who has had altogether too much of this world's pleasures come these lines from the Song of Deborah and Barak:

> She put her hand to the nail,
> and her right hand to the workman's hammer;
> and with the hammer she smote Sisera,
> she smote off his head,
> when she had pierced and stricken through his temples.
> At her feet he bowed, he fell, he lay down:
> at her feet he bowed, he fell:
> where he bowed, there he fell down dead.
>
> (Judges 5:26–27)

The point I am trying to make may be emphasized by quoting the Jerusalem Version:

> She stretched out her hand to seize the peg,

her right hand to seize the workman's mallet.

She struck Sisera, crushed his head,
pierced his temple and shattered it.
At her feet he tumbled, he fell, he lay;
at her feet he tumbled, he fell.
Where he tumbled, there he fell dead.

Keeping in mind that Jael had only one chance to drive the peg clear through Sisera's head and into the ground, this eleven-fold repetition of the act would seem rather excessive, were we judging descriptive writing. The very repetition, however, as Frye indicates in *The Great Code*, serves to bring out the oracular and authoritative nature of the Song: "The more poetic, repetitive, and metaphorical the texture," he writes, comparing the original Song with the newer prose account found in Judges 4, "the more the sense of external authority surrounds it; the closer the texture comes to continuous prose, the greater the sense of the human and familiar" (Frye, p. 214).

The omission of the central act of the story from Avison's poem gives it a radically different shape from that of the Song, whose last eight verses begin with the blessing of Jael, continue with the description of her hospitality and her assassination of Sisera, then describe the waiting of Sisera's mother and the princesses, and conclude with the moralizing praise of Yahweh. Avison's poem shows us Sisera alive and Sisera dead, but not the killing of Sisera, and it certainly does not express anywhere the fierce joy of the Singer in the act itself. In a sense, Jael's part in this action is missing from the poem, and so, like an audience watching a performance of *Oedipus Rex*, we see the events leading up to the bloody act and the events that follow, but the actual hammering of the peg through the forehead of Sisera happens, as it were, offstage. Caught like the figures on Keats's Grecian urn, Sisera is forever accepting milk and butter and, in the next breath, lying

Sprawled like a glutton . . .
Pegged to the dust under the smothering tentskins . . . .

In this Keatsian sense, as in his flight from battle, from defeat and into ambush, Sisera is truly

. . . a new alien
In time.

Less obvious than this omission is Avison's rearrangement of the other elements of the Song. She begins and ends with Sisera's mother, who in the Song is the object of sarcastic irony, mentioned only at the end, immediately after the description of Sisera's violent death:

> The mother of Sisera looked out at a window,
> and cried through the lattice,
> Why is his chariot so long in coming?
> why tarry the wheels of his chariots?
>
> (Judges 5:28)

By beginning with the end of the Song, with the enemies of Yahweh, and, in particular, with Sisera's mother, Avison draws our attention to the tragedy and grief of Sisera's death, rather than to the ironic exultation in the Song at expectations soon to be dashed:

> They are gathering, doubtless, sharing the spoil:
> a girl, two girls for each man of war;
> a garment, two dyed garments for Sisera;
> a scarf, two embroidered scarves for me!
>
> (Judges 5:30; JV)

chant Sisera's mother and the princesses. Avison mentions the spoils of Sisera only once, and then immediately juxtaposes to line 4 images of defeat, which ironically transfer the brilliant colour and handiwork of the expected garments to "the sacred torrent," the Kishon, so that the river itself becomes a monumental scarf of blood in the landscape. Echoing in our minds is Elijah's slaughter of the priests of Baal, the sun god, on the shores of the same river (1 Kings 18:40), as well as the prayer of the psalmist as he recalls the battle against Sisera:

> God, do not remain silent;
> do not be unmoved, O God, or unresponsive!
> See how your enemies are stirring,
> see how those who hate you rear their heads.

Weaving a plot against your people,
conspiring against those you protect, they say,
"Come, we will finish them as a nation,
the name of Israel shall be forgotten!"

Treat them like Midian and Sisera, like Jabin at the river
Kishon,
wiped out at En-dor,
they served to dung the ground.

(Psalms 83:1, 9–10; JV)

The reality of defeat is brought home by Avison's creation of five distinct and alternating landscapes: two suggesting fertility and wealth; two, sterility and death; and one combining the two. The last is the land of the Kishon, source of water in a dry land, but here, despite the images, a sewer of death. The other landscapes are the dream landscape in Sisera's mind; the dead vineyard into which he stumbles; Jael's land of milk and olives; and the brown landscape in which Sisera's mother waits in vain for her son, a landscape enclosing the poem. Sisera, escaping from Barak, is caught in one of the desert landscapes, in a "thorny thicket," like the ram sacrificed for Isaac – and the image, indeed, recalls the "rams-horn thickets" of "Not the Sweet Cicely . . . ." Metaphorically, he is washed up by the Kishon onto the shores of a spoiled landscape without spoils, emerging from a dead vineyard (even more sterile than the "gardenless gardens" of "Not the Sweet Cicely . . ."), to find a woman for whom olives ripen and the sun shines. Dreaming of ripe fruit, sated with milk and butter, Sisera finally returns to the dust, which, indifferently below the window of his mother and beneath the tent of Jael, underlies the whole poem like a palimpsest, waiting for some sign. Here it receives its first mark, the sign of Jael's hammer. The "haze-white" evening itself takes on the colour and texture of a dead vineyard; the image moves from air and sky to the ground as the evening becomes the scored sign of Sisera's defeat. Keeping in mind that the name "Sisera" means "leader," we are left with the image of the mother in a leaderless world, staring at two lines whose hieroglyphic shape she can see but whose ironies she cannot understand.

Within the Song of Deborah and Barak, Jael plays her divinely allotted part as an instrument of divine retribution and as fulfillment of Deborah's prophecy. In the Bible, she becomes a type of

Mary, the only other woman in the Old or New Testaments to be praised in a similar fashion, as "Blessed . . . among women" (Luke 1:42). In the poem, her part, in one sense of the word, is that of another voice singing in counterpoint to an ancient melody. It is also a part, a role, in a tragedy, which she acts out differently from the Jael in the Book of Judges: we are told, for example, that she "envied Sisera's cheerless voice." Why? This is an extraordinary emotion here, entirely absent from the biblical accounts. Does she envy Sisera's knowledge of utter defeat? Avison does not tell us: the line sits in the poem like an obscure emblem of some other reality — a reality in which Sisera's mother can wait indefinitely, and Deborah can turn into blessing an act that violates the most fundamental code of hospitality, let alone the prohibition against murder. The Song ends with a celebration of Yahweh and of Israel's triumph:

> So let all thine enemies perish, O Lord;
> but let them that love him
> be as the sun when he goeth forth in his might.
>
> (Judges 5:31)

The biblical story's conclusion is brief: "And the land had rest forty years." Avison's poem ends, not with celebration or rest, not with the blessedness of the heroine, but with the lingering image of the mother of the enemy staring forever at a meaningless world.

Certainly there is a context of redemption for the poem. In the mythic Song, Jael takes her place with Deborah and Barak as a saviour of Israel. But the context remains the ground against which the figure of the poem stands out in sharp relief. The bewildered stare of Sisera's mother must be set against the blessedness of Jael, and Sisera, suffering the thorns and briars of a dead garden, then nailed to the ground, is somehow closer to a suffering Christ than Jael is to Christ's mother. The ironic perspective of the poet evokes a sympathy for both assassin and victim that cuts across the sharp divisions of humanity in the Song of Deborah and Barak and comes much closer to the spirit of the Gospels.

If "Jael's Part" offers a kind of no-man's-land between the harsh certainties of the Old Testament and the certainty of redemption in the New, "The Bible to be Believed" crosses this gap and recombines the two. The poem was first published (and examined) in my study of Avison under its original title, "On Believing the Bible."[5]

A comparison of the later with the earlier version gives us an insight not only into the ways in which she uses the Bible, but also into the growth of her imagination.

The fundamental metaphor in the poem – one might say, in all of Avison's poetry – is the *Logos*, the Word made flesh. Jesus is incarnate as reborn language, the original Word of Creation. Avison's reading of the Bible really begins with the Gospel of St. John:

> In the beginning was the Word,
> and the Word was with God,
> and the Word was God . . . .
>
> All things were made by him;
> and without him was not any thing made that was made.
>
> In him was life;
> and the life was the light of men.
>
> And the light shineth in darkness;
> and the darkness comprehended it not.
>
> (John 1:1, 3–5)

The later version of the poem sharpens the typological reading of the Old Testament, relating Old and New Testaments more closely, especially to the central act of the New Testament: Crucifixion and Resurrection. Avison adds "He reads" to line 5, so that the first three stanzas more clearly depict Jesus reading the Old Testament as a twelve-year-old in the Temple, questioning the teachers and astonishing them with his answers to their questions (Luke 2: 42–50). The first two lines establish the paradoxical word/Word relation: the incarnate Word reads of his own predecessors, of his own types. Language again becomes the instrument of creation as the second Adam's lexicon unlocks itself in his mind, sculpturing, rather than gouging out, the form of the shaper himself, like Maurits Escher's paradoxical hands, each drawing the other, a divine and creative version of the demonic and devouring *Ourobouros*.

The third line is as paradoxical as the first two. One may read: "What happens, *means*" or: "What *happens*, means." The first reading expresses the epistemological content of the word/Word;

the second, the ontological process. If we recall that Avison is deeply influenced by the story of Moses and the Burning Bush, with its revelation of Yahweh as "I am that I am"; if we then reflect that *Yahweh* means "he is," or, as Frye puts it, if we think of God "as a verb" (Frye, p. 17), we begin to see in this line of philosophical compression of her whole attitude towards the Bible and God.

Goethe's Faust, contemplating the same verse of St. John, comes to the conclusion that he can impossibly rate the Word this highly, and attempts his own translation: "*I'm Anfang war der Sinn*" – "in the beginning was the mind"; but dissatisfied with that idea, settles for a moment on "*I'm Anfang war die Kraft*" (I, 1233) – "in the beginning was power." Finally, he comes to the conclusion that "*I'm Anfang war die Tat*" (I, 1237) – "in the beginning was the act." Faust may, in fact, at this very point be falling "into the power of Mephistopheles, the spirit of denial," as Frye puts it (Frye, p. 18), but this Faustian "translation" is curiously parallel to Avison's idea of the Word as simultaneously acting and meaning. The difference between Faust and Avison lies in the difference between Faust's concept of *die Tat* and Avison's concept of "what happens." Faust, tired of contemplation and reflection, wants experience, not words; Avison, however, interprets John 1:1 as both act and word: the life, death, and resurrection of Jesus and the relation of Old and New Testaments come under one heading, as a sacramental unified field, as it were, in which Creation and Redemption are one act of will existing outside time – or, more exactly, at the intersection of time and eternity. Thus the Word, embedded in history and reading history, is independent of history, speaking with equal clarity through ancient or contemporary apocalypses.

The structure of the second stanza of version two suggests three items in Jesus' reading: Moses (Exodus 2), Isaiah (Isaiah 6:6–8), and the "anointed twelve-year-old" – who is Jesus himself ("Messiah" is "the anointed one": Luke 7:38; Mark 14:3–9; Matt. 26:7–13, and Mark 16:1). Line 8 is both object of the verb and subject, in apposition to "He." The stanza thus expresses the kind of paradox we find in stanza 1, and which is missing in version one of the poem. We read it first on the literal level, but quickly see both its moral and its anagogic meanings: Moses is the instrument of Yahweh in the deliverance of Israel from bondage; Isaiah, redeemed by the seraphic fire, is Yahweh's instrument in the conversion and redemption of Israel. Formed by his reading of these stories, Jesus begins to act out their antitypes. He reads them *and* himself, the incarnation of Gospels that have yet to be written. The content of the reading includes both Jesus as reader and what he reads; the meaning lies in the very act, in what is happening *now*, that moment in Avison's poetry that, time and again, recapitulates T. S. Eliot's "still point of the turning world."

Avison's focusing of her fundamental metaphors is equally clear in stanza 3 of the second version. The most significant change is in her substitution of "sword" for "word," which completes the metaphor of honing and is related to sculpturing, ritual sacrifice, and the hewing of the doorway leading out of the tomb. Whether the *word* of line 10 in the first version was a typographical error, the change eliminates one example of the Word/word metaphor but adds an implicit allusion to St. Paul's catalogue of the armour and weaponry of the believer:

> . . . take the helmet of salvation, and the sword of the Spirit, which is the word of God.
>
> (Ephesians 6:17)

We are also reminded of the metaphor in Hebrews:

> . . . the word of God is quick, and powerful, and sharper than any two edged sword, piercing even to the dividing asunder of soul and spirit, and of the joints and marrow, and is a discerner of the thoughts and intents of the heart.
>
> (4:13)

This metaphorical identification of "sword" and "word" is not, of course, the only biblical allusion in this stanza. We are reminded of Jesus' description of the nature of his mission, which, on a spiritual level, is as ruthless as Jael's part in the redemption of Israel:

> Think not that I am come to send peace on earth: I came not to send peace, but a sword . . .
>
> (Matt. 10:34)

a mission anticipated by Simeon's prophecy to Mary:

> Behold, this child is set
> for the fall and rising again of many in Israel,
> and for a sign which shall be spoken against,

(Yea, a sword shall pierce through thy own soul also),
that the thoughts of many hearts may be revealed.
(Luke 2:34–35)

The function of this sword is to divide son from father, mother from daughter; this is one consequence of declaring holiness and "coming clear" not mentioned in the poem. Instead, Avison concentrates on what lies beyond the sword: the sharply dividing Word reunites Cain with Abel, Isaac with Abraham; and the anagogic sacrifice of Isaac is re-enacted with a critical difference: the second, antitypical Isaac is his own sacrificial lamb, as he becomes in another poem, "Waking and Sleeping: Christmas" (*s*, 96). Here Isaac is saved by the "branched ram"; the adjective means "horned," of course, but recalls also Zechariah's prophecy of the messianic leader, "my servant the Branch," or in Greek, "rising Sun" (Zechariah 3:8), both of which anticipate the coming of Christ.

The world of stanzas 4 and 5 is a version of that Peaceable Kingdom described by Isaiah, in which all animals and all humans are alive within the Word, in a *Now* embodying the elements of communion, the spikenard and myrrh of anointing, burial and resurrection, a Now that is an act of will or, more exactly, the abdication of will in the Garden, the will to choose the course no man would. In her poem "Then" (*s*, 98) Avison specifically relates Isaiah's Peaceable Kingdom to the Incarnation, in lines echoing Christopher Smart:

The leopard and the kid
  are smoothness (fierce)
  and softness (gentle)
        and will lie down together.
Then, storm and salt and largeness, known, in time,
        will be within the wholely pure,
              the unimaginable!

. . . .

Here, then, prophetically,
in the strange peace of the outcast
on the manger hay
lies a real baby:

    all-cherishing, the unsourced,
    the never fully celebrated
    well-spring of That Day.

"And in that day there shall be a root of Jesse, which shall stand for an ensign of the people," says Isaiah (11:10). *That* day is the prophetic eschatalogical *Then* arising from the *Now* of Incarnation; it is the moment when the grain and grapes of Cain the murderer are transformed into the bread and wine of the sacrificial lamb:

> In time the paschal lamb
> before the slaying did
> what has made new the wine
> and broken bread

writes Avison in "For the Murderous: The Beginning of Time" (*s*, 49). This is the unsafe moment of yet another, "He Couldn't be Safe (Isaiah 53:5)" (*s*, 52), a commentary on this verse made famous by Handel:

> . . . he was wounded for our transgressions,
> he was bruised for our iniquities:
> the chastisement of our peace was upon him;
> and with his stripes we are healed.
>
> (Isaiah 53:5)

The "covenanting song" of stanza 6 in version two is a parody of the Covenant implicit in God's promise to Abraham (Genesis 22:15–18) because it would mean the submission of the will of Jesus to that of the Tempter. Jesus is being tempted to make a "covenant of death," as Isaiah puts it in a passage underlying another problematic poem, "Stone's Secret" (*s*, 21–22), in which the prophet speaks out against evil counsellors at the court of Judah, types of the Tempter, and prophesies the founding of the New Jerusalem — typologically, the coming of Messiah (Isaiah 28:15–16). The prophet's long poem containing the oracle is directed against perversions of the true word of God, against parodies of the prophetic language; and the oracle itself is echoed in St. Paul's Letter to the Ephesians, in which he describes Jesus as "the chief corner stone" of the Church (2:20), "sculptured," Avison would add, by his very reading of prophets like Isaiah.

The anagogic relation of Old to New Testament is also implied in the allusion to Ezekiel's vision of the valley of dry bones, which anticipates the forty days of Jesus in the wilderness to the Temptation. The dry bones of Ezekiel's vision represent Israel exiled and dispersed; the promise of Yahweh is resurrection and return:

> Behold, O my people,
> I will open your graves,
> and cause you to come up out of your graves,
> and bring you into the land of Israel.
>
> Moreover, I will make a covenant of peace with them;
> it shall be an everlasting covenant with them:
> and I will place them, and multiply them,
> and will set my sanctuary in the midst of them for evermore.
>
> (37:12, 26)

This stanza is especially complex in its allusions. If we take as given that Avison is referring to the Temptation of Jesus, we must read the original story in the spirit in which it is written, i.e., in an anagogic sense. The forty days and forty nights in the wilderness are a re-enactment of Israel's forty years of wandering, as becomes clear in Jesus' answer to Satan's first temptation:

> If thou be the Son of God, command that these stones be made bread.
> But he answered and said,
> It is written,
> Man shall not live by bread alone,
> But by every word that proceedeth out of the mouth of God.
>
> (Matt. 4:3–4)

The point Avison makes about this sparring, in which both Jesus and the Devil cite Scripture, is that Satan's relation to the Word is entirely external, while Jesus is both sayer and incarnation of the Word.

The first version of this stanza is centred on human failings, on the human desire to distance oneself from the immediacy of the Word by "wash[ing] out" its effect in ritualized worship. Version two is centred on the Word himself/itself, repeating in another fashion the paradoxes of stanza I. Here the "wash[ing] out" is more crucial to the development of the Word/word, and the object of the metaphoric verb much more illusive in its meanings than anything in the comparable stanza of version one. On the simplest level, the "brand on the dry bone" is the mark of death, of the fall of the first Adam, and the temptation Jesus faces is to renege on his mission as the second Adam to redeem the first. On a more complicated level, there may be a conscious or unconscious echo of a prophetic vision to which I have already referred, that of Zechariah:

> And he shewed me Joshua the high priest
> standing before the angel of the Lord,
> and Satan standing at his right hand to resist him.
> And the Lord said unto Satan,
> The Lord rebuke thee, O Satan;
> even the Lord that hath chosen Jerusalem rebuke thee:
> is not this a brand plucked out of the fire?
>
> (3:1–2)

Joshua, representing the Jewish people (typologically, the Church), is the brand, this ember that recalls Isaiah's burning coal of line 7. Again, as in the vision of Ezekiel, the promise of God is redemption, the one in the form of physical resurrection out of the valley of dry bones, the other in the form of the Messianic "Branch" mentioned above.

Whether Avison herself had this particular allusion in mind, the effect of the line is a commingling of at least two metaphors: the fire metaphor, usually associated in the Old Testament with divine purification, and the bone metaphor, part of the greater metaphor of resurrection and restoration. Both are prophetic, i.e., expressing in human form the Word of God; the temptation of Jesus is to deny both the human and the divine halves of himself, to deny not only the prophetic word but also himself, the Branch, the Rising Sun, the Morning Star, the Resurrection, the Word as incarnation of the prophetic texts of the Old Testament.

Throughout the poem, there is a tension, on the one hand, between words and acts that exist in time, and, on the other, the Word and the Act that exist outside time. For the human race, time begins, as Avison indicates in "For the Murderous: The Beginning of Time," when one man expresses his resentment against God by killing his brother. Such an act can only be redeemed by another act within time, the slaying of the Lamb. This is historical and temporal, but for Avison that moment is the eternal *now*:

> The line we drew, you crossed,
> and cross out, wholly forget,

at the faintest stirring of what
you know is love, is One
whose name has been, and is
and will be, the
I AM.

("The Word"; *D*, 151)

Jesus escapes time by "hewing out" of the stone tomb the "one crevice-gate" (a metaphor missing from version one), sculpturing his own being out of death. This "gate" is essentially the same as the "door" in the poem "Person" (*D*, 146): his own nature, temporally human, eternally divine:

This door that is "I AM"
seemed to seal my tomb
. . . .
there was no knob, or hinge . . . .

"I am." The door
was flesh; was there.
. . . .
So drenched with Being and created new
. . . .
. . . forth
shining, unseen, draws near
the Morning Star.

The tone of the second version of the poem, and indeed its *kerygmatic* emphasis, are changed from the first by Avison's removal of the penultimate stanza of the original, which establishes a close personal relation between poet and Word/word. This is a real loss, because in its simplicity of language, its freedom from the clichés of the stanza that succeeded it, the stanza is a powerful and direct personal statement, the last of a series in the original version, all of which are excised in version two. However, these cuts, including the last, integrate the tone of the second version, and together with the many other changes (most of which improve the poem), focus the poem on the Word rather than on a personal relation of poet to Word.

Partly because of the omission of this stanza, but also because of subtle changes in diction, syntax, and punctuation, the final stanza moves to a different conclusion from that of version one. The effect of the first version is to emphasize the "sealing-up" (not merely "sealing") of the "living word" – a metaphor that, so to speak, leaves the Word in the tomb, especially because of the full stop at the end of the second line. The paradox of the last two lines is therefore not as strong as in version two, where it follows the colon. In the latter, Avison changes the metaphor from entombment to a royal and divine confirmation. And, instead of the anticlimactic final two lines of version one, with the vague and abstract participle "peace-imparting," she moves logically from "word" to "voiceful" and then, in the final line, first to "free" and then to the image that supersedes "sealing": "opening-out," an image expressing again the bursting forth introduced by the revised penultimate stanza. The repetition of "all" reminds us of the two uses of that word in revised stanza 5, and emphasizes, far more than the first version, the universality of the Word. The heaviest stress in the final line is on "out," so that diction, imagery, and rhythm work together in the second version to convey a radically different and more vital sense of rebirth.

The poem thus begins with the images of reading and sculpturing and ends with the images of speaking and "opening-out," a movement from inside to outside, from receiving to giving, from an image of inert rock to an image of blossoming. The encompassing action of the poem is that of a divine Pygmalion sculpturing the word/Word in its/his final form in a unity of action, meaning, and the divine will.

The effect of version two is, on the whole, more distant, more impersonal, but also more liturgical, more anagogic. The language itself, diction and syntax, is more measured; no quoted statements or questions interrupt the relentless sequence of statements. In Frye's sense of a "proclaiming rhetoric" (Frye, p. 18), Avison's poem is *kerygmatic*: its final purpose is a revelation towards which metaphor serves as an instrument.

This is perhaps the most explicit statement of Avison's relation to the Bible, not only because of what it says, but also because its extensive revision indicates her continuing, growing, and imaginative response to the most profound source of her thought and imagery. A thorough analysis of her use of the Bible would require much more space than is available here; but this examination of three levels of her creative relation to the Bible, ranging from the use of allusion and metaphor to a *kerygmatic* commentary, offers a useful model for further study. If "Not the Sweet Cicely of Gerardes Herball" portrays an unredeemed world, and "Jael's Part" a world in which the ironies of redemption undercut the triumph of the original Song, "The Bible to be Believed" takes us out of the deserts of the spirit and into the Peaceable Kingdom in which the meaningless signs — the rabbinical glosses, the lost maps, the nameless territories, the dead vineyard, and the leaderless "warcars" — are transcended in a new dispensation. Here sign, act, meaning, and person are unified in Avison's imagination into one coherent word/ Word.

NOTES

[1] One might mention critics like Lawrence M. Jones, William New, George Bowering, Frank Davey, Daniel Doerksen, D. G. Jones, R. J. Merrett, James Neufeld, Ants Reigo, David Kent, and J. M. Kertzer; and, in particular, the analysis of "Dispersed Titles" by Joseph Zezulka and William Aide's "An Immense Answering of Human Skies: The Poetry of Margaret Avison."

[2] See Appendix 2.

[3] Northrop Frye, *The Great Code* (New York: Harcourt Brace Jovanovich, 1981), p. 15.

[4] James Strong, *A Concise Dictionary of the Words in the Greek Testament* (Madison, 1890), p. 42.

[5] Margaret Avison, "On Believing the Bible," in Ernest Redekop, *Margaret Avison* (Toronto: Copp Clark, 1970), pp. 144–45; and "The Bible to be Believed," in *s*, 56–57.

Appendix I

Not the Sweet Cicely of Gerardes Herball

(i.e., ORIENTAL MYRRH, NOT ENGLISH MYRRH)

Myrrh, bitter myrrh, diagonal,
Divides my gardenless gardens
Incredibly as far as the eye reaches
In this falling terrain.
Low-curled in rams-horn thickets,
With hedge-solid purposefulness
It unscrolls, glistening,
Where else the stones are white,
Sky blue.
No beetles move. No birds pass over.
The stone house is cold.
The cement has crumbled from the steps.
The gardens here, or fields,
Are weedless, not from cultivation but from
Sour unfructifying November gutters,
From winds that bore no fennel seeds,
Finally, from a sun purifying, harsh, like
Sea-salt.
The stubbled grass, dragonfly-green,
Between the stones, was not so tended.
Mild animals with round unsmiling heads
Cropped unprotested, unprotesting
(After the rind of ice
Wore off the collarbones of shallow shelving rock)
And went their ways.

The bitter myrrh
Cannot revive a house abandoned.
Time has bleached out the final characters
Of a too-open Scripture.
Under the staring day
This rabbinical gloss rustles its
Leaves of living darkness.

With the maps lost, the voyages

Cancelled by legislation years ago,
This is become a territory without name.
No householder survives
To marvel on the threshold
Even when the evening myrrh raises
An aromatic incense for
Far ivory nostrils
Set in the vertical plane of ancient pride.

(*WS*, 22–23)

Jael's Part

The mother of Sisera in late afternoon,
Bewildered by the stirless dust,
Cried out, leaning and peering from the window
For Sisera and his spoils.

Its ancient flood weltered with rich embroideries
Dark Kishon billowed to the bloodening sun.

Flotsam of that defeat,
Sisera, out of the Day of Judges, paced
The darkening vineyard, a new alien
In time. The thorny thicket of the vinestems,
Ravaged and leafless, blackened under night.
But the metallic green of the horizon
Stirred in his mind gentle and terrible dreams
Of morning-mists, and a valleyside
Purpose with fruit; dreams he had never known
Till now, under the dense dead briary branches.

Sisera's brow, withering with the vision that
Outstripped the Day of Judges, Jael saw.
And to her the olives ripened
And the day hung heavy upon them
And every stone on the ground cast its sharp shadow.
And Jael envied Sisera's cheerless voice
When he came to her, and bade her pour him water.
Milk she brought, and butter
In a lordly dish.

And in her haze-white evening,
Sprawled like a glutton, Sisera
Lay on the tentfloor of Heber the Kenite
Pegged to the dust under the smothering tentskins
By Jael, blessed above women
The wife of Heber the Kenite.

And Sisera's mother stood and stared where the wheels
Of the leaderless warcar scored the leafbrown evening.

(*WS*, 76–77)

VERSION 1 (FIRST PUBLISHED 1970)

On Believing the Bible
towards parable depth

Margaret Avison
(enclosed in a letter to the author)

The word read by the living Word
gouged out its shaper's form.
What happens, means — no meaning blurred
by water nor sunswarm.

— One first born Egyptian
was not quite three years old,
one was a scrawny musician, one
a tubby twelve-year-old.

As the Word dwelt on that word
it honed a true heart's word:

what it costs to declare
holiness slowly coming clear . . .

Ancient names, eon-shrivelled eyes,
within the word, open, on mysteries:

"Murderer, wanderer,
hearken who gulps your night."
""'Look son, though you never question, know you're
safe

from the sacrificial knife . . ."
high on a hill, looking to his father,
wordless, another wanderer
stares upon night.

The Word created, cherishing,
throbbing doves, lamb, sea-whale,
grapes and bread-grain; word-bare is even
such life, unless One will

('It's human to get it wrong.
Mightn't it be so?
Wash out in ritual praise and song
this hitting home. Not go
my mile beyond the horizon-long
openness to woe?')

The Word was moved
too deeply to be bound
in time. So the beloved
wound, and know the wound.

There was a dark word, a smothering,
none knew but he and I.
He took the cup and drank it in
from me; so he must die.

Final silencing endured
sealed up the living word.
Now therefore He is free, voiceful, to be heard,
our peace-imparting Lord.

VERSION 2 (*s*, 56–57)

The Bible to be Believed

The word read by the living Word
sculptured its shaper's form.
What happens, means. The meanings *are not* blurred
by *Flood – or fiery atom.*

He reads: a Jewish-Egyptian
firstborn, not three years old;
a coal-seared poet-statesman;
an anointed twelve-year-old.

The Word dwells on *this* word
honing His heart's *sword*,
ready at knife-edge to declare
holiness, *and come* clear.

Anćient names, eon-*brittled* eyes,
within the word, open on mysteries:
the estranged murderer, *exiled, hears at last*
his kinsman's voice;
the child, confidingly questioning, so close
to the awful ritual knife,
is stilled by another, looking to His Father –
the saving one, not safe.

The Word *alive cherishes all:*
doves, lambs – or whale –
beyond old rites or emblem burial.
Grapes, bread, *and fragrant oil:*
all that means, is real
now, only as One *wills.*

Yes, he was tempted to wash out
in *covenanting* song
the brand on the dry bone;
he heard the tempter quote
the texts he meant and went embodying.

The Word was moved
too *vitally* to be entombed
in time. *He has hewn out*
of it one crevice-gate.

His final silencing endured
has sealed the living word:
now therefore He is voiceful, to be heard,
free, and *of all opening-out* the Lord.

Appendix 2

Quotations from, and references and allusions to, specific biblical texts in *Winter Sun*, *The Dumbfounding*, and *sunblue*:

[page • *poem* • Old Testament • New Testament]

Winter Sun

22–23 • *Not the Sweet Cicely of Gerardes Herball* • Canticles (*passim*) • Matt. 2:11; Mark 15:23; John 19:39

28 • *Unbroken Lineage* • • Matt. 27; Mark 15; Luke 23; John 18–19

29 • *Butterfly Bones* • Gen. 2:19

30 • *Jonathan, o Jonathan* • 2 Sam. 1:19–27

31–32 • *Meeting Together of Poles and Latitudes (In Prospect)* • • Matt. 27:19; John 19:13; Acts 18:12–17; 25:6–17; Rom. 14:10; 2 Cor. 5:10

33 • *The Fallen, Fallen World* • Gen. 28:11–19; Isa. 14:12; Job 38:12 • Luke 1:78; 2 Pet. 1:19

53 • *Easter* • • Resurrection

55–57 • *Intra-Political* • Gen. 1 • Matt. 17:2; Mark 9:2

58 • *Watershed* • Job 38:12 • Luke 1:78

60 • *Apocalyptic?* • • Revelation/Apocalypse

61 • *Apocalyptics* • • Revelation/Apocalypse; John 10

74 • *R.I.P.* • • Revelation 21

76–77 • *Jael's Part* • Judges 4:11–5:31

78 • *Span* • 1 Sam. 2:12–5:18

81–82 • *The Mirrored Man* • Gen. 19; Gen. 1; Canaan/Promised Land; Deuteronomy (*passim*)

83–84 • *Birth Day* • Genesis 1

88–89 • *The Agnes Cleves Papers* • 1 Samuel 17

The Dumbfounding

118 • *Ps. 19* • Psalms 19

120–23 • *A Story* • Matt. 13:18; Mark 4:14

125–27 • *A Child: Marginalia on an Epigraph* • (Mt. 18:3; Lk. 9:48)

130 • *For Tinkers Who Travel on Foot* • • Hebrews 2:14, 15 (mentioned in Bunyan's *Memoirs, Works.* Edinburgh: Blackie & Son, 1866, I, xx.)

131–39 • *The Earth That Falls Away* • Ps. 27:9; Neh. 1:6; Exod. 24:17 • Matt. 27:27; Luke 22:64; James 3:6; 5:6, 8

140–41 • *Branches* • • Acts 9:3–9; Luke 22:64

143–44 • *In Truth* • • Rev. 5:8; 14:2; 15:2; 4:3; 21:11, 18, 19

146 • *Person* • Exod. 3:14; Job 38:7 • Rev. 2:28; 22:16; 1 Pet. 1:19

150–51 • *The Word* • Exod. 3:14 • Luke 5:11; 14:53; Matt. 20:27; Crucifixion

152–53 • *The Dumbfounding* • • John 6:19–21; Mark 8:22–25; Last Supper; Golgotha; Crucifixion; Resurrection

154–56 • *Searching and Sounding* • • Gethsemane; Golgotha; Matt. 27:33; Mark 15:22; John 19:17

158–59 • *For Dr. and Mrs. Dresser* • • Last Supper

160–61 • *The Christian's Year in Miniature* • Ps. 23; 121; Isa.

29:16; 45:9; 64:8 • Rom. 9:20–21; John 19:39–41; 14:2

173 • *Janitor Working on a Threshold* • Malachi 4:2 • Matt. 25:40

177 • *Hot June* • Ps. 69:9

182–83 • *Christmas: Anticipation* • • Luke 1

sunblue

11 • SKETCH: *Overcast Monday* • Isa. 61:3

21 • *Stone's Secret* • Isa. 11; 66:12; Ps. 118:22; Isa. 48:18; 28:16 • Luke 19:40; Matt. 21:42; Luke 20:17–18; Acts 4:11; Eph. 2:20; 1 Pet. 2:7

27 • *Highway in April* • • John 11:43

34 • *A Lament* • Gen. 3

35 • *The Evader's Meditation* • • James 1:22–25; 2 Cor. 3:18

43–44 • *Sestina (1964)* • 1 Sam. 13–14

45 • *Embezzler (I): His Act* • • Luke 16:1–15

46 • *Embezzler (II): A Classic Case?* • • Luke16:1–15

47 • *Embezzler (III): ". . . wiser than the children of light"?* • • Luke 16:8

48 • *Embezzler (IV): The Wastrel Begins to Hope* • • Luke 16:1–15

49 • *For the Murderous: The Beginning of Time* • Gen. 4:3–4 • Last Supper; Crucifixion

50 • *All Out;* OR, *Oblation* • 2 Sam. 23:13–17; 1 Chron. 11:17–19

51 • *Dryness and Scorch of Ahab's Evil Rule . . .* • 1 Kings 17:7; 1 Kings 17

52 • *He Couldn't be Safe* • Isa. 53:5

53 • *To Emmaus* • • Luke 24:13

54 • *As a Comment on Romans 1:10 . . . .* • Ps. 16:8 • Rom. 1:10; Acts 2:25–26; Matt. 27:51; Mark 15:38; Luke 23:45

55 • *The Circuit* • Ps. 19:6 • Phil. 2:5–11; Matt. 27:51; Mark

Muse of Danger

MARGARET AVISON

THE IMPULSE to write a poem occurs in human context — and can be a pulsation in darkness or in light. Poetry in itself is neither "evil" nor "good," in other words.

No fool-proof formula exists for using a poetic impulse to God's glory. The child of God claims the victory of Christ, and yet lives embattled from moment to moment, falling often and constantly knowing no power except through forgiveness. Even so the believer can dedicate his gifts and acknowledge God as their source, and yet can experience much daily struggle in using them. As with poetry itself, the writer of poetry is neither "evil" nor "good," in other words.

Such expressions as "a Christian poem" or "Christian literature" or "Christian works of art" involve shorthand that can be seriously misleading. They imply that good subject matter will ensure good art, or that a dedicated Christian who writes will by virtue of his dedication understand the art of writing well. But it is the word of God alone, the being of God alone, that is good without any admixture — light without any shadow of darkness at all.

In this light all our actions are empowered and judged, including the act of writing a poem. In the steady light of that assertion, we will see some of the questions cleared up that arise when Christians discuss the writing of poems.

CHOOSING THE SUBJECT

First, let the writer who feels the impulse to write poetry accept the activity involved, the fact of the impulse, and himself as writer. No subject matter is ruled out, or in, in advance for the writer (whether Christian or not). No specific "content" can be prescribed for a poem. Moreover, no special training in literature can ensure the writing of poetry.

Yet a poem is not written out of a verbal nowhere. And once a poem is written it takes its place in the context of literature by the very fact of its existence. The body of poetry at large is the range where a writer of poems is free to read, and where as poet he is responsible. When a writer gives his life to the Lord, he admits God's right over every aspect of his energy, imagination, use of time and communication. But there is no conflict for a Christian plumber, for example, where he dedicates his day to the Lord and then goes whole-heartedly about his job, and also whole-heartedly needs and responds to his children's love and their needs. Similarly there need be no conflict between a believing writer's will to serve God and his impulse to write a poem, involving as it can a total absorption in this process for as long as it goes on.

PLAYING IT SAFE

In fact there *are* points of acute conflict in the experience of most Christian writers. The propositions of doctrine are in words, and there is a verbal world that is "safe." To seek subjects within it, and avoid hazarding statements outside the territory that has been clearly defined, is a natural urge for someone who longs to be used as a channel for communicating the faith, and wants to avoid empty words. Yet this continual checking on one's sure anchorage in each statement is a denial of the writer's spontaneity. Moreover, if only sure words are needed, the Bible is enough.

But in His strange and marvelous mercy, God nonetheless lets the believer take a necessary place as a living witness, in behaviour with family and classmate and stranger, in conversation, or in a poem. Thus each of us may find the Word in His newness through every way and every day. The poem can no more be a "safe" venture than a direct human encounter can. Here, too, the believer is fully involved, all the more fully because of his faith.

The faith still retains first place. Its claims conflict with artistic drives just because both are compelling. This difficulty is real. The writer must accept the plain fact of his total involvement as a writer, as stated above. But the second fact for a Christian writer to accept is the tentative nature of his mortal involvement, in art as in anything else. For all our acts except one (the act of worship) are acts in mortal time. The eternal dimension may alter any of our commitments except one (our commitment to the living Son of God).

IDENTITY AND FAITH

This seems to demand of the writer an absolute artistic identity, and then advises him to weasel out on it. Experience will press home the paradox, however, so it may as well be openly stated. What, practically is involved here?

Writers are sure to know some temptations peculiar to their craft — e.g. writing instead of acting. But as with Shakespeare's Lear, writers can find opportunities to use literature to deepen human awareness. At other times action may be required as when God appoints an hour for two friends to share an anxiety, a joyful discovery or a sorrow. It is a lifelong discipline to learn both to act on impulses to action, and to write when an insight is given to be shared in words.

There is no set of "safe" or "preferred" subjects for Christian poets. Nor is there a set of "safe" or "preferred" daily experiences. You would be presuming to know better than the Gift-giver to preset your range and exclude some truths of experience from expression or to refuse to record some explorings that go on from the sources of poetic energy within.

Poetry is a great boon in testing honesty. Shadows of unsureness, shreds of lingering mist, emotional colorlessness, unexamined phases, empty words: these show up for what they are in a poem. ("'Fool,' said my Muse to me, 'Look in thy heart, and write.'" This is how a Renaissance Christian gentleman urged himself towards the art of poetry.[1]) It is true that a Christian writer may have a strong anticipation of what he wants his poems to be so that they measure up to the rich meaning opened to him through Jesus Christ. But to list the fruit of the Spirit is not straightway to bear it. And poems share something of the mysterious timing of organic processes of growth.

WORDS AND EXPERIENCE

Most writers discover for themselves the distinction between devotional reality and literature. The experience of beauty is not alien to the worshiper's awareness of God (although it is possible for beauty to be cold, and cruel, and arrogant). Certainly out of a morning hour of Bible meditation and prayer, words may be breathed that rise from the deeps and hold the promise of communicative loveliness. Yet how often they need revising, later on, before they are ready for others' eyes. Fervour in worship can so far exceed the power of our words that the words alone will not convey the experience to anyone else. The Christian writer should remind himself to give careful scrutiny to any poems written out of such experiences before making them public. And he should accept poetic impulse from every area of experience, and avoid looking for his "inspiration" only from the moments least accessible to lisping human terms.

IS ONE POETIC FORM "RIGHT"?

No pre-determined range of experience is "right" for a Christian poet's subject matter, and there are no "right" forms. The culturally excellent is not necessarily the spiritually valid. Dante's *terza rima*, Milton's blank verse, the simple lyric forms of devotional writers in the seventeenth century, the psalmist's parallelism of thought, and the nineteenth century hymnwriter's rhymed stanzas: all have been explicit vehicles for poetry of faith. And each of these forms had its cultural roots and ramifications in many a secular form of speech and writing.

The believer asserts that the Creator called form out of chaos, and draws orderliness out of the otherwise incoherent. These assertions often lure him to seek some definite principles of order (rhyme, regular measure, logic) as necessary to the poetry he will approve. But to do so is to limit the poet. The known, already recognized means of ordering words in poems are not necessarily better than other means that may still be discovered.

Before continuing with the discussion of inter-related form and content, a side issue should be faced. Hymns and songs are a special genre of poetry. Because Christian writers are often responsive to hymns, they tend to identify poetic form with the regular, repetitive word patterns required by the hymn tunes commonly used in congregational singing. Thus a particularly difficult form is often the one first attempted. It is difficult because a repeat without loss of freshness is in itself a forbidding technical undertaking. Good current hymnology involves double awareness, both musical and verbal. And local traditions are confining unless the practitioner is able to work with an awareness of the total context. This is not to discourage anyone from hymn-writing, but only to prevent anyone from backing into it with shut eyes, and to keep him from forcing his poetry into a form inappropriate to it. The hymn-form, *per se*, is not godly in some special fashion.

WHOLEHEARTED USE OF WORDS

The packaging and the goods packaged may be easily distinguished in a store, but not when words are involved. When you speak, a listener hears much more than the dictionary words you use. There is an individual identity conveyed. Words are in a particular language family, and are learned in a particular family by a particular infant. Then they gather meaning over the years from school, through TV, conversations and reading. You pronounce words the way people in your home region pronounce them. And the way your own mouth and teeth and breathing work make them peculiarly your own. (I have always pictured Edmund Spenser as having a space between his two front teeth, so that "f" would fan a gentle airflow over his lips – his speech seems to me thus individual.) A person's unique flesh-and-blood force is in his own words, in his way of sounding them and using them. His words reveal his family and the time and place he is abroad on the earth. The natural rhythm, the flow or biting off or slow shaping of word, reflect temperament and mood. The "mundane context" of the words becomes, and in a sense is, their sound and sequence. Moreover, the reading of the Bible and the experience of prayer are both part of the "context of language" for a Christian, so that for the believer the language context also can become extramundane.

In prose, a writer or speaker may work against these personal and extramundane powers in language, seeking a detached, logical statement. In contrast, a poet chooses to accept the full halo of values in the words he uses. He accepts the personal identity they reveal. He develops his sense of their echoes across developing centuries, the double or triple meanings, the suggestiveness of vowel-sound and rhythm. No potential effect of any word is irrelevant to the poem where it occurs.

Thus the poet uses language as an artist's raw material. Consequently, his words have potential effect at every level – not only the intentional or logical levels. Poetry is the *whole-hearted* use of language, then. Let the Christian plunge in if he is given potentialities in reading and writing – and so discover.

The practice of poetry is as dangerous as this next hour of life, whoever you are. Yet its advantages are great.

NOTE

1 Sir Philip Sidney, Sonnet I from *Astrophel and Stella* (1591).

Bibliography of Margaret Avison

FRANCIS MANSBRIDGE

PART I

Works by Margaret Avison

PART II

Works on Margaret Avison

PART I

Works by Margaret Avison

A Books (Poetry, History, Compilation, Translation, and Biography), Broadsides, Criticism, and Manuscripts

POETRY

A1 *Winter Sun*. London: Routledge and Kegan Paul, 1960. 98 pp.
——. Toronto: Univ. of Toronto Press, 1960. 98 pp.

Includes "The Agnes Cleves Papers" (B44), "All Fools' Eve" (B45), "The Apex Animal" (B34), "Apocalyptic?", "Apocalyptics," "The Artist," "Atlantis and the Department Store," "Banff" (B12), "Birth Day," "Butterfly Bones; or, a Sonnet Against Sonnets," "Chronic," "Civility a Bogey; or, Two Centuries of Canadian Cities" (B53), "A Conversation," "Death," "Dispersed Titles" (B55), "Easter," "Extra-Political: The Thorned Speaks (While Day Horses Afar)," "The Fallen, Fallen World," "Far off from University" (B51), "A Friend's Friend," "From a Provincial" (B40), "Grammarian on a Lakefront Park Bench," "Hiatus" (B38), "Identity," "Intra-Political: An Exercise in Political Astronomy," "Jael's Part," "Jonathan, o Jonathan," "Meeting together of Poles and Latitudes (In Prospect)" (B48), "The Mirrored Man," "Mordent for a Melody," "New Year's Poem" (B42), "Not the Sweet Cicely of Gerardes Herball (i.e. Oriental Myrrh, not English Myrrh)," "November 23," "On the Death of France Darte Scott (Upon the Birth of Twin Sons Who Later Died)," "Our Working Day may be Menaced," "Prelude" (B52), "Public Address," "R.I.P.," "Rich Boy's Birthday through a Window" (B46), "Rigor Viris" (B26), "Rondeau Redoublé," "September Street," "Snow" (B49), "Span," "Stray Dog, near Ecully" (B47), "The Swimmer's Moment," "Tennis" (B50), "Thaw," "To Professor X, Year Y" (B56), "Unbroken Lineage," "Unfinished After-Portrait (or: Stages of Mourning)," "Voluptuaries and Others" (B43),

"Watershed," and "The World Still Needs."

A2 *The Dumbfounding*. New York: Norton, 1966. 99 pp.
Includes "The Absorbed," "And Around," "The Artist" (A1), "Bestialities" (B85), "Black-White Under Green: May 18, 1965," "Branches," "Canadian/Inverted," "A Child: Marginalia on an Epigraph (Mt. 18:3; Lk. 9:48)," "The Christian's Year in Miniature," "Christmas: Anticipation," "Controversy," "The Dumbfounding" (B80), "The Earth That Falls Away" (B86), "First," "Five Breaks" (B84), "For Dr. and Mrs. Dresser," "For Tinkers Who Travel on Foot" (B61), "From a Provincial" (B40), "Hot June" (B73), "In a Season of Unemployment" (B62), "In Eporphyrial Harness" (B77), "In Time" (B63), "In Truth," "Janitor Working on Threshold," "July Man," "Lonely Lover," "Many As Two," "Meeting Together of Poles and Latitudes (in Prospect)" (B48), "Micro-Metro," "Miniature Biography of One of My Father's Friends Who Died a Generation Ago," "The Mourner," "A Nameless One" (B81), "Natural/Unnatural" (B65), "Of Tyranny, in One Breath: (translated from a Hungarian poem by Gyula Illyés, 1956)," "Old . . . Young. . . . ," "Once," "Pace," "Person," ". . . Person, or A Hymn on and to the Holy Ghost," "A Prayer Answered by Prayer," "Ps. 19," "Report from the Pedestrians' Outpost" (B66), "Riding and Waves" (B72), "A Sad Song," "Searching and Sounding," "Simon: finis" (B78), "The Store Seeds" (B79), "A Story," "The Swimmer's Moment" (A1), "Thaw" (A1), "Transit" (B69), "Twilight" (B59), "Two Mayday Selves," "The Two Selves," "Unspeakable" (B88), "Until Silenced: To I. A.," "Urban Tree," "Walking Behind, en Route, in Morning, in December," "The Word," and "Words."

A3 *Sliverick*. Ganglia Mini Memo Series, No. 23. Toronto: Ganglia, 1969. 4 pp.
Includes "Sliverick" (B103).

A4 *sunblue*. Hantsport, N.S.: Lancelot, 1978. 105 pp.
Includes "Absolute," "All Out; OR Oblation (as defined in 2 Sam. 23, 13–17 & 1 Chron. II, 17–19)" (B92), "As a Comment on Romans 1:10 – ," "As Though," "Backing into Being" (B113), "Bereaved," "The Bible to Be Believed"

(B101), "A Blurt on Gray," "Christmas Approaches, Highway 401," "Christmas: Becoming," "The Circuit (Phil. 2, 5–11)," "City Park in July," "Contemplatives; OR, Internal Combustion," "Contest," "Creative Hour," "Dryness and Scorch of Ahab's Evil Rule," "The Effortless Point," "Embattled Deliverance" (B114), "Embezzler (I): His Act (Luke 16)," "Embezzler (II): A Classic Case?", "Embezzler (III): '. . . wiser than the children of light'?", "Embezzler (IV): The Wastrel Begins to Hope," "Emmanuel," "The Engineer and the Asparagus," "The Evader's Meditation," "For the Murderous: The Beginning of Time," "From a Public Library Window," "From Age to Age: Found Poem," "Grass Roots," "He Couldn't be Safe (Isaiah 53:5)" (B95), "Hid Life," "Highway in April," "Hope," "Intercession," "Into the Vineyard: A Vision," "Kahoutek," "A Lament," "Let Be," "Light (I)" (B108), "Light (II)" (B110), "Light (III)," "Listening," "March" (B115), "March Morning" (B111), "Midsummer Christmas" (B107), "Morning Bus," "Needy," "Neighbours?", "On?", "On Goodbye," "Oughtiness Ousted," "Poem on the Astronauts in Apollo XIII's Near-Disaster, written April 17–18, 1970, for the newspaper" (B104), "Ps. 80:1 – 'Thou that dwellest between the cherubim, shine forth!'", "Released Flow," "Research," "Scarface," "Sestina (1964)," "The Seven Birds (College Street at Bathurst): SKETCH," "SKETCH: A Childhood Place," "SKETCH: A Work Gang on Sherbourne and Queen, across from a Free Hostel for Men," "SKETCH: Cement Worker on a Hot Day," "SKETCH: Child in Subway," "SKETCH: CNR London to Toronto (I)," "SKETCH: CNR London to Toronto (II)" [2 poems pp. 15–16], "SKETCH: End of a Day: OR, I as a Blurry," "SKETCH: From Train Window (Leamington to Windsor) in March,""SKETCH: Overcast Monday," "SKETCH: Thaws," "SKETCH: Weekend," "Slow Advent" (B96), "Sounds Carry" (B116), "Speleologist" (B117), "Stone's Secret," "Strong Yellow, for Reading Aloud," "Technology is Spreading," "Then," "Thirst" (B118), "To a Pioneer in Canadian Studies; And to all in Such Pedantry," "To Emmaus," "To not know when it is the worst is worst," "Transients," "Until Christmas," "Us Artists – Before Public Was, or Grants; OR, Can Litter," "Waking and Sleeping: Christmas," "Water and Worship: An Open-Air Service on the Gatineau

River," "We are not poor, not Rich," "We the Poor who are Always with us" (B112), "'While as yet no leaves may fall,'" "Wonder: A Street-car Sketch," and "A Work-Up."

A5 *Winter Sun/The Dumbfounding: Poems 1940–66*. Modern Canadian Poets. Toronto: McClelland and Stewart, 1982. 191 pp.

Includes "The Absorbed" (A2), "The Agnes Cleves Papers" (B44), "All-Fools' Eve" (B45), "And Around" (A2), "The Apex Animal" (B39), "Apocalyptic?" (A1), "Apocalyptics" (A1), "The Artist" (A1), "Atlantis and the Department Store" (A1), "Banff" (B12), "Bestialities" (B85), "Birth Day" (A1), "Black-White Under Green: May 18, 1965" (A2), "Branches" (A2), "Butterfly Bones OR Sonnet Against Sonnets" (A1), "Canadian/Inverted" (A2), "A Child: Marginalia on an Epigraph (Mt. 18:3; Lk. 9:48)" (A2), "The Christian's Year in Miniature" (A2), "Christmas: Anticipation" (A2), "Chronic" (A1), "Civility a Bogey OR Two Centuries of Canadian Cities" (B53), "Controversy" (A2), "A Conversation" (A1), "Death" (A1), "Dispersed Titles" (B55), "The Dumbfounding" (B80), "The Earth That Falls Away" (B86), "Easter" (A1), "Extra-Political: The Thorned Speaks (While Day Horses Afar)" (A1), "The Fallen, Fallen World" (A1), "Far Off from University" (B51), "First" (A2), "Five Breaks" (B84), "For Dr. and Mrs. Dresser" (A2), "For Tinkers Who Travel on Foot" (B61), "A Friend's Friend" (A1), "From a Provincial" (B40), "Grammarian on a Lakefront Park Bench" (A1), "Hiatus" (B38), "Hot June" (B73), "Identity" (A1), "In a Season of Unemployment" (B62), "In Eporphyrial Harness" (B77), "In Time" (B63), "In Truth" (A2), "Intra-Political: An Exercise in Political Astronomy" (A1), "Jael's Part" (A1), "Janitor Working on Threshold" (A2), "Jonathan, o Jonathan" (A1), "July Man" (A2), "Lonely Lover" (A2), "Many As Two" (A2), "Meeting Together of Poles and Latitudes (In Prospect)" (B48), "Micro-Metro" (A2), "Miniature Biography of One of My Father's Friends Who Died a Generation Ago" (A2), "The Mirrored Man" (A1), "Mordent for a Melody" (A1), "The Mourner" (A2), "A Nameless One" (B81), "Natural/Unnatural" (B65), "New Year's Poem" (B42), "Not the Sweet Cicely of Gerardes Herball (i.e., Oriental Myrrh, Not English Myrrh" (A1), "November 23" (A1), "Of Tyranny, in One Breath (translated from a Hungarian poem by Gyula Illyés,

1956.)" (A2), "Old . . . Young. . . ." (A2), "On the Death of France Darte Scott: Upon the Birth of Twin Sons Who Later Died" (A1), "Once" (A2), "Our Working Day May Be Menaced" (A1), "Pace" (A2),"Person" (A2), ". . . Person OR A Hymn on and to the Holy Ghost" (A2), "A Prayer Answered by Prayer" (A2), "Prelude" (B52), "Public Address" (A1), "Ps. 19" (A2), "R.I.P." (A1), "Report from the Pedestrian's Outpost" (B66), "Rich Boy's Birthday Through a Window" (B46), "Riding and Waves" (B72), "Rigor Viris" (B26), "Rondeau Redoublé" (A1), "A Sad Song" (A2), "Searching and Sounding" (A2), "September Street" (A1), "Simon: finis" (B78), "Snow" (B49), "Span" (A1), "The Store Seeds" (B79), "A Story" (A2), "Stray Dog, Near Ecully" (B47), "The Swimmer's Moment" (A1), "Tennis" (B50), "Thaw" (A1), "To Professor X, Year Y" (B56), "Transit" (B69), "Twilight" (B59), "Two Mayday Selves" (A2), "Unbroken Lineage" (A1), "Unfinished After-Portrait OR Stages of Mourning" (A1), "Unspeakable" (B88), "Until Silenced: To I. A. (A Pakistani Scholar, Who Quoted and Interpreted Some Lines of Rumi's Poetry for Me in the Afternoon of February 15, 1965)" (A2), "Urban Tree" (A2), "Voluptuaries and Others" (B43), "Walking Behind, en Route, in Morning, in December" (A2), "Watershed" (A1), "The Word" (A2), "Words" (A2), and "The World Still Needs" (A1).

HISTORY

A6 *History of Ontario*. Illus. Selwyn Dewdney. Toronto: Gage, 1951. 138 pp.

COMPILATIONS

A7 *Books About Russia*. Toronto: Canadian Institute of International Affairs, 1943. 19 pp.

A8 *The Research Compendium: Reviews and Abstracts of Graduate Research 1942–1962*. Toronto: Univ. of Toronto Press, 1964. 265 pp.

Published in celebration of the fiftieth anniversary of the School of Social Work at the University of Toronto, this book includes introductory essays by Margaret Avison and Albert

Rose, and abstracts by Avison of all theses accepted by the University of Toronto School of Social Work from 1942 to 1962.

TRANSLATION

A9 ——, and Ilona Duczyńska, trans. *Acta Sanctorum and Other Tales*. By Jozef Lengyel. Introd. Ilona Duczyńska. London: Peter Owen, 1970. 256 pp.

Avison collaborated with Ilona Duczyńska in the translation; but asked not to have her name listed on the title page on religious grounds. Duczyńska mentions this in her Introduction.

BIOGRAPHY

A10 Willinsky, A. J. *A Doctor's Memoirs*. Toronto: Macmillan, 1960.

A foreword states that Avison acted as Willinsky's "amanuensis." She "helped to bring his materials into final order."

BROADSIDES

A11 *Factoring*. Thornhill, Ont.: Village, 1959. 1 leaf.

Designed and printed by Gus Rueter.

A12 "Hid Life." Dreadnaught Broadside, National Book Festival, 1982. 1 leaf.

CRITICISM

A13 "The Style of Byron's *Don Juan* in Relation to the Newspapers of His Day." M.A. Thesis Toronto 1964.

MANUSCRIPTS

A14 Margaret Avison Papers
Scott Library Archives
York University
Downsview, Ontario

This collection includes correspondence with bill bissett, Frederick Bock, Barry Callaghan, bpNichol, and others; typescripts of poetry by bill bissett, Frederick Bock, bpNichol, Al Purdy, and others; notes on Karl Polanyi's life; reviews of Avison's works; published poetry and prose by Avison; miscellaneous clippings and photographs; and printed music ca. World War I. A "List of Books and Periodicals Given to York University by Margaret Avison (1984)" has been prepared by David A. Kent and is available from the Scott Library Archives.

A15 Canadian Miscellany
McLennan Library
McGill University
Montreal, Quebec

The McLennan Library holds rough and fair copies of "The Fallen, Fallen World" from *Winter Sun*.

A16 Manuscript Collection
Thomas Fisher Rare Book Library
University of Toronto
Toronto, Ontario

This collection holds the ms. of an unpublished poem by Avison entitled "For Professor Endicott: an address," dated 16 April 1968, a letter from Gertrude Stein, written 23 June 1945 (1 leaf), and a letter from e. e. cummings, written 16 April 1950 (1 leaf).

A17 The Cid Corman Collection
Archives and Special Collections
Harriet Irving Library
University of New Brunswick
Fredericton, New Brunswick

The Archives and Special Collections Section has 5 letters from Avison to Cid Corman, written 26 June 1953 (2 leaves), 27 July 1953 (1 leaf), 18 Aug. 1953 (1 leaf), 13 Oct. 1953 (1 leaf), and 1 Dec. 1953 (1 leaf).

A18 Earle Birney Collection
Thomas Fisher Rare Book Library
University of Toronto
Toronto, Ontario

The collection contains 2 letters from Earle Birney to Avison, written 15 March 1950 (1 leaf) and 12 April 1950 (1 leaf); and 2 letters from Avison to Birney, written 2 April 1950 (1 leaf) and 7 Feb. 1951 (1 leaf).

A19 The Alan Crawley Papers
Queen's University Archives
Queen's University
Kingston, Ontario

The collection contains a letter from Avison to Alan Crawley, written 14 June 1952 (3 leaves).

A20 Lilly Library
University of Indiana
Bloomington, Indiana

The collection contains a letter from Avison to Henry Rago (then editor of *Poetry* [Chicago]), written 30 Dec. 1963, and proofs of *Winter Sun*.

A21 F.R. Scott Papers
Public Archives of Canada
Ottawa, Ontario

The collection contains eleven letters from Avison to F.R. Scott dated 16 Jan. 1955 to 29 Dec. 1957.

A22 Margaret Avison
Apt. 1215
877 Yonge Street
Toronto, Ontario

Most of Avison's manuscripts are in her possession. Since they are uncatalogued, no short list follows.

B Contributions to Periodicals and Books (Poems, Translations and Adaptations, Reprinted Anthology Contributions: A Selection, Essays, Book Reviews, Movie Reviews, Letters, and Short Stories) and Audio-Visual Material

Note: When an item is reprinted in one of Avison's books, this fact is noted in the entry through one of the following abbreviations:

The Dumbfounding .... *Dumb.*
Sliverick .... *Sliv.*
sunblue .... *sun.*
Winter Sun .... *WS*
Winter Sun/The Dumbfounding: Poems 1940–66 .... *WS/D*

POEMS

B1 "An Argument for Joy." *Hermes* [Humberside Collegiate], 1932, p. 111.

B2 "The Prairie." *Hermes* [Humberside Collegiate], 1932, p. 121.

B3 "Star Time." *Hermes* [Humberside Collegiate], 1932, p. 114.

B4 "To an Apple-Core." *Hermes* [Humberside Collegiate], 1932, p. 119.

B5 "Back Pew." *Acta Victoriana* [Victoria College, Univ. of Toronto], 61, No. 3 (Dec. 1936), 9.

B6 "Dirge." *Acta Victoriana* [Victoria College, Univ. of Toronto], 61, No. 4 (Jan. 1937), 5.

B7 "Mr. Noah Sir . . . ." *Acta Victoriana* [Victoria College, Univ. of Toronto], 61, No. 5 (Feb. 1937), 21.

B8 "Loose Ends." *Acta Victoriana* [Victoria College, Univ. of

Toronto], 62, No. 2 (Dec. 1937), 12.

B9 "Having Once Looked." *Acta Victoriana* [Victoria College, Univ. of Toronto], 63, No. 2 (Dec. 1938), 7.

B10 "Or Ever the Golden Bowl." *Acta Victoriana* [Victoria College, Univ. of Toronto], 63, No. 2 (Dec. 1938), 3.

B11 "Gatineau." *Acta Victoriana* [Victoria College, Univ. of Toronto], 64, No. 2 (Dec. 1939), frontispiece. Rpt. in *Canadian Poetry Magazine*, 4, No. 3 (Dec. 1939), 19.

B12 "Alberta." *Acta Victoriana* [Victoria College, Univ. of Toronto], 64, No. 4 (Feb. 1940), 18. *WS* (revised – "Banff"); *WS/D*.

B13 "Ontario." *Acta Victoriana* [Victoria College, Univ. of Toronto], 64, No. 4 (Feb. 1940), 15.

B14 "Yonge Street." *Acta Victoriana* [Victoria College, Univ. of Toronto], 64, No. 5 (March 1940), 6.

B15 "Break of Day." *The Canadian Forum*, Nov. 1942, p. 243.

B16 "I Saw One Walking." *The Canadian Forum*, Nov. 1942, p. 229.

B17 "The Butterfly." In *The Book of Canadian Poetry: A Critical and Historical Anthology.* Ed. and introd. A. J. M. Smith. Chicago: Univ. of Chicago Press, 1943, p. 429. Rpt. Toronto: Gage, 1943, p. 429.

B18 "Maria Minor." In *The Book of Canadian Poetry: A Critical and Historical Anthology.* Ed. and introd. A. J. M. Smith. Chicago: Univ. of Chicago Press, 1943, p. 428. Rpt. Toronto: Gage, 1943, p. 428.

B19 "Neverness or The One Ship Beached on One Far Distant Shore." In *The Book of Canadian Poetry: A Critical and Historical Anthology.* Ed. and introd. A. J. M. Smith. Chicago: Univ. of Chicago Press, 1943, pp. 426–28. Rpt. Toronto:

Gage, 1943, pp. 426–28.

B20 "Old Adam." In *The Book of Canadian Poetry: A Critical and Historical Anthology.* Ed. and introd. A. J. M. Smith. Chicago: Univ. of Chicago Press, 1943, p. 429. Rpt. Toronto: Gage, 1943, p. 429.

B21 "Optional." *The Canadian Forum*, Jan. 1943, p. 307.

B22 "The Past and the Break." *Manitoba Arts Review*, 3, No. 4 (Fall 1943), 30.

B23 "This Is the Season." *Manitoba Arts Review*, 3, No. 4 (Fall 1943), 31.

B24 "Mutable Hearts." *The Canadian Forum*, Oct. 1943, p. 155.

B25 "The Valiant Vacationist." *The Canadian Forum*, Dec. 1944, p. 205. Rpt. in *The Human Voice* [New York], Aug. 1966, n. pag.
See B257.

B26 "Rigor Viris." *The Canadian Forum*, Nov. 1945, p. 191. *WS*; *WS/D*.

B27 "Geometaphysics." *Poetry* [Chicago], 70 (Sept. 1947), 318–19.

B28 "The Iconoclasts." *Poetry* [Chicago], 70 (Sept. 1947), 319–20.

B29 "The Party." *Poetry* [Chicago], 70 (Sept. 1947), 323.

B30 "Perspective." *Poetry* [Chicago], 70 (Sept. 1947), 320–21. Rpt. in *Quarry*, 18, No. 2 (Winter 1969), 20.

B31 "Song but Oblique to '47." *Poetry* [Chicago], 70 (Sept. 1947), 322.

B32 "Another Christmas." *Contemporary Verse*, No. 26 (Fall 1948), p. 5.

B33 "Christmas." *Contemporary Verse*, No. 26 (Fall 1948), p. 3.

B34 "The Road." *Contemporary Verse*, No. 26 (Fall 1948), p. 4.

B35 "The Coward." *here and now*, 1, No. 3 (Jan. 1949), 68.

B36 "Omen." *here and now*, 1, No. 3 (Jan. 1949), 68.

B37 "Song of the Flaming Sword." *Contemporary Verse*, No. 35 (Summer 1951), p. 16.

B38 "Hiatus." *Poetry* [Chicago], 80 (April 1952), 15. *WS*; *WS/D*.

B39 "The Apex Animal." *Kenyon Review*, 18 (Spring 1956), 263–64. *WS*; *WS/D*.

B40 "From a Provincial." *Kenyon Review*, 18 (Spring 1956), 263. *WS*; *Dumb.*; *WS/D*.
See B260.

B41 "Knowledge of Age." *Kenyon Review*, 18 (Spring 1956), 265.

B42 "New Year's Poem." *Kenyon Review*, 18 (Spring 1956), 264–65. *WS*; *WS/D*.
See B261.

B43 "Voluptuaries and Others." In *The Book of Canadian Poetry: A Critical and Historical Anthology.* Ed. and introd. A. J. M. Smith. 3rd ed. Toronto: Gage, 1957, pp. 476–77. *WS*; *WS/D*.
See B270.

B44 "The Agnes Cleves Papers." *Origin*, Ser. 1, No. 20 (Winter 1957), pp. 99–109. *WS*; *WS/D*.
See B259.

B45 "All Fools' Eve." *Poetry* [Chicago], 91 (Dec. 1957), 173. *WS*; *WS/D*.

B46 "Rich Boy's Birthday through a Window." *Poetry* [Chicago], 91 (Dec. 1957), 175. *WS*; *WS/D* ("Rich Boy's Birthday

Through a Window").

B47 "Stray Dog, Near Ecully: Commune de Rhône." *Poetry* [Chicago], 91 (Dec. 1957), 174. *WS* ("Stray Dog, near Ecully"); *WS/D* ("Stray Dog, Near Ecully").

B48 "Meeting Together of Poles & Latitudes: in Prospect." In *The Penguin Book of Canadian Verse*. Ed. and introd. Ralph Gustafson. Harmondsworth, Eng.: Penguin, 1958, pp. 214–15. *WS* ["Meeting together of Poles and Latitudes (In Prospect)"]; *Dumb.* ["Meeting Together of Poles and Latitudes (in Prospect)"]; *WS/D* ["Meeting Together of Poles and Latitudes (In Prospect)"].

B49 "Snow." In *The Penguin Book of Canadian Verse*. Ed. and introd. Ralph Gustafson. Harmondsworth, Eng.: Penguin, 1958, p. 214. *WS*; *WS/D*.
See B266.

B50 "Tennis." In *The Penguin Book of Canadian Verse*. Ed. and introd. Ralph Gustafson. Harmondsworth, Eng.: Penguin, 1958, pp. 213–14. *WS*; *WS/D*.
See B233.

B51 "June as Christmas." *Combustion*, No. 8 (Nov. 1958), p. 4. *WS* ("Far off from University"); *WS/D* ("Far Off from University").

B52 "Prelude." *Poetry* [Chicago], 93 (March 1959), 366–68. *WS*; *WS/D*.

B53 "Civility a Bogey — Two Centuries of Canadian Cities." *Queen's Quarterly*, 66 (Summer 1959), 275–76. *WS* ("Civility a Bogey; or, Two Centuries of Canadian Cities"); *WS/D* ("Civility a Bogey OR Two Centuries of Canadian Cities").

B54 "Factoring." *The Canadian Forum*, Aug. 1959, p. 110.

B55 "Dispersed Titles." *Winter Sun*. Toronto: Univ. of Toronto Press, 1960, pp. 3–7. Rpt. in *The Human Voice* [New York], Aug. 1966, n. pag. *WS/D*.

B56 "To Professor X, Year Y." *Winter Sun*. Toronto: Univ. of Toronto Press, 1960, p. 34. Rpt. in *The Human Voice* [New York], Aug. 1966, n. pag. *WS/D*.

B57 "Chestnut Tree – Three Storeys Up." In *Poetry 62*. Ed. Eli Mandel and Jean-Guy Pilon. Preface Eli Mandel. Toronto: Ryerson, 1961, pp. 10–11.

B58 "Unseasoned." In *Poetry 62*. Ed. Eli Mandel and Jean-Guy Pilon. Preface Eli Mandel. Toronto: Ryerson, 1961, pp. 14–15.

B59 "Twilight." *Waterloo Review* [London, Ont.], No. 6 (Winter 1961), p. 27. *Dumb.*; *WS/D*.

B60 "Diminuendo." *Origin*, Ser. 2, No. 4 (Jan. 1962), pp. 17–18.

B61 "For Tinkers Who Travel on Foot." *Origin*, Ser. 2, No. 4 (Jan. 1962), p. 5. *Dumb.*; *WS/D*.

B62 "In a Season of Unemployment." *Origin*, Ser. 2, No. 4 (Jan. 1962), p. 19. *Dumb.*; *WS/D*.
See B235.

B63 "In Time." *Origin*, Ser. 2, No. 4 (Jan. 1962), p. 1. *Dumb.*; *WS/D*.

B64 "The Local & the Lakefront." *Origin*, Ser. 2, No. 4 (Jan. 1962), pp. 3–4.

B65 "Natural/Unnatural." *Origin*, Ser. 2, No. 4 (Jan. 1962), pp. 20–21. *Dumb.* (revised); *WS/D*.

B66 "Report from the Pedestrians' Outpost." *Origin*, Ser. 2, No. 4 (Jan. 1962), p. 2. *Dumb.*; *WS/D*.

B67 "Streetcar." *Origin*, Ser. 2, No. 4 (Jan. 1962), pp. 6–7.

B68 "To a Period." *Origin*, Ser. 2, No. 4 (Jan. 1962), pp. 12–13.

B69 "Transit." *Origin*, Ser. 2, No. 4 (Jan. 1962), p. 16. *Dumb.*; *WS/D*.

B70 "The Typographer's Ornate Symbol at the End of a Chapter or Story." *Origin*, Ser. 2, No. 4 (Jan. 1962), pp. 14–15.

B71 "Waking Up." *Origin*, Ser. 2, No. 4 (Jan. 1962), p. 8.

B72 "Why Not?". *Origin*, Ser. 2, No. 4 (Jan. 1962), p. 9. Rpt. ("Riding and Waves") in *Chatelaine*, Oct. 1972, p. 104. Rpt. in *Right on* (*Jubal* Section) [California], March 1975, p. 5. *Dumb.*; *WS/D.*

B73 "Hot June." *The Canadian Forum*, March 1963, p. 286. *Dumb.*; *WS/D.*

B74 "Unspeakable." *Evidence*, No. 7 (Summer 1963), p. 85. Rpt. in *Canadian Poetry*, 29 (Feb. 1966), 12. *Dumb.*; *WS/D.*

B75 "Hialog." *Ganglia*, Ser. 1, No. 1 (1964), n. pag.

B76 "Holiday Plans for the Whole Family." In *Poetry of Mid-Century 1940–1960*. Ed. and introd. Milton Wilson. New Canadian Library Original, No. 04. Toronto: McClelland and Stewart, 1964, p. 110.

B77 "In Eporphyrial Harness." *Ganglia*, Ser. 1, No. 1 (1964), n. pag. *Dumb.*; *WS/D.*

B78 "Simon (finis)." In *Poetry of Mid-Century 1940–1960*. Ed. and introd. Milton Wilson. New Canadian Library Original, No. 04. Toronto: McClelland and Stewart, 1964, p. 111. *Dumb.* ("Simon: finis"); *WS/D.*

B79 "The Store Seeds." *Ganglia*, Ser. 1, No. 1 (1964), n. pag. *Dumb.*; *WS/D.*
See B267.

B80 "The Dumbfounding." *His*, Feb. 1964, [back cover]. *Dumb.*; *WS/D.*
See B258.

B81 "A Nameless One." *Desert Review*, Spring 1964, p. 4. *Dumb.*; *WS/D.*

B82 "From a Continuing Tribute: To Karl Polanyi." *The Canadian Forum*, June 1964, p. 52.

B83 "Grad Camp, 1964." *Crux*, 2, No. 2 (1965), 8–9.

B84 "Five Breaks." *The Literary Review* [Fairleigh Dickinson Univ., Teaneck, N.J.], [Canada Number], 8 (Summer 1965), 515–16. *Dumb.*; *WS/D.*

B85 "Bestealities/OR/Any Number Can Play." *BlewOintment* [Vancouver], 3, No. 1 (Nov. 1965), n. pag. *Dumb.* ("Bestialities"); *WS/D.*
See B240.

B86 "The Earth That Falls Away." *Island* [Toronto], No. 6 – *Combflustion*, No. 15 (1966), pp. 62–69. *Dumb.*; *WS/D.*
See B243.

B87 "A Medical-Psychological Decision. (Anagoge?)." *Ganglia*, Ser. 1, No. 5 (1966), n. pag.

B88 "Unspeakable." *Canadian Poetry*, 29 (Feb. 1966), 12. *Dumb.*; *WS/D.*

B89 "Despondency." *Adam International Review*, Nos. 313–14–15 (1967), p. 10.

B90 "March: College-Bathurst Corner." *BlewOintment* [Vancouver], 5, No. 1 (Jan. 1967), n. pag.

B91 "To Jacques Ellul." *BlewOintment* [Vancouver], 5, No. 1 (Jan. 1967), n. pag.

B92 "All Out or Oblation." *The Catalyst*, No. 1 (Autumn 1967), p. 21. Rpt. (revised – "All Out") in *BlewOintment* [Vancouver], 6, No. 2 (Aug. 1968), n. pag. *sun.* [revised – "All Out; OR Oblation (as defined in 2 Sam. 23, 13–17 & 1 Chron. II, 17–19)"].

B93 "Go On I'm Listening." *Crux*, 5, No. 3 (1968), 28.

B94 "Having," *Credo*, No. 5 (April 1968), p. 6.

B95 "He Couldn't be Safe." *His*, Dec. 1968, p. 42. *sun*. ["He Couldn't Be Safe (Isaiah 53:5)"].

B96 "Slow Advent and Christmas: Time." *Christianity Today*, 6 Dec. 1968, p. 9. *sun*. (revised – "Slow Advent").

This poem is also used by the American Inter-Varsity Christian Fellowship on a greeting card.

B97 "'Canada': Shooting Schedule." In *Notes for a Native Land*. Ed. and introd. Andy Wainwright. Ottawa: Oberon, 1969, pp. 78–79.

B98 "Childhood Fields Near Ponoka." *IS.*, No. 7 (1969), n. pag.

B99 "Missionaries: Sequence." *Crux*, 6, No. 2 (1969), 24.

B100 "The Useless Using." *IS.*, No. 7 (1969), n. pag.

B101 "On Believing the Bible." In *Margaret Avison*. By Ernest Redekop. Studies in Canadian Literature, No. 9. Toronto: Copp Clark, 1970, pp. 144–45. Rpt. in *Michigan Quarterly Review*, 22 (Summer 1983), 393–94. *sun*. (revised – "The Bible to Be Believed").

B102 "Hoping: on reading Mr. Kent's 'The House of Christmas.'" In *In Memoriam: H. Harold Kent*. Toronto: 1972, p. 19.

B103 "Sliverick." *ellipse*, No. 17 (1975), p. 109. Rpt. partly trans. Jerry Ofo in *ellipse*, No. 17 (1975), p. 108. *Sliv.*

B104 "April 17–18, 1970 (Apollo XIII)." *The Telegram* [Toronto], 25 April 1970, p. 51. Rpt. in *Margaret Avison*. By Ernest Redekop. Studies in Canadian Literature, No. 9. Toronto: Copp Clark, 1970, p. 146. *sun*. (revised – "Poem on the Astronauts in Apollo XIII's Near-Disaster, written April 17–18, 1970, for the newspaper").

B105 "Because Somebody Said 'They Dress So Well.'" *Impulse*, 1, No. 1 (1971), 15.

B106 "Immobility / Rest / . . . ." *Impulse*, 1, No. 1 (1971), 16.

B107 "Christmas from Summertime Seen." *Exile*, 1, No. 2 (1972), 105. *sun*. (revised – "Midsummer Christmas").

B108 "Light I." *Exile*, 1, No. 2 (1972), 103. *sun*. [revised – "Light (I)"].

B109 "Part of a Debate." *Crux*, Fall 1972, p. 17.

B110 "Light II." *Exile*, 1, No. 2 (1972), 104. *sun*. ["Light (II)"].

B111 "March Morning in London, Ont." *Applegarth's Folly* [London, Ont.], No. 1 (Summer 1973), p. 110. *sun*. (revised – "March Morning").

B112 "We the Poor Who Are Always with Us." In *Canadian Anthology*. Ed. and preface Carl F. Klinck and Reginald E. Watters. 3rd ed., Toronto: Gage, 1974, p. 452. *sun*. (revised – "We the Poor who are Always with us").

B113 "Backing into Being." *The Second Mile* [Hantsport, N.S.], Aug. 1977, p. 12. *sun*.

B114 "Embattled Deliverance." *The Second Mile* [Hantsport, N.S.], Aug. 1977, p. 14. *sun*.

B115 "March." *The Second Mile* [Hantsport, N.S.], Aug. 1977, p. 13. *sun*.

B116 "Sounds Carry." *The Second Mile* [Hantsport, N.S.], Aug. 1977, p. 10. *sun*.

B117 "Speleologist." *The Second Mile* [Hantsport, N.S.], Aug. 1977, p. 11. *sun*.

B118 "Thirst." *The Second Mile* [Hantsport, N.S.], Aug. 1977, p. 13. *sun*.

B119 "About a New Anthology Again . . . ." In *Poets of Canada*. Ed. and preface John Robert Colombo. Edmonton: Hurtig,

1978, pp. 153–54.

B120 "A Hearing." In *The Country of the Risen King: An Anthology of Christian Poetry.* Ed. Merle Meeter. Grand Rapids, Mich.: Baker Book House, 1978, pp. 10–11.

B121 "No Matter What." In *The Country of the Risen King: An Anthology of Christian Poetry.* Ed. Merle Meeter. Grand Rapids, Mich.: Baker Book House, 1978, p. 15.

B122 "Thinking Back." *Acta Victoriana* [Victoria College, Univ. of Toronto], [Centennial 1878–1978], 102, No. 2 (Fall 1978), 42.

B123 "Known." In *In Celebration: Anemos.* Poems for Denise Levertov on her sixtieth birthday. Palo Alto: Matrix Press, 198?. Rpt. in *Poetry Canada Review*, 7, No. 1 (Autumn 1985), 9.

B124 "And the World was There." *Exile*, 9, Nos. 2, 3, & 4 (1984), 293.

B125 "Goal far and Near." *Exile*, 9, Nos. 2, 3, & 4 (1984), 304.

B126 "Incentive." *Exile*, 9, Nos. 2, 3, & 4 (1984), 302.

B127 "Ineradicable Promise." *Exile*, 9, Nos. 2, 3, & 4 (1984), 303.

B128 "Loss." *Exile*, 9, Nos. 2, 3, & 4 (1984), 295.

B129 "nose-thrills/ nose-drills/ nostrils . . . ." *Exile*, 9, Nos. 2, 3, & 4 (1984), 294.

B130 "Nothing else for it." *Exile*, 9, Nos. 2, 3, & 4 (1984), 301.

B131 "O, None of that." *Exile*, 9, Nos. 2, 3, & 4 (1984), 299.

B132 "Paraphrase of Ephesians 2: 1–6." *Exile*, 9, Nos. 2, 3, & 4 (1984), 300.

B133 "Patience." *Exile*, 9, Nos. 2, 3, & 4 (1984), 297.

B134 "A sad poem on a sad summer." *Exile*, 9, Nos. 2, 3, & 4 (1984), 305.

B135 "Setting for the Portrait." *Exile*, 9, Nos. 2, 3, & 4 (1984), 292.

B136 "Sky." *Exile*, 9, Nos. 2, 3, & 4 (1984), 298.

B137 "A small music on a spring morning." *Exile*, 9, Nos. 2, 3, & 4 (1984), 296.

B138 "Coming Back." *Poetry Canada Review*, 7, No. 1 (Autumn 1985), 9.

TRANSLATIONS AND ADAPTATIONS

B139 "Ode to Bartok." *The New Reasoner*, 1, No. 5 (Summer 1958), 69–72.

Adapted to English from the literal translation by Ilona Duczyńska of a poem by Gyula Illyés.

B140 "Ars Poetica." In *The Plough and the Pen: Writings from Hungary 1930–1956*. Ed. Ilona Duczyńska and Karl Polanyi. Foreword W. H. Auden. Toronto: McClelland and Stewart, 1963, pp. 169–70.

Adapted to English from work sheets including "the literal translation and word identifications, the rhyme and assonance patterns, number of syllables and rhythmic pictures" by Ilona Duczyńska of a poem by Attila József.

B141 ——, and Eustace Ross. "Nightmare and Dawn." In *The Plough and the Pen: Writings from Hungary 1930–1956*. Ed. Ilona Duczyńska and Karl Polanyi. Foreword W. H. Auden. Toronto: McClelland and Stewart, 1963, pp. 188–89.

Adapted to English from work sheets including "the literal translation and word identifications, the rhyme and assonance patterns, number of syllables and rhythmic pictures" by Ilona Duczyńska of a poem by Zoltán Zelk.

B142 "Debris." In *The Plough and the Pen: Writings from Hungary 1930–1956*. Ed. Ilona Duczyńska and Karl Polanyi. Foreword W. H. Auden. Toronto: McClelland and Stewart, 1963, pp. 183–84.

Adapted to English from work sheets including "the literal translation and word identifications, the rhyme and assonance patterns, number of syllables and rhythmic pictures" by Ilona Duczyńska of a poem by László Benjamin.

B143 "Farm, at Dark, on the Great Plain." In *The Plough and the Pen: Writings from Hungary 1930–1956*. Ed. Ilona Duczyńska and Karl Polanyi. Foreword W. H. Auden. Toronto: McClelland and Stewart, 1963, pp. 199–203.

Adapted to English from work sheets including "the literal translation and word identifications, the rhyme and assonance patterns, number of syllables and rhythmic pictures" by Ilona Duczyńska, or Karl Polanyi, of a poem by Ferenc Juhász.

B144 "Here on This Earth." In *The Plough and the Pen: Writings from Hungary 1930–1956*. Ed. Ilona Duczyńska and Karl Polanyi. Foreword W. H. Auden. Toronto: McClelland and Stewart, 1963, pp. 185–86.

Adapted to English from work sheets including "the literal translation and word identifications, the rhyme and assonance patterns, number of syllables and rhythmic pictures" by Ilona Duczyńska of a poem by Zoltán Zelk.

B145 "The Plough Moves." In *The Plough and the Pen: Writings from Hungary 1930–1956*. Ed. Ilona Duczyńska and Karl Polanyi. Foreword W. H. Auden. Toronto: McClelland and Stewart, 1963,pp. 173–74.

Adapted to English from work sheets including "the literal translation and word identifications, and rhyme and assonance patterns, number of syllables and rhythmic pictures" by Ilona Duczyńska of a poem by Gyula Illyés.

B146 "Wayfaring Seaman." In *The Plough and the Pen: Writings from Hungary 1930–1956*. Ed. Ilona Duczyńska and Karl Polanyi. Foreword W. H. Auden. Toronto: McClelland and Stewart, 1963, p. 190.

Adapted to English from work sheets including "the literal translation and word identifications, the rhyme and assonance patterns, number of syllables and rhythmic pictures" by Ilona Duczyńska of a poem by Lajos Tamási.

B147 "The Butterfly" and "Rigor Viris." In *Other Canadians: An Anthology of New Poetry in Canada 1940–1946*. Ed. John Sutherland. Montreal: First Statement, 1947, pp. 29–30.

B148 "The Butterfly." In *Canadian Poems 1850–1952*. Ed. Louis Dudek and Irving Layton. 2nd ed. Toronto: Contact, 1952, p. 97.

B149 "Christmas." In *Twentieth Century Canadian Poetry: An Anthology with Introduction and Notes*. Ed. and introd. Earle Birney. Toronto: Ryerson, 1953, p. 44.

B150 "Rigor Viris." In *Canadian Poetry in English*. Rev. and enl. ed. Ed. Bliss Carman, Lorne Pierce, and V. B. Rhodenizer. Foreword Lorne Pierce. Toronto: Ryerson, 1954, p. 437.

B151 "The Butterfly," "Maria Minor," "Neverness, or The One Ship Beached on One Far Distant Shore," "Perspective," "*Rigor viris*," "[The Simple Horizontal]," and "Voluptuaries and Others." In *The Book of Canadian Poetry: A Critical and Historical Anthology*. Ed. and preface A. J. M. Smith. 3rd ed. Toronto: Gage, 1957, pp. 471–77.

B152 "Knowledge of Age" and "Perspective." In *The Penguin Book of Canadian Verse*. Ed. and introd. Ralph Gustafson. Harmondsworth, Eng.: Penguin, 1958, pp. 212–13.

B153 "The Butterfly," "Meeting Together of Poles & Latitudes: In Prospect," "New Year's Poem," "Perspective," "Stray Dog, near Ecully, Valley of the Rhône," and "Watershed." In *The Oxford Book of Canadian Verse: In English and French*. Ed. and introd. A. J. M. Smith. Toronto: Oxford Univ. Press, 1960, pp. 354–60.

B154 "Chestnut Tree — Three Storeys Up," "Twilight," "The Two Selves," and "Unseasoned." In *Poetry 62*. Ed. Eli Mandel and Jean-Guy Pilon. Preface Eli Mandel. Toronto: Ryerson, 1961, pp. 10–15.

B155 "Ode to Bartók." In *The Plough and the Pen: Writings from Hungary 1930–1956*. Ed. Ilona Duczyńska and Karl Polanyi. Foreword W. H. Auden. Toronto: McClelland and Stewart, 1963, pp. 69–72.

Adapted to English from work sheets including "the literal translation and word identifications, the rhyme and assonance patterns, numbers of syllables and rhythmic pictures" by Ilona Duczyńska of a poem by Gyula Illyés.

B156 "All Fools' Eve," "Birth Day," "Dispersed Titles," "From a Provincial," "The Iconoclasts," "Intra-Political: An Exercise in Political Astronomy," "The Local & the Lakefront," "Meeting Together of Poles and Latitudes (In Prospect)," "Mordent for a Melody," "On the Death of France Darte Scott: Upon the Birth of Twin Sons Who Later Died," "Perspective," "Snow," "Thaw," "To Professor X, Year Y," "The Valiant Vacationist," "Voluptuaries and Others," and "Waking Up." In *Poetry of Mid-Century 1940–1960*. Ed. and introd. Milton Wilson. New Canadian Library Original, No. O4. Toronto: McClelland and Stewart, 1964, pp. 84–110.

B157 "The Apex Animal," "The Butterfly," "Butterfly Bones; or, Sonnet Against Sonnets," "Civility a Bogey, or, Two Centuries of Canadian Cities," "Far Off from University," "Mordent for a Melody," "Neverness, or, The One Ship Beached on One Far Distant Shore," and "New Year's Poem." In *Canadian Anthology*. Ed. and preface Carl F. Klinck and Reginald E. Watters. Rev. ed. Toronto: Gage, 1966, pp. 434–40.

B158 "Thaw." In *Great Canadian Writing: A Century of Imagination*. Ed. and introd. Claude Bissell. Toronto: Canadian Centennial, 1966, p. 115.

B159 "A Conversation." In *A Century of Canadian Literature/Un Siècle Littérature Canadienne*. Ed. Gordon Green and Guy Sylvestre. Toronto: Ryerson, 1967, pp. 506–07.

B160 "For Dr and Mrs Dresser," "In a Season of Unemployment," "Intra-Political: An Exercise in Political Astronomy," "A Story," "Voluptuaries and Others," and "The Word." In

Modern Canadian Verse: In English and French. Ed. and preface A. J. M. Smith. Toronto: Oxford Univ. Press, 1967, pp. 207–19.

B161 "The Absorbed," "Black-White Under Green: May 18, 1965," "In a Season of Unemployment," "July Man," "A Nameless One," "Pace," "The Swimmer's Moment," "To Professor X, Year Y," "Voluptuaries and Others," and "The World Still Needs." In *20th Century Poetry and Poetics*. Ed. and preface Gary Geddes. Toronto: Oxford Univ. Press, 1969, pp. 366–77.

B162 "The Absorbed," "Birth Day," "Black-White Under Green: May 18, 1965," "In a Season of Unemployment," "July Man," "A Nameless One," "New Year's Poem," "Pace," "Snow," "The Swimmer's Moment," "To Professor X, Year Y," "Voluptuaries and Others," and "The World Still Needs." In *15 Canadian Poets*. Ed. and preface Gary Geddes and Phyllis Bruce. Toronto: Oxford Univ. Press, 1970, pp. 128–43.

B163 "Butterfly Bones; or, Sonnet Against Sonnets" and "New Year's Poem." In *A Little Treasury of Modern Poetry*. Ed. and introd. Oscar Williams. 3rd ed. New York: Scribner, 1970, pp. 661–62.

B164 "Sliverick." In *THE COSMIC CHEF GLEE AND PERLOO MEMORIAL SOCIETY UNDER THE DIRECTION OF CAPTAIN POETRY PRESENTS AN EVENING OF CONCRETE*. Ed. bpNichol. Ottawa: Oberon, 1970, p. 74.

B165 "Black-White Under Green: May 18, 1965," "The Dumbfounding," "For Dr. and Mrs. Dresser," "For Tinkers Who Travel on Foot," "In a Season of Unemployment," "Ps. 19," "Searching and Sounding," "A Story," "The Swimmer's Moment," "The Two Selves," "The Word," and "Words." In *6 Days: An Anthology of Canadian Christian Poetry*. Ed. H. Houtman. Toronto: Wedge, 1971, pp. 119–39.

B166 "All Fools' Eve," "Death," "New Year's Poem," "R.I.P.," "Snow," "To Professor X, Year Y," and "The Two Selves." In *Eight More Canadian Poets*. Ed. and introd. Eli Mandel. Toronto: Holt, Rinehart and Winston, 1972, pp. 8–13.

B167 "A Story." In *Listen! Songs and Poems of Canada*. Ed. and introd. Homer Hogan. Methuen Canadian Literature Series. Toronto: Methuen, 1972, pp. 153–55.

B168 "Mutable Hearts." In *Forum: Canadian Life and Letters 1920–70. Selections from* The Canadian Forum. Ed. and preface J. L. Granatstein and Peter Stevens. Toronto: Univ. of Toronto Press, 1972, pp. 214–15.

B169 "Apocalyptic?", "The Butterfly," "Butterfly Bones; or, Sonnet Against Sonnets," "The Dumbfounding," "First," "Grammarian on a Lakefront Parkbench," "Neverness, or The One Ship Beached on One Far Distant Shore," "New Year's Poem," "Snow," "The Swimmer's Moment," and "Waking Up." In *The Evolution of Canadian Literature in English: 1945–70*. Ed. and introd. Paul Denham. Preface Mary Jane Edwards. Toronto: Holt, Rinehart and Winston, 1973, pp. 88–98.

B170 "For Tinkers Who Travel on Foot," "Tennis," and "The Two Selves." In *The Norton Anthology of Modern Poetry*. Ed. Richard Ellmann and Robert O'Clair. New York: Norton, 1973, pp. 957–59.

B171 "In a Season of Unemployment," "Snow," and "Twilight." In *The Oxford Anthology of Canadian Literature*. Ed. and preface Robert Weaver and William Toye. Toronto: Oxford Univ. Press, 1973, pp. 14–16.

B172 "The Apex Animal," "Butterfly Bones; or, Sonnet Against Sonnets," "'The Earth That Falls Away'" (excerpt), "New Year's Poem," "Perspective," and "The World Still Needs." In *Canadian Anthology*. Ed. and preface Carl F. Klinck and Reginald E. Watters. 3rd ed. Toronto: Gage, 1974, pp. 447–51.

B173 "A Story" and "The Word." In *The Peaceable Kingdom*. Literature: Uses of the Imagination Series. Ed. Alvin A. Lee, Hope Arnott Lee, and W. T. Jewkes. Sup. ed. Northrop Frye. New York: Harcourt, Brace, Jovanovich, Inc., 1974, pp. 82–84, 244–45.

B174 "Black-White Under Green: May 18, 1965," "The Dumbfounding," and "Thaw." In *The Norton Anthology of Poetry.* Ed. Alexander W. Allison, Herbert Barrows, Caesar R. Blake, Arthur J. Carr, Arthur M. Eastman, and Hubert M. English, Jr. Rev. ed. New York: Norton, 1975, pp. 1184–87.

B175 "For Dr and Mrs Dresser," "Janitor Working on Threshold," "Knowledge of Age," "Meeting Together of Poles and Latitudes: In Prospect," ". . . Person, or a Hymn on and to the Holy Ghost," "Perspective," "Snow," and "Tennis." In *The Penguin Book of Canadian Verse*. 3rd ed. Ed. and introd. Ralph Gustafson. Harmondsworth, Eng.: Penguin, 1975, pp. 225–29.

B176 "The Local & the Lakefront," "Natural/Unnatural," "The Typographer's Ornate Symbol," "Waking Up," and "Why Not?". In *The Gist of Origin*. Ed. and introd. Cid Corman. New York: Grossman, 1975, pp. 191–96.

B177 "The Absorbed," "The Dumbfounding," "Five Breaks," "In Eporphyrial Harness," "Jonathan, O Jonathan," "July Man," "Miniature Biography," "Natural/Unnatural," "September Street," "Twilight," "Watershed," and "Words." In *Canadian Poetry: The Modern Era*. Ed. and preface John Newlove. Toronto: McClelland and Stewart, 1977, pp. 32–45.

B178 "All Out or Oblation," "Circuit," "The Dumbfounding," "For Tinkers Who Travel on Foot," "A Hearing," "Hymn on and to the Holy Ghost," "No Matter What," "Sestina for Professor William Blissett," and "The Word." In *The Country of the Risen King: An Anthology of Christian Poetry.* Ed. Merle Meeter. Grand Rapids, Mich.: Baker Book House, 1978, pp. 7–15.

B179 "Butterfly Bones: or, Sonnet Against Sonnets," "The Dumbfounding," "From a Provincial," "The Iconoclasts," "Meeting Together of Poles and Latitudes (In Prospect)," "A Nameless One," "Perspective," "Snow," and "The Swimmer's Moment." In *Literature in Canada*. Vol. II. Ed.

and preface Douglas Daymond and Leslie Monkman. Toronto: Gage, 1978, 346–54.

B180 "All Fools' Eve," "Hiatus," "In Time," "Natural/ Unnatural," "Two Mayday Selves," "Transit," and "The World Still Needs." In *News and Weather: Seven Canadian Poets*. Ed. and foreword August Kleinzahler. Coldstream. Ilderton, Ont.: Brick, 1982, pp. 17–26.

B181 "The Apex Animal," "Black-White Under Green: May 18, 1965," "Butterfly Bones; or Sonnet Against Sonnets," "Easter," "The Mirrored Man," "Strong Yellow, for Reading Aloud:", "The Swimmer's Moment," and "Voluptuaries and Others." In *Canadian Poetry*. Ed. Jack David and Robert Lecker. Introd. George Woodcock. New Press Canadian Classics. Toronto/Downsview, Ont.: General/ECW, 1982. Vol. I, 267–76.

B182 "Civility a Bogey," "The Dumbfounding," "In a Season of Unemployment," "Meeting Together of Poles and Latitudes (In Prospect)," "A Nameless One," "New Year's Poem," "Snow," "Thaw," and "Unspeakable." In *The New Oxford Book of Canadian Verse: In English*. Ed. and introd. Margaret Atwood. Toronto: Oxford Univ. Press, 1982, pp. 195–204.

B183 "The Apex Animal," "The Butterfly," "Butterfly Bones; or Sonnet Against Sonnets," "Light (I)," "Light (II)," "Light (III)," "Meeting Together of Poles and Latitudes (In Prospect)," "Neverness, or, The One Ship Beached on One Far Distant Shore," "Perspective," "Snow," "Strong Yellow, for Reading Aloud," and "Tennis." In *An Anthology of Canadian Literature in English*. Ed. and introd. Donna Bennett and Russell Brown. Vol. II. Toronto: Oxford Univ. Press, 1983, 33–43.

ESSAYS

B184 "Among Those Present." *Acta Victoriana* [Victoria College, Univ. of Toronto], 61, No. 2 (Nov. 1936), 12–13.

B185 "The Bob." *Acta Victoriana* [Victoria College, Univ. of Toronto], 63, No. 1 (Nov. 1938), 32.

B186 "Conferences at Potsdam." *The Nations Have Declared: The Documents Issued by The United Nations*, Pt. III (Oct. 1945), pp. 25–27.

B187 "The International Court." *The Nations Have Declared: The Documents Issued by The United Nations*, Pt. III (Oct. 1945), p. 22.

B188 Introduction. *The Nations Have Declared: The Documents Issued by The United Nations*, Pt. III (Oct. 1945), pp. 3–4.

B189 "San Francisco Conference on International Organization." *The Nations Have Declared: The Documents Issued by The United Nations*, Pt. III (Oct. 1945), pp. 5–7.

B190 "The Trial of War Criminals." *The Nations Have Declared: The Documents Issued by The United Nations*, Pt. III (Oct. 1945), pp. 35–36.

B191 "Poets in Canada." *Poetry* [Chicago], 94 (June 1959), 182–85.

B192 "Twentieth Century Witchcraft." *Crux*, 2, No. 1 (1965), 2–6.

B193 "What Knox Church Means to Me." *Faith for Today*, 6, No. 1 (Fall 1966), 5–7.

B194 "I Wish I Had Known." In *I Wish I Had Known*. Ed. M. H. London: Scripture Union, 1968, pp. 86–89.
Signed: "Angela Martin."

B195 "Muse of Danger." *His*, March 1968, pp. 33–35.

B196 "Who Listens and How Come?". *Crux*, 6, No. 2 (1969), 4–5.

B197 "She Showed His Love." *The Glad Tidings*, Jan. 1970, pp. 22–24.

B198 ". . . at least we are together . . . ." *Crux*, 8, No. 2 (1970–71),

15–19.

B199 Autobiographical Note. In *6 Days: An Anthology of Canadian Christian Poetry*. Ed. H. Houtman. Toronto: Wedge, 1971, pp. 140–41.

BOOK REVIEWS

B200 Rev. of *New Poems*, by Dylan Thomas. *The Canadian Forum*, Sept. 1943, p. 143.

B201 Rev. of *Day and Night*, by Dorothy Livesay. *The Canadian Forum*, June 1944, p. 67.

B202 Rev. of *The Soldier, a Poem*, by Conrad Aiken. *The Canadian Forum*, Jan. 1945, p. 241.

B203 Rev. of *Here and Now*, by Irving Layton. *The Canadian Forum*, May 1945, pp. 47–48.

B204 Rev. of *The Task*, by Robert Bhain Campbell. *The Canadian Forum*, Dec. 1945, p. 223.

B205 Rev. of *Selected Poems*, by Kenneth Patchen; and *Residence on Earth and Other Poems*, by Pablo Neruda. *The Canadian Forum*, April 1947, pp. 21–22.

B206 Rev. of *The Rocking Chair and Other Poems*, by A. M. Klein. *The Canadian Forum*, Nov. 1948, p. 191. Rpt. in *A. M. Klein*. Ed. and introd. Tom Marshall. Critical Views on Canadian Writers, No. 4. Toronto: Ryerson, 1970, pp. 55–58.

B207 Rev. of *The Canticle of the Rose: Selected Poems 1920–1947*, by Edith Sitwell. *The Canadian Forum*, Feb. 1950, pp. 262–63.

B208 Rev. of *The Red Heart*, by James Reaney. *The Canadian Forum*, Feb. 1950, p. 264.

B209 Rev. of *Χαιρε: Seventy-One Poems*, by e. e. cummings. *The Canadian Forum*, Jan. 1951, p. 240.

B210 Rev. of *Collected Poems*, by W. B. Yeats. *The Canadian Forum*, Feb. 1951, p. 261.

B211 Rev. of *The Dead Seagull*, by George Barker. *The Canadian Forum*, Feb. 1951, p. 262.

B212 "Turning New Leaves." Rev. of *Selected Essays*, by T. S. Eliot. *The Canadian Forum*, March 1951, pp. 282–84.

B213 Rev. of *Boswell's London Journal*, ed. Frederick A. Pottle. *The Canadian Forum*, June 1951, p. 70.

B214 Rev. of *William Stukely: An Eighteenth Century Antiquarian*, by Stuart Piggot. *The Canadian Forum*, July 1951, p. 94.

B215 Rev. of *A Vagrant and Other Poems*, by David Gascoyne. *The Canadian Forum*, Aug. 1951, p. 119.

B216 Rev. of *A Crisis in English Poetry, 1880–1940*, by V. de S. Pinto. *The Canadian Forum*, March 1952, pp. 284–85.

B217 Rev. of *Collected Poems*, by Conrad Aiken. *The Canadian Forum*, July 1954, p. 92.

B218 "Poetry Chronicle." Rev. of *Let Us Compare Mythologies*, by Leonard Cohen; *Selected Poems*, by Raymond Souster; *The Bull Calf and Other Poems*, by Irving Layton; *The Hangman Ties the Holly*, by Anne Wilkinson; *Friday's Child*, by Wilfred Watson; *Even Your Right Eye*, by Phyllis Webb; and *Collected Poems*, by William Empson. *The Tamarack Review*, No. 1 (Autumn 1956), pp. 78–85.

B219 "Callaghan Revisited." Rev. of *Morley Callaghan's Stories*, by Morley Callaghan. *The Canadian Forum*, Feb. 1960, pp. 276–77. Rpt. in *Morley Callaghan*. Ed. and introd. Brandon Conron. Critical Views on Canadian Writers, No. 10. Toronto: McGraw-Hill Ryerson, 1975, pp. 74–77.

B220 "Turning New Leaves." Rev. of *Terror in the Name of God*, by Simma Holt. *The Canadian Forum*, March 1965, pp. 280–81.

MOVIE REVIEWS

B221 Rev. of *The Lady Vanishes*. *Acta Victoriana* [Victoria College, Univ. of Toronto], 63, No. 4 (Feb. 1939), 32–33.

B222 Rev. of *Moonlight Sonata*. *Acta Victoriana* [Victoria College, Univ. of Toronto], 63, No. 5 (March 1939), 33–34.

LETTERS

B223 Letter. *The Canadian Forum*, June 1945, p. 65.

Avison's previous critical review of Irving Layton's *Here and Now* had caused Layton to respond with characteristic vigour. Avison's response immediately follows Layton's reply (C4), explaining the premises behind her judgement.

B224 Letter to Cid Corman. 9 March 1961. Printed in *Origin*, Ser. 2, No. 4 (Jan. 1962), pp. 10–11.

B225 Letter to bpNichol. In *bp/Journeying and the Returns*. By bpNichol. Toronto: Coach House, 1967, n. pag.

SHORT STORIES

B226 "The Wind Passeth Over It." *Acta Victoriana* [Victoria College, Univ. of Toronto], 62, No. 3 (Jan. 1938), 1–3.

B227 "Cyrleen." *Acta Victoriana* [Victoria College, Univ. of Toronto], 63, No. 2 (Dec. 1938), 9–11.

B228 "Bats and Footmarks." *Acta Victoriana* [Victoria College, Univ. of Toronto], 65, No. 2 (Nov. 1940), 15.

B229 "Night Edition." *The Canadian Forum*, Feb. 1953, pp. 253–54.

AUDIO-VISUAL MATERIAL

B230 "Excerpt from Work in Progress." Narr. Margaret Avison. In *Six Toronto Poets*. Folkways Records, FL 9086, 1958. (L.p.; 2 min., 50 sec.)

B231 "Not the Sweet Cicely of Gerardes Herball." Narr. Margaret Avison. In *Six Toronto Poets*. Folkways Records, FL 9086, 1958. (L.p.; 1 min., 50 sec.) Rerecorded. Narr. Margaret Avison. *Canadian Poets*. Toronto: CBC Archives, T1678, 27 Aug. 1967. (2 min., 3 sec.)

See *WS* ["Not the Sweet Cicely of Gerardes Herball (i.e. Oriental Myrrh, not English Myrrh)"] and *WS/D* ["Not the Sweet Cicely of Gerardes Herball (i.e., Oriental Myrrh, Not English Myrrh)"].

B232 "Our Working Day May Be Menaced." Narr. Margaret Avison. In *Six Toronto Poets*. Folkways Records, FL 9086, 1958. (L.p.; 2 min., 5 sec.)

See *WS* and *WS/D*.

B233 "Tennis." Narr. Margaret Avison. In *Six Toronto Poets*. Folkways Records, FL 9086, 1958. (L.p.; 55 sec.)

See *WS*, *WS/D*, and B50.

B234 "For Dr. and Mrs. Dresser." In "A Selection of the Poetry of Margaret Avison and Margaret Atwood." Narr. Joan Gregson, Phyllis Malcolm Stewart, and Faith Ward. Host A. J. M. Smith. Prod. Peter Donkin. *Anthology*. CBC Radio, 1 Dec. 1966. (1 min., 42 sec.) Rerecorded. Narr. Margaret Avison. *Canadian Poets*. Toronto: CBC Archives, T1679, 27 Aug. 1967. (2 min., 2 sec.)

In the 1966 tape, Smith also comments on Avison's work (C28). See *Dumb.* and *WS/D*.

B235 "In a Season of Unemployment." In "A Selection of the Poetry of Margaret Avison and Margaret Atwood." Narr. Joan Gregson, Phyllis Malcolm Stewart, and Faith Ward. Host A. J. M. Smith. Prod. Peter Donkin. *Anthology*. CBC Radio, 1 Dec. 1966. (1 min., 15 sec.)

Smith also comments on Avison's work (C28). See *Dumb.*, *WS/D*, and B62.

B236 "A Story." In "A Selection of the Poetry of Margaret Avison and Margaret Atwood." Narr. Joan Gregson, Phyllis Malcolm Stewart, and Faith Ward. Host A. J. M. Smith. Prod. Peter Donkin. *Anthology*. CBC Radio, 1 Dec. 1966. (4 min., 16 sec.) Rerecorded. Narr. Margaret Avison. *Canadian Poets*. Toronto: CBC Archives, T1678, 27 Aug. 1967. (4 min., 11 sec.)

In the 1966 tape, Smith also comments on Avison's work (C28). See *Dumb.* and *WS/D*.

B237 "The Word." In "A Selection of the Poetry of Margaret Avison and Margaret Atwood." Narr. Joan Gregson, Phyllis Malcolm Stewart, and Faith Ward. Host A. J. M. Smith. Prod. Peter Donkin. *Anthology*. CBC Radio, 1 Dec. 1966 (1 min., 55 sec.)

Smith also comments on Avison's work (C28). See *Dumb.* and *WS/D*.

B238 "The Absolute the Day." Narr. Margaret Avison. *Poetry Reading*. Montreal: Sir George Williams Univ., 27 Jan. 1967. (1 min., 13 sec.)

B239 "The Absorbed." Narr. Margaret Avison. *Poetry Reading*. Montreal: Sir George Williams Univ., 27 Jan. 1967. (2 min., 10 sec.) Rerecorded. Narr. Margaret Avison. *Modern Canadian Poetry*. CBC Television Extension, 11 June 1967. (2 min., 5 sec.)

Includes an interview (C122). See also *Dumb.* and *WS/D*.

B240 "Bestialities." Narr. Margaret Avison. *Poetry Reading*. Montreal: Sir George Williams Univ., 27 Jan. 1967. (44 sec.)

See *Dumb.*, *WS/D*, and B85 ("Bestealities/OR/ Any Number Can Play").

B241 "Black-White Under Green." Narr. Margaret Avison. *Poetry Reading*. Montreal: Sir George Williams Univ., 27 Jan. 1967. (2 min., 10 sec.)

See *Dumb.* and *WS/D*.

B242 "[The boy with the brilliant promise . . .]." Narr. Margaret Avison. *Poetry Reading*. Montreal: Sir George Williams Univ., 27 Jan. 1967. (25 sec.)

B243 "The Earth That Falls Away." Narr. Margaret Avison. *Poetry Reading*. Montreal: Sir George Williams Univ., 27 Jan. 1967. (9 min., 6 sec.) Rerecorded. Narr. Margaret Avison. Toronto:

CBC Archives, 16 Sept. 1974. (11 min., 20 sec.)
See *Dumb.*, *WS/D*, and B86.

B244 "[Grey by water . . .]." Narr. Margaret Avison. *Poetry Reading*. Montreal: Sir George Williams Univ., 27 Jan. 1967. (40 sec.)

B245 "He Couldn't be Safe." Narr. Margaret Avison. *Poetry Reading*. Montreal: Sir George Williams Univ., 27 Jan. 1967. (39 sec.)
See *sun*.

B246 "[Inside the TTC . . .]." Narr. Margaret Avison. *Poetry Reading*. Montreal: Sir George Williams Univ., 27 Jan. 1967. (2 min.)

B247 "Insomniac's Report." Narr. Margaret Avison. *Poetry Reading*. Montreal: Sir George Williams Univ., 27 Jan. 1967. (45 sec.) Rerecorded. Narr. Margaret Avison. *Canadian Poets*. Toronto: CBC Archives, T1678, 27 Aug. 1967. (42 sec.)

B248 "Is That You/Me Standing on My/Your Foot?". Narr. Margaret Avison. *Poetry Reading*. Montreal: Sir George Williams Univ., 27 Jan. 1967. (1 min.)

B249 "[A junk truck stopped beside my bus . . .]." Narr. Margaret Avison. *Poetry Reading*. Montreal: Sir George Williams Univ., 27 Jan. 1967. (2 min., 20 sec.)

B250 "[No instant morality . . .]." Narr. Margaret Avison. *Poetry Reading*. Montreal: Sir George Williams Univ., 27 Jan. 1967. (55 sec.)

B251 "October 21, 1966." Narr. Margaret Avison. *Poetry Reading*. Montreal: Sir George Williams Univ., 27 Jan. 1967.

B252 "Of Tyranny, in One Breath." Narr. Margaret Avison. *Poetry Reading*. Montreal: Sir George Williams Univ., 27 Jan. 1967. (6 min., 25 sec.) Rerecorded. Narr. Margaret Avison. *Canadian Poets*. Toronto: CBC Archives, T1678, 27 Aug. 1967. (6 min., 44 sec.)

See *Dumb.* and *WS/D.*

B253 "The Seven Birds." Narr. Margaret Avison. *Poetry Reading*. Montreal: Sir George Williams Univ., 27 Jan. 1967. (54 sec.) Rerecorded. Narr. Margaret Avison. *Canadian Poets*. Toronto: CBC Archives, T1679, 27 Aug. 1967. (59 sec.)
See *sun*. ["The Seven Birds (College Street at Bathurst): SKETCH"].

B254 "Thaw." Narr. Margaret Avison. *Poetry Reading*. Montreal: Sir George Williams Univ., 27 Jan. 1967. (1 min., 7 sec.) Recorded. Narr. Margaret Avison. *Canadian Poets*. Toronto: CBC Archives, T1678, 27 Aug. 1967. (1 min., 14 sec.)
See *WS* and *WS/D*.

B255 "To Professor X, Year Y." Narr. Margaret Avison. *Poetry Reading*. Montreal: Sir George Williams Univ., 27 Jan. 1967. (1 min., 59 sec.)
See *WS* and *WS/D*.

B256 "Two Mayday Selves." Narr. Margaret Avison. *Poetry Reading*. Montreal: Sir George Williams Univ., 27 Jan. 1967. (1 min., SEC.)
See *Dumb.* and *WS/D*.

B257 "The Valiant Vacationist." Narr. Margaret Avison. *Poetry Reading*. Montreal: Sir George Williams Univ., 27 Jan. 1967. (3 min., 2 sec.) Rerecorded. Narr. Margaret Avison. *Canadian Poets*. Toronto: CBC Archives, T1678, 27 Aug. 1967. (2 min., 56 sec.)
See B25.

B258 "The Dumbfounding." Narr. Margaret Avison. *Modern Canadian Poetry.* CBC Television Extension, 11 June 1967. (2 min., 12 sec.)
Includes an interview (C122). See also *Dumb.*, *WS/D*.

B259 "The Agnes Cleves Papers." Narr. Margaret Avison. *Canadian Poets*. Toronto: CBC Archives, T1678, 27 Aug. 1967. (21 min., 24 sec.)

See *WS*, *WS/D*, and B44.

B260 "From a Provincial." Narr. Margaret Avison. *Canadian Poets*. Toronto: CBC Archives, T1678, 27 Aug. 1967. (53 sec.)
See *WS*, *Dumb.*, *WS/D*, and B40.

B261 "New Year's Poem." Narr. Margaret Avison. *Canadian Poets*. Toronto: CBC Archives, T1678, 27 Aug. 1967. (1 min., 18 sec.)
See *WS*, *WS/D*, and B42.

B262 "On the Death of France Darte Scott (Upon the Birth of Twin Sons Who Later Died)." Narr. Margaret Avison. *Canadian Poets*. Toronto: CBC Archives, T1678, 27 Aug. 1967. (57 sec.)
See *WS* and *WS/D*.

B263 "Poem with Footnotes for October." Narr. Margaret Avison. *Canadian Poets*. Toronto: CBC Archives, T1678, 27 Aug. 1967. (51 sec.)

B264 "Searching and Sounding." Narr. Margaret Avison. *Canadian Poets*. Toronto: CBC Archives, T1678, 27 Aug. 1967. (3 min., 53 sec.)
See *Dumb.* and *WS/D*.

B265 "September Street." Narr. Margaret Avison. *Canadian Poets*. Toronto: CBC Archives, T1678, 27 Aug. 1967. (1 min., 19 sec.)
See *WS* and *WS/D*.

B266 "Snow." Narr. Margaret Avison. *Canadian Poets*. Toronto: CBC Archives, T1678, 27 Aug. 1967. (41 sec.)
See *WS*, *WS/D*, and B49.

B267 "The Store Seeds." Narr. Margaret Avison. *Canadian Poets*. Toronto: CBC Archives, T1678, 27 Aug. 1967. (41 sec.)
See *Dumb.*, *WS/D*, and B79.

B268 "Streetcar, or Evil, Though God Is Sovereign." Narr. Margaret Avison. *Canadian Poets*. Toronto: CBC Archives, T1679, 27 Aug. 1967. (1 min., 50 sec.)
See *sun.* ("Wonder: A Street-car Sketch").

B269 "A Triad Ballad Cycle." Narr. Margaret Avison. *Canadian Poets*. Toronto: CBC Archives, T1678, 27 Aug. 1967. (38 sec.)

B270 "Voluptuaries and Others." Narr. Margaret Avison. *Canadian Poets*. Toronto: CBC Archives, T1678, 27 Aug. 1967. (2 min., 4 sec.)
See *WS*, *WS/D*, and B43.

B271 "Butterfly Bones; or, a Sonnet Against Sonnets." Narr. Margaret Avison. In "Canadian Poets Reading." *Anthology*. Supervising prod. Alex Smith. Ed. Robert Weaver. CBC Radio, 6 Nov. 1971.
See *WS* and *WS/D*.

B272 "Micro-Metro." Narr. Margaret Avison. Toronto: CBC Archives, 16 Sept. 1974. (1 min., 25 sec.)
See *Dumb.* and *WS/D*.

B273 "Old . . . Young . . . ." Narr. Margaret Avison. Toronto: CBC Archives, 16 Sept. 1974. (31 sec.)
See *Dumb.* and *WS/D*.

B274 "Pace." Narr. Margaret Avison. Toronto: CBC Archives, 16 Sept. 1974. (43 sec.)
See *Dumb.* and *WS/D*.

B275 "A Sad Song." Narr. Margaret Avison. Toronto: CBC Archives, 16 Sept. 1974. (51 sec.)
See *Dumb.* and *WS/D*.

PART II

Works on Margaret Avison

Book, Articles and Sections of Books, Theses and Dissertations, Interviews, Poems about Margaret Avison, and Awards and Honours

BOOK

C1 Redekop, Ernest. *Margaret Avison*. Studies in Canadian Literature, No. 9. Toronto: Copp Clark, 1970. 152 pp.

ARTICLES AND SECTIONS OF BOOKS

C2 Smith, A. J. M. "Margaret Avison (1918–)." In *The Book of Canadian Poetry: A Critical and Historical Anthology*. Ed. and preface A. J. M. Smith. Toronto: Gage, 1943, p. 426. 2nd ed., 1948, p. 441. 3rd ed., 1957, p. 471.

C3 Frye, Northrop. "Canada and Its Poetry." *The Canadian Forum*, Dec. 1943, p. 210. Rpt. in *The Making of Modern Poetry: Essential Articles on Contemporary Canadian Poetry in English*. Ed. Louis Dudek and Michael Gnarowski. Toronto: Ryerson, 1967, p. 96. Rpt. in *The Bush Garden: Essays on the Canadian Imagination*. By Northrop Frye. Toronto: House of Anansi, 1971, p. 142. Rpt. in *Forum: Canadian Life and Letters 1920–70. Selections from* The Canadian Forum. Ed. and preface J. L. Granatstein and Peter Stevens. Toronto: Univ. of Toronto Press, 1972, p. 220.

C4 Layton, Irving. Letter. *The Canadian Forum*, June 1945, p. 65.

C5 Sutherland, John. "Introduction: The Old and the New. 1 –

Mr. Smith and the 'Tradition.'" In *Other Canadians; An Anthology of the New Poetry of Canada 1940–1946*. Ed. John Sutherland. Montreal: First Statement, 1947, p. 10. Rpt. ("Introduction to *Other Canadians*") in *The Making of Modern Poetry in Canada: Essential Articles on Contemporary Canadian Poetry in English*. Ed. Louis Dudek and Michael Gnarowski. Toronto: Ryerson, 1967, p. 52. Rpt. ("Mr. Smith and the 'Tradition'") in *Essays, Controversies and Poems*. By John Sutherland. Ed. and introd. Miriam Waddington. New Canadian Library Original, No. 81. Toronto: McClelland and Stewart, 1972, p. 61.

C6 Ghiselin, Brewster. "The Architecture of Vision." *Poetry* [Chicago], 70 (Sept. 1947), 324–28.

C7 Pacey, Desmond. *Creative Writing in Canada: A Short History of English-Canadian Literature*. Toronto: Ryerson, 1952, p. 141. (Revised) 2nd ed., 1961, pp. 153, 240–41, 251.

C8 Birney, Earle. Notes. In *Twentieth Century Canadian Poetry: An Anthology*. Ed. and introd. Earle Birney. Toronto: Ryerson, 1953, p. 153.

C9 Frye, Northrop. "Preface to an Uncollected Anthology." Sec. II, The Royal Society of Canada, Toronto. 11 June 1956. Printed (expanded) in *Studia Varia: Royal Society of Canada, Literary and Scientific Papers*. Ed. G. D. Murray. Toronto: Univ. of Toronto Press, 1957, p. 35. Rpt. (abridged) in *Canadian Anthology*. Ed. Carl F. Klinck and Reginald E. Watters. Toronto: Gage, 1966, p. 523. Rpt. (expanded, original) in *The Bush Garden: Essays on the Canadian Imagination*. By Northrop Frye. Toronto: House of Anansi, 1971, p. 179. Rpt. in *Contexts of Canadian Criticism: A Collection of Critical Essays*. Ed. Eli Mandel. Patterns of Literary Criticism, No. 9. Chicago: Univ. of Chicago Press, 1971, p. 197. Rpt. in *Canadian Anthology*. Ed. Carl F. Klinck and Reginald E. Watters, 3rd ed. Toronto: Gage, 1974, p. 603. Rpt. in *Contexts of Canadian Criticism: A Collection of Critical Essays*. Ed. Eli Mandel. Rev. ed. Toronto: Univ. of Toronto Press, 1977, p. 197.

C10 Daniells, Roy. "Literature: 1. Poetry and the Novel." In *The Culture of Contemporary Canada*. Ed. Julian Park. Ithaca, N.Y.: Cornell Univ. Press, 1957, pp. 59–60.

C11 Wilson, Milton. "*Other Canadians and After.*" Association of Canadian University Teachers of English, Univ. of Alberta, Edmonton, Alta. June 1958. Printed in *The Tamarack Review*, No. 9 (Autumn 1958), pp. 90, 92. Rpt. in *Masks of Poetry: Canadian Critics on Canadian Verse*. Ed. and introd. A. J. M. Smith. New Canadian Library Original, No. 03. Toronto: McClelland and Stewart, 1962, pp. 136, 138. Rpt. in *Irving Layton: The Poet and His Critics*. Ed. and introd. Seymour Mayne. Toronto: McGraw-Hill Ryerson, 1978, pp. 73–74, 76.

C12 Dudek, Louis. "Patterns of Recent Canadian Poetry." *Culture*, 19, No. 4 (Dec. 1958), 405–06. Rpt. in *The Making of Modern Poetry in Canada: Essential Articles on Contemporary Canadian Poetry in English*. Ed. Louis Dudek and Michael Gnarowski. Toronto: Ryerson, 1967, p. 277. Rpt. in *Selected Essays and Criticism*. By Louis Dudek. Ottawa: Tecumseh, 1978, p. 101.

C13 Wilson, Milton. "The Poetry of Margaret Avison." *Canadian Literature*, No. 2 (Autumn 1959), pp. 47–58. Rpt. in *A Choice of Critics: Selections from* Canadian Literature. Ed. George Woodcock. Toronto: Oxford Univ. Press 1966, pp. 321–22.

C14 Frye, Northrop. "Letters in Canada: 1959. Poetry." *University of Toronto Quarterly*, 29 (April 1960), 458. Rpt. (revised — "Letters in Canada: Poetry 1952–1960: Valedictory") in *Masks of Poetry: Canadian Critics on Canadian Verse*. Ed. and introd. A. J. M. Smith. New Canadian Library Original, No. 03. Toronto: McClelland and Stewart, 1962, p. 106. Rpt. (revised, excerpt — "from 'Letters in Canada' *University of Toronto Quarterly: 1959*") in *The Bush Garden: Essays on the Canadian Imagination*. By Northrop Frye. Toronto: House of Anansi, 1971, p. 124.

C15 Smith, A. J. M. "Eclectic Detachment: Aspects of Identity on Canadian Poetry." *Canadian Literature*, No. 9 (Summer

1961), pp. 6, 12. Rpt. in *Towards a View of Canadian Letters: Selected Critical Essays 1928–1971*. By A. J. M. Smith. Vancouver: Univ. of British Columbia Press, 1973, pp. 22, 28.

C16 Finnigan, Joan. "Canadian Poetry Finds Its Voice in a Golden Age." *The Globe Magazine* [*The Globe and Mail*] [Toronto], 20 Jan. 1962, p. 12. Rpt. ("Joan Finnigan") in *The Making of Modern Poetry in Canada: Essential Articles on Contemporary Canadian Poetry in English*. Ed. Louis Dudek and Michael Gnarowski. Toronto: Ryerson, 1967, pp. 235–40.

C17 Pacey, Desmond. "Contemporary Canadian Poetry (1962)." *The Canadian Forum*, April 1962, p. 18. Rpt. in *Essays in Canadian Criticism 1939–1969*. By Desmond Pacey. Toronto: Ryerson, 1969, p. 217.

C18 Birney, Earle. "CPM, 27: 1946–1948." *Canadian Author & Bookman*,39, No. 2 (Winter 1963), 4. R1946–48: Retrospective Article") in *Spreading Time: Remarks on Canadian Writing and Writers, Book* I: *1904–1949*. By Earle Birney. Montreal: Véhicule, 1980, p. 128.

C19 "Margaret Avison (1918–)." In *Écrivains Canadiens/ Canadian Writers: A Biographical Dictionary*. Ed. Guy Sylvestre, Brandon Conron, and Carl F. Klinck. Toronto: Ryerson, 1964, p. 4. Rpt. in *Canadian Writers/Écrivains Canadiens: A Biographical Dictionary*. Rev. and enl. ed. Ed. Guy Sylvestre, Brandon Conron, and Carl F. Klinck. Toronto: Ryerson, 1966, p. 4.

C20 Woodcock, George. "Away from Lost Worlds." In *On Contemporary Literature*. Ed. and introd. Richard Kostelanetz. New York: Avon, 1964, pp. 100, 107. Rpt. (revised — "Culture and the Death of Colonialism") in *Canada and the Canadians*. By George Woodcock. Toronto: Oxford Univ. Press, 1970, p. 254. Rpt. (revised — "Away from Lost Worlds: Notes on the Development of a Canadian Literature") in *Odysseus Ever Returning: Essays on Canadian Writers and Writing*. Ed. George Woodcock. Introd. W. H. New. New Canadian Library, No. 71. Toronto: McClelland and Stewart, 1970, pp. 4, 10. Rpt. in *Readings in Commonwealth*

Literature. Ed. William Walsh. Oxford: Clarendon, 1973, pp. 212, 218.

C21 Beattie, Munro. "Poetry: 1950–1960." In *Literary History of Canada: Canadian Literature in English*. Gen. ed. and introd. Carl F. Klinck. Toronto: Univ. of Toronto Press, 1965, pp. 808–11. 2nd ed., 1976. Vol. II, 320–23.

C22 Frye, Northrop. "Conclusion." In *Literary History of Canada: Canadian Literature in English*. Gen. ed. and introd. Carl F. Klinck. Toronto: Univ. of Toronto Press, 1965, p. 844. Rpt. in *The Bush Garden: Essays on the Canadian Imagination*. By Northrop Frye. Toronto: House of Anansi, 1971, p. 244.

C23 Jones, D. G. "The Sleeping Giant, or the Uncreated Conscience of the Race." Association of Canadian University Teachers of English, Univ. of British Columbia, Vancouver, B.C. June 1965. Printed in *Canadian Literature*, No. 26 (Autumn 1965), pp. 6–7, 14, 19. Rpt. in *A Choice of Critics: Selections from* Canadian Literature. Ed. George Woodcock. Toronto: Oxford Univ. Press, 1966, pp. 7, 22–23. Rpt. in *Butterfly on Rock: A Study of Themes and Images in Canadian Literature*. By D. G. Jones. Toronto: Univ. of Toronto Press, 1970, pp. 16, 23, 30.

C24 McPherson, Hugo. "Canadian Literature: Present Declarative." *English*, 15 (Autumn 1965), 214.

C25 Watters, R. E. "Margaret Avison (1918–   )." In *Canadian Anthology*. Ed. Carl F. Klinck and Reginald E. Watters. Rev. ed. Toronto: Gage, 1966, p. 560. (Revised) 3rd ed., 1974, p. 651.

C26 Klinck, Carl F., and Reginald E. Watters. "Margaret Avison (1918–   )." In *Canadian Anthology*. Ed. Carl F. Klinck and Reginald E. Watters. Rev. ed. Toronto: Gage, 1966, p. 434. 3rd ed., 1974, p. 447.

C27 Watters, Reginald Eyre, and Inglis Freeman Bell. *On Canadian Literature 1806–1960: A Check List of Articles, Books and Theses on English-Canadian Literature, Its Authors and Language.* Toronto: Univ. of Toronto Press, 1966, pp. 38, 72.

C28 Smith, A. J. M. Host. *Anthology.* Prod. Peter Donkin. CBC Radio, 1 Dec. 1966.

C29 "Avison, Margaret 1918– ." In *Contemporary Authors: A Bio-Bibliographical Guide to Current Authors and Their Works.* Ed. James Ethridge and Barbara Kopala. Vols. XVII–XVIII. Detroit: Gale, 1967, 33. Rpt. (expanded) in First Revision. Ed. Clare D. Kinsman. Vols. XVII–XX. Detroit: Gale, 1976, 42.

C30 Story, Norah. "Avison, Margaret (1918–)." In her *The Oxford Companion to Canadian History and Literature.* Toronto: Oxford Univ. Press, 1967, p. 43.

C31 Story, Norah. "Poetry in English." In her *The Oxford Companion to Canadian History and Literature.* Toronto: Oxford Univ. Press, 1967, pp. 648, 650.

C32 Purdy, Al. "Canadian Poetry in English since 1867." *Journal of Commonwealth Literature*, No. 3 (July 1967), p. 29.

C33 Jones, Laurence M. "A Core of Brilliance: Margaret Avison's Achievement." *Canadian Literature*, No. 38 (Autumn 1968), pp. 50–57.

C34 New, William H. "A Wellspring of Magma: Modern Canadian Writing." *Twentieth Century Literature*, 14 (Oct. 1968), 126–27.

C35 Geddes, Gary. "Margaret Avison (b. 1918)." In *20th Century Poetry and Poetics.* Ed. Gary Geddes. Toronto: Oxford Univ. Press, 1969, pp. 575–76. 2nd ed., 1973, p. 616.

C36 Manning, Gerald. "Margaret Avison's 'Perspective': An Interpretation." *Quarry*, 18, No. 2 (Winter 1969), 21–24.

C37 Dudek, Louis. "2. Poetry in English." *Canadian Literature*, No. 41 (Summer 1969), p. 118. Rpt. in *The Sixties: Writers and Writing of the Decade. A Symposium to Celebrate the Tenth Anniversary of* Canadian Literature. Ed. George Woodcock. Vancouver: Univ. of British Columbia Press, 1969, p. 118. Rpt. in *Readings in Commonwealth Literature*. Ed. William Walsh. Oxford: Clarendon, 1973, p. 264. Rpt. ("Poetry of the Sixties") in *Selected Essays and Criticism*. By Louis Dudek. Ottawa: Tecumseh,1978, pp. 278–79.

C38 Geddes, Gary, and Phyllis Bruce. "Margaret Avison." In *15 Canadian Poets*. Ed. Gary Geddes and Phyllis Bruce. Toronto: Oxford Univ. Press, 1970, pp. 266–68. Rpt. in *15 Canadian Poets Plus 5*. Ed. Gary Geddes and Phyllis Bruce. Toronto: Oxford Univ. Press, 1978, pp. 379–80.

C39 Jones, D. G. *Butterfly on Rock: A Study of Themes and Images in Canadian Literature*. Toronto: Univ. of Toronto Press, 1970, pp. 137, 139, 164, 165, 179–80.

C40 Smith, A. J. M. "Avison, Margaret (Kirkland)." In *Contemporary Poets of the English Language*. Ed. Rosalie Murphy. New York: St. Martin's, 1970, pp. 42–44. Rpt. in *Contemporary Poets*. Rev. ed. Ed. James Vinson. New York: St. Martin's, 1975, pp. 49–50. 3rd ed., 1980, pp. 52–53.

C41 Mandel, Eli. "Modern Canadian Poetry." *Twentieth Century Literature*, 16 (July 1970), 177. Rpt. in *Another Time*. By Eli Mandel. Three Solitudes: Contemporary Literary Criticism in Canada, No. 3. Erin, Ont.: Porcépic, 1977, p. 83.

C42 New, William H. "The Mind's Eyes (I's), (Ice): The Poetry of Margaret Avison." *Twentieth Century Literature*, 16 (July 1970), 185–202. Rpt. in *Articulating West: Essays on Purpose and Form in Modern Canadian Literature*. By William H. New. Three Solitudes: Contemporary Literary Criticism in Canada, No. 1. Toronto: new, 1972, pp. 234–58. Rpt. (abridged) in *Contemporary Literary Criticism: Excerpts from Criticism of the Works of Today's Novelists, Poets, Playwrights, and Other Creative Writers*. Ed. Carolyn Riley. Vol. IV. Detroit: Gale, 1975, 36.

C43 Djwa, Sandra. "Canadian Poetry and the Computer." *Canadian Literature*, No. 46 (Autumn 1970), pp. 44, 45, 54.

C44 Reference Division, McPherson Library, University of Victoria, B.C., comp. "Avison, Margaret 1918- ." In their *Creative Canada: A Biographical Dictionary of Twentieth Century Creative and Performing Artists*. Vol. 1. Toronto: Univ. of Toronto Press, 1971, 15.

C45 Atwood, Margaret. *Survival: A Thematic Guide to Canadian Literature*. Toronto: House of Anansi, 1972, pp. 65, 246.

C46 Lee, Dennis. "Modern Poetry." In *Read Canadian: A Book about Canadian Books*. Ed. Robert Fulford, David Godfrey, and Abraham Rotstein. Introd. Robert Fulford. Toronto: James Lewis and Samuel, 1972, p. 232.

C47 Watters, Reginald Eyre. "Avison, Margaret Kirkland, 1918– ." In his *A Checklist of Canadian Literature and Background Materials, 1628–1960*. 2nd ed. Toronto: Univ. of Toronto Press, 1972, p. 10.

C48 Redekop, Ernest. "The Only Political Duty: Margaret Avison's Translations of Hungarian Poems." *The Literary Half-Yearly* [Univ. of Mysore, India], [Canadian Number], 13, No. 2 (July 1972), 157–70.

C49 Shain, Merle. "Some of Our Best Poets Are Women." *Chatelaine*, Oct. 1972, pp. 103, 104.

C50 Denham, Paul. Introduction. In *The Evolution of Canadian Literature in English: 1945–70*. Ed. Paul Denham. Preface Mary Jane Edwards. Toronto: Holt, Rinehart and Winston, 1973, pp. 8, 9.

C51 Gnarowski, Michael. "Avison, Margaret, 1918- ." In his *A Concise Bibliography of English Canadian Literature*. Toronto: McClelland and Stewart, 1973, p. 11. 2nd rev. ed., 1978, p. 12.

C52 Hassan, Ihab. "Canadian Literature: Poetry in English." In

World Literature Since 1945: Critical Surveys of the Contemporary Literatures of Europe and the Americas. Ed. Ivar Ivask and Gero von Wilpert. New York: Frederick Ungar Publishing Co., 1973, p. 132.

C53 Strickland, David. "*Quotations*" *from English Canadian Literature*. Modern Canadian Library. Toronto: Pagurian, 1973, pp. 52, 126, 145, 154, 166.

C54 T[oye]., W[illiam]. E. "Margaret Avison (1918–)." In *Supplement to The Oxford Companion to Canadian History and Literature*. Ed. William Toye. Toronto: Oxford Univ. Press, 1973, pp. 7–8.

C55 Waterston, Elizabeth. *Survey: A Short History of Canadian Literature*. Methuen Canadian Literature Series. Toronto: Methuen, 1973, pp. 9, 13, 140, 146–47.

C56 Jones, D. G. "Myth, Frye and Canadian Writers." *Canadian Literature*, No. 55 (Winter 1973), p. 11.

C57 Bowering, George. "Avison's Imitation of Christ the Artist." *Canadian Literature*, No. 54 (Autumn 1973), pp. 56–69. Rpt. (abridged) in *Contemporary Literary Criticism: Excerpts from Criticism of the Works of Today's Novelists, Poets, Playwrights, and Other Creative Artists*. Ed. Carolyn Riley and Barbara Harte. Vol. II. Detroit: Gale, 1974, 29. Rpt. (expanded, original) in *A Way with Words*. By George Bowering. Ottawa: Oberon, 1982, pp. 5–23.

C58 Davey, Frank. "Margaret Avison (1918–)." In his *From There to Here: A Guide to English Canadian Literature since 1960*. Vol. II of *Our Nature – Our Voices*. Erin, Ont.: Porcépic, 1974, pp. 37–40.

C59 Doerksen, D. W. "Search and Discovery: Margaret Avison's Poetry." *Canadian Literature*, No. 60 (Spring 1974), pp. 7–20. Rpt. in *Poets and Critics: Essays from* Canadian Literature *1966–1974*. Ed. George Woodcock. Toronto: Oxford Univ. Press, 1974, pp. 123–37. Rpt. (abridged) in *Contemporary Literary Criticism: Excerpts from Criticism of the Work of*

Today's Novelists, Poets, Playwrights, and Other Creative Writers. Ed. Carolyn Riley. Vol. IV. Detroit: Gale, 1975, 36–37.

C60 Jones, D. G. "Cold Eye and Optic Heart: Marshall McLuhan and Some Canadian Poets." *Modern Poetry Studies*, 5 (Autumn 1974), 175, 178–79, 181–82, 183, 184, 185, 186.

C61 Farley, T. E. *Exiles and Pioneers: Two Visions of Canada's Future 1825–1975*. Ottawa: Borealis, 1976, pp. 136, 145.

C62 McCullagh, Joan. *Alan Crawley and* Contemporary Verse. Foreword Dorothy Livesay. Vancouver: Univ. of British Columbia Press, 1976, pp. 32, 46, 49.

C63 Merrett, R. J. "'The Ominous Centre': The Theological Impulse in Margaret Avison's Poetry." *White Pelican*, 5, No. 2 (1976), 12–24.

C64 Seymour-Smith, Martin. "Margaret Avison." *Who's Who in Twentieth Century Literature* (1976).

C65 Neufeld, James. "Some Pivot for Significance in the Poetry of Margaret Avison." *Journal of Canadian Studies*, 11, No. 2 (May 1976), 35–42.

C66 Cohn-Sfectu, Ofelia. "Margaret Avison: the All-Swallowing Moment." *English Studies in Canada*, 2 (Fall 1976), 339–44.

C67 Moisan, Clément. "Rina Lasnier et Margaret Avison." *Liberté*, 18, No. 6 (nov./déc. 1976), 21–33. Rpt. (abridged — "Poésie de la clandestinité: Rina Lasnier — Margaret Avison") in *Poésie des frontières: étuide comparée des poésies canadienne et québécoise*. By Clément Moisan. Collection constantes, No. 38. Québec: Hurtubise HMH, 1979, pp. 115–27. Rpt. ("Poetry of Clandestiny: Rina Lasnier — Margaret Avison") in *A Poetry of Frontiers: Comparative Studies in Quebec/Canadian Literature*. By Clément Moisan. Trans. George Lang and Linda Weber. Victoria: Porcépic, 1983, pp. 64–74.

C68 Frye, Northrop. "Haunted by Lack of Ghosts: Some Patterns in the Imagery of Canadian Poetry." In *The Canadian Imagination: Dimensions of a Literary Culture*. Ed. and introd. David Staines. Cambridge, Mass.: Harvard Univ. Press, 1977, pp. 38–39.

C69 McClung, M. G. *Women in Canadian Literature*. Preface George Woodcock. Women in Canadian Life. Toronto: Fitzhenry & Whiteside, 1977, p. 42.

C70 Reeves, John. "John Reeves: Photojournalist." *Toronto Life: Photography Guide*, Spring 1977 – *Toronto Life*, May 1977, p. 25. Rpt. (revised – "Literary Portraits: Margaret Avison") in *Canadian Fiction Magazine*, Nos. 34–35 (1980), pp. 74–75.

C71 Reigo, Ants. "Margaret Avison and the Gospel of Vision." *CV/II*, 3, No. 2 (Summer 1977), 14–19.

C72 Zezulka, J. M. "Refusing the Sweet Surrender: Margaret Avison's 'Dispersed Titles.'" *Canadian Poetry: Studies, Documents, Reviews*, No. 1 (Fall/Winter1977), pp. 44–53.

C73 Mansbridge, Francis. "Margaret Avison: A Checklist." *Canadian Library Journal*, 34 (Dec. 1977), 431–36.

C74 Stevens, Peter. "Avison, Margaret Kirkland (1918–)." In his *Modern English-Canadian Poetry: A Guide to Information Sources*. Vol. XV of *American Literature, English Literature and World Literatures in English*. Detroit: Gale, 1978, pp. 13, 20, 107–09.

C75 Mallinson, Jean. "Ideology and Poetry: An Examination of Some Recent Trends in Canadian Criticism." *Studies in Canadian Literature*, 3 (Winter 1978), 99–100.

C76 Cohn-Sfectu, Ofelia. "To Live in Abundance of Life: Time in Canadian Literature." *Canadian Literature*, No. 76 (Spring 1978), pp. 25–36.

C77 Taylor, Michael. "Snow Blindness." *Studies in Canadian Literature*, 3 (Summer 1978), 288–90.

C78 Zichy, Francis. "Each in His Prison / Thinking of the Key:

Images of Confinement and Liberation in Margaret Avison." *Studies in Canadian Literature*, 3 (Summer 1978), 232–43.

C79 Marshall, Tom. *Harsh and Lovely Land: The Major Canadian Poets and the Making of a Canadian Tradition.* Vancouver: Univ. of British Columbia Press, 1979, pp. xii, xiv, 20, 58, 71, 75, 77, 78, 90, 92, 107, 109, 110, 111, 112, 115, 119, 128, 150, 154, 168, 171, 172, 174, 176, 177, 178, 179.

C80 Moisan, Clément. *Poésie des frontières: étude comparée des poésies canadienne et québécoise.* Collection constantes, No. 38. Québec: Hurtubise HMH, 1978, pp. 16, 77, 91, 101n., 239n., 285, 294, 297, 298, 300, 324, 327. Rpt. *A Poetry of Frontiers: Comparative Studies in Quebec/Canadian Literature.* By Clément Moisan. Trans. George Lang and Linda Weber. Victoria: Porcépic, 1983, pp. 34–35, 171, 183, 190, 193, 207.

C81 Pacey, Desmond. *Essays: Canadian Literature in English.* Ed. and preface A. L. McLeod. Foreword H. H. Anniah Gowda. Powre above Powres, No. 4. Mysore, India: Centre for Commonwealth Literature and Research, Univ. of Mysore, 1979, pp. 131, 134–35, 136.

C82 Redekop, Ernest. "Margaret Avison." In *Commonwealth Literature.* Ed. James Vinson. Introd. William Walsh. London: Macmillan, 1979, pp. 24–25.

C83 Woodcock, George. "Poetry." In *Literary History of Canada: Canadian Literature in English.* Gen. ed. and introd. Carl F. Klinck. Toronto: Univ. of Toronto Press, 1979, Vol. III, 314.

C84 Lecker, Robert. "Exegetical Blizzard." *Studies in Canadian Literature*, 4 (Winter 1979), 180–84.

C85 Pollock, Zailig. "A Response to Michael Taylor's 'Snow Blindness.'" *Studies in Canadian Literature*, 4 (Winter 1979), 177–79.

C86 Marshall, Tom. "Major Canadian Poets IV: Margaret Avison." *The Canadian Forum*, March 1979, pp. 20–33. Rpt.

(revised) in *Harsh and Lovely Land: The Major Canadian Poets and the Making of a Canadian Tradition*. By Tom Marshall. Vancouver: Univ. of British Columbia Press, 1979, pp. 99–106.

C87 Hutcheon, Linda. "'Snow Storm of Paper': The Act of Reading in Self-Reflexive Canadian Verse." *Dalhousie Review*, 59 (Spring 1979), 118–27.

C88 Kertzer, J. M. "Margaret Avison: Power, Knowledge and the Language of Poetry." *Canadian Poetry: Studies, Documents, Reviews*, No. 4 (Spring/Summer 1979), pp. 29–44.

C89 Zichy, Francis. "A Response to Robert Lecker's 'Exegetical Blizzard' and Michael Taylor's 'Snow Blindness.'" *Studies in Canadian Literature*, 4 (Summer 1979), 147–54.

C90 Kertzer, J. M. "Margaret Avison's Portrait of a Lady: 'The Agnes Cleves Papers.'" *Concerning Poetry*, 12, No. 2 (Fall 1979), 17–24.

C91 Jeffrey, David L. "Margaret Avison: Sonnets and Sunlight." *Calvinist Contact*, 19 Oct. 1979, pp. 3, 4.

C92 Kertzer, Jon. "Margaret Avison." In *Profiles in Canadian Literature*. Vol. II. Ed. and foreword Jeffrey M. Heath. Toronto: Dundurn, 1980, 33–40.

C93 Redekop, Ernest H. "sun/Son light/Light: Avison's elemental *Sunblue*." *Canadian Poetry: Studies, Documents, Reviews*, No. 7 (Fall/Winter 1980), pp. 21–37.

C94 Aide, William. "An Immense Answering of Human Skies: The Poetry of Margaret Avison." In *The Human Elements*. 2nd ser. Ed. and introd. David Helwig. Ottawa: Oberon, 1981, pp. 51–76.

C95 Anderson, Mia. "'Conversation with the Star Messenger': An Enquiry into Margaret Avison's *Winter Sun*." *Studies in Canadian Literature*, 6 (1981), 82–132.

C96 Atwood, Margaret. Introduction. In *The New Oxford Book of Canadian Verse: In English*. Ed. Margaret Atwood. Toronto: Oxford Univ. Press, 1982, pp. xxvi, xxix.

C97 Kent, David. "Margaret Avison 1918- ." In *Canadian Poetry*. Ed. Jack David and Robert Lecker. Introd. George Woodcock. New Press Canadian Classics. Toronto/Downsview, Ont.: General/ECW, 1982, Vol. 1, 318–20.

C98 Woodcock, George. "Canadian Poetry: *An Introduction to Volume One*." In *Canadian Poetry*. Ed. Jack David and Robert Lecker. New Press Canadian Classics. Toronto/Downsview, Ont.: General/ECW, 1982, Vol. 1, 18, 19, 29.

C99 Woodcock, George. "Canadian Poetry: *An Introduction to Volume Two*." In *Canadian Poetry*. Ed. Jack David and Robert Lecker. New Press Canadian Classics. Toronto/Downsview, Ont.: General/ECW, 1982, Vol. 2, 13.

C100 Bentley, D. M. R. "Drawers of Water; Notes on the Significance and Scenery of Fresh Water in Canadian Poetry." *CV/II*, 6, No. 4 (Aug. 1982), 27–28.

C101 Lane, M. Travis. "Contemporary Canadian Verse: The View from Here." *University of Toronto Quarterly*, 52 (Winter 1982–83), 184.

C102 Bennett, Donna, and Russell Brown. "Margaret Avison, b. 1918." In *An Anthology of Canadian Literature in English*. Ed. Donna Bennett and Russell Brown. Vol. 2. Toronto: Oxford Univ. Press, 1983, 32–33.

C103 Ho[s]ek, Chaviva. "Poetry in English: 1950 to 1982." In *The Oxford Companion to Canadian Literature*. Ed. William Toye. Toronto: Oxford Univ. Press, 1983, p. 663.

C104 Sullivan, Rosemary. "Avison, Margaret (b. 1918)." In *The Oxford Companion to Canadian Literature*. Ed. William Toye. Toronto: Oxford Univ. Press, 1983, p. 34.

C105 "Avison, Margaret." In *Who's Who in Canadian Literature*.

Ed. Gordon Ripley and Anne V. Mercer. Toronto: Reference Press, 1983, p. 12.

C106 Stouck, David. "Margaret Avison." In his *Major Canadian Writers: A Critical Introduction*. Lincoln, Nebraska: Univ. of Nebraska Press, 1984, pp. 212–27.

C107 Gnarowski, Michael. "Avison, Margaret." *The Canadian Encyclopedia*. Vol. I. Foreword by Mel Hurtig. Introd. James H. Marsh. Edmonton: Hurtig, 1985, p. 123.

C108 McDougall, R.L. "Literature in English." *The Canadian Encyclopedia*. Vol. II. Foreword by Mel Hurtig. Introd. James H. Marsh. Edmonton: Hurtig, 1985, p. 1019.

THESES AND DISSERTATIONS

C109 Ade, Janet Elizabeth. "The Poetry of Margaret Avison: Technique and Theme." M.A. Thesis Toronto 1966.

C110 Djwa, Sandra Anna. "Metaphor, World View and the Continuity of Canadian Poetry: A Study of the Major English Canadian Poets with a Computer Concordance to Metaphor." Diss. British Columbia 1968.

C111 Munro, Jane Patricia. "Seas, Evolution and Images of Continuing Creation in English-Canadian Poetry." M.A. Thesis Simon Fraser 1970.

C112 Williamson, Hendrika. "Man and Mandala: The Poetry of Margaret Avison." M.A. Thesis Simon Fraser 1971.

C113 Klus, Christopher. "The Religious Poetry of Margaret Avison: An Examination of *The Dumbfounding*." M.A. Thesis McMaster 1972.

C114 Mansbridge, Francis. "The Poetry of Margaret Avison and Raymond Souster." Diss. Ottawa 1975.

C115 Sherwood, Lyn Elliot. "Innocence and Experience: An

Analysis of the Sun Image in Some Modern Canadian Poetry." M.A. Thesis Carleton 1977.

C116 Armstrong, E. Jane Jackman. "Margaret Avison's Poetry." M.A. Thesis Carleton 1980.

C117 Lehman, Victoria Evelyn. "The Poet as Isolated Visionary in the Work of Margaret Avison and A. M. Klein." M.A. Thesis Queen's 1980.

C118 Cohn-Sfectu, Ofelia. "To Live in Abundance of Life: A Study of Time in Five Canadian Authors." Diss. McMaster 1981.

C119 McColm, Sheila Clare. "Metaphorical Style and Thought in the Poetry of Margaret Avison and Michael Ondaatje." M.A. Thesis Western Ontario 1981.

C120 St. Pierre, Jeannette. "Avison and the Metaphysicals." M.A. Thesis McMaster 1982.

INTERVIEWS

C121 Murray, Peggy. "She Wants an Award for the Readers." *The Telegram* [Toronto], 27 Feb. 1961, p. 25.

C122 Webb, Phyllis. "Poets Here, Now and Then." Interview with Margaret Avison and Alfred Purdy. *Modern Canadian Poetry.* CBC Television Extension, 11 June 1967. (8 min., 30 sec.)

C123 Bolette, John, Claudette Jones, and Mike Caroline. "A Conversation with Margaret Avison." Dir. Bert Laale. Prod. Instructional Media Centre. Host John Margeson. Scarborough, Ont.: Scarborough College, Univ. of Toronto, 001085, 1971. (Videocassette; black-and-white; 17 min.)

C124 Anderson, Allan. "Poets of Canada: 1920 to the Present." Interview with Milton Acorn, Margaret Atwood, Margaret Avison, Earle Birney, George Bowering, Victor Coleman, Leonard Cohen, Joan Finnigan, John Glassco, George Jonas, Irving Layton, Dorothy Livesay, Gwendolyn MacEwen, Eli

Mandel, Alden Nowlan, Michael Ondaatje, P. K. Page, Al Purdy, James Reaney, and A. J. M. Smith. *Anthology.* Supervising prod. Alex Smith. Ed. Robert Weaver. CBC Radio, 15 May 1971. (3 min., 2 sec.)

C125 Anderson, Allan. "Poets of Canada: 1920 to the Present." Interview with Margaret Atwood, Margaret Avison, Nelson Ball, Victor Coleman, Northrop Frye, John Glassco, Irving Layton, Dennis Lee, Dorothy Livesay, Gwendolyn MacEwen, Eli Mandel, Anne Marriott, John Newlove, Glen Siebrasse, Francis Sparshott, Peter Stevens, Miriam Waddington, Milton Wilson, and George Woodcock. *Anthology.* Supervising prod. Alex Smith. Ed. Robert Weaver. CBC Radio, 19 June 1971 (44 sec.)

C126 Anderson, Allan. "Poets of Canada: 1920 to the Present." Interview with Milton Acorn, Margaret Avison, Henry Beissel, Earle Birney, George Bowering, John Robert Colombo, Frank Davey, Ronald Everson, Joan Finnigan, John Glassco, Phyllis Gotlieb, David Helwig, George Johnston, George Jonas, Irving Layton, Anne Marriott, John Newlove, Alden Nowlan, Michael Ondaatje, James Reaney, Miriam Waddington, and Robert Weaver. *Anthology.* Supervising prod. Alex Smith. Ed. Robert Weaver. CBC Radio, 26 June 1971. (55 sec.)

C127 Nederlanden, Harry der. "Margaret Avison: The Dumbfoundling" [sic]. *Calvinist Contact*, 19 Oct. 1979, pp. 1, 3, 4.

C128 Chunn, Ian. "Interview: Margaret Avison." *The Strand* [Victoria College, Univ. of Toronto], 26 Jan. 1983, p. 5.

C129 Meyer, Bruce, and Brian O'Riordan. "Margaret Avison: Conversion & Meditation." *Poetry Canada Review*, 7, No. 1 (Autumn 1985), 8–9.

POEMS ABOUT MARGARET AVISON

C130 Bowering, George. "Margaret Avison." In his *Curious*. Toronto: Coach House, 1973, p. 42. Rpt. in his *Selected Poems*. Vancouver: Talonbooks, 1980, p. 113.

C131 Galt, George. "For Margaret Avison." *Applegarth's Folly* [London, Ont.], No. 2 (1975), p. 136.

AWARDS AND HONOURS

C132 Guggenheim Fellowship (1956).

C133 Governor-General's Award for Poetry for *Winter Sun* (1960).

C134 Doctor of Letters, York University (1985).

C135 Order of Canada (1985).

SELECTED BOOK REVIEWS

Winter Sun

D1 House, Vernal. "A Bow to Margaret Avison." *The Globe Magazine [The Globe and Mail]* [Toronto], 30 July 1960, p. 9.

D2 Woodcock, George. "Two Accomplished Poets Share Ironically Tragic View of Life." Rev. of *Winter Sun*, by Margaret Avison; and *You, Emperors, and Others: Poems 1957–1960*, by Robert Penn Warren. *The Vancouver Sun*, 17 Sept. 1960, p. 5.

D3 Endicott, N. J. "Recent Verse." Rev. of *Winter Sun*, by Margaret Avison; *Lost Dimension*, by Fred Cogswell; and *Eyes Without a Face*, by Kenneth McRobbie. *Canadian Literature*, No. 6 (Autumn 1960), pp. 60–62.

D4 Mandel, Eli. Rev. of *Winter Sun*. *Queen's Quarterly*, 67 (Winter 1960–61), 704–05.

D5 Atwood, Margaret. "Some Sun for This Winter." *Acta Victoriana* [Victoria College, Univ. of Toronto], 85, No. 2 (Jan. 1961), 18–19. Rpt. in *Second Words: Selected Critical Prose*. By Margaret Atwood. Toronto: House of Anansi, 1982, pp. 21–23.

D6 Smith, A. J. M. "Critical Improvisations on Margaret Avison's *Winter Sun*." *The Tamarack Review*, No. 18 (Winter 1961), pp. 81–86. Rpt. in *Towards a View of Canadian Letters: Selected Critical Essays 1928–1971*. By A. J. M. Smith. Vancouver: Univ. of British Columbia Press, 1973, pp. 142–45.

D7 Reaney, James. "Turning New Leaves (1)." *The Canadian Forum*, March 1961, p. 284.

D8 Kennedy, X. J. "Five Poets in Search of Six Lines." Rev. of *Winter Sun*, by Margaret Avison; *Wilderness of Ladies*, by

Eleanor Ross Taylor; *Walls and Distances*, by David Galler; *Outlanders*, by Theodore Weiss; and *The Drunk in the Furnace*, by W. S. Merwin. *Poetry* [Chicago], 98 (May 1961), 118–19.

D9 Slater, Joseph. "All's Well in the World of Verse." *Saturday Review*, 6 May 1961, pp. 30, 47.

D10 Wilson, Milton. "Letters in Canada: 1960. Poetry." *University of Toronto Quarterly*, 30 (July 1961), 380–83.

D11 Bates, Ron. "Review of Recent Canadiana." *Alphabet*, No. 3 (Dec. 1961), p. 42.

The Dumbfounding

D12 Smith, A. J. M. "Margaret Avison's New Book." *The Canadian Forum*, Sept. 1966, pp. 132–34.

D13 Carruth, Hayden. "In Spite of Artifice." *The Hudson Review*, 19 (Winter 1966–67), 697.

D14 Gibbs, Robert. Rev. of *The Dumbfounding. The Fiddlehead*, No. 70 (Winter 1967), pp. 70–71. Rpt. (abridged) in *Contemporary Literary Criticism: Excerpts from Criticism of the Works of Today's Novelists, Poets, Playwrights, and Other Creative Writers*. Ed. Carolyn Riley and Barbara Harte. Vol. II. Detroit: Gale, 1974, 29.

D15 Harrison, Keith. "Poetry Chronicle." Rev. of *The Dumbfounding*, by Margaret Avison; *A Christ of the Ice-Floes*, by David Wevill; *The L. S. D. Leacock*, by Joe Rosenblatt; *The Circle Game*, by Margaret Atwood; and *The Silver Wire*, by George Bowering. *The Tamarack Review*, No. 42 (Winter 1967), pp. 76–77.

D16 Pacey, Desmond. "Canadian Literature 1966: A Good to Middling Year." *Commentator* [Toronto], No. 11 (Jan. 1967), p. 25.

D17 MacCallum, Hugh. "Letters in Canada: 1966. Poetry."

University of Toronto Quarterly, 36 (July 1967), 354–57.

D18 Tillinghast, R. "Seven Poets." *Poetry* [Chicago], 110 (July 1967), 265–66.

D19 Colombo, John Robert. "Avison and Wevill." Rev. of *The Dumbfounding*, by Margaret Avison; and *A Christ of the Ice-Floes*, by David Wevill. *Canadian Literature*, No. 34 (Autumn 1967), pp. 72–76.

D20 Helwig, David. "Canadian Poetry: Seven Recent Books." *Queen's Quarterly*, 74 (Winter 1967), 759–61.

D21 Moran, Ronald. "Quality and Quantity: A Chronicle of the Poetry Explosion." *The Southern Review* [Baton Rouge, La.], 4 (Summer 1968), 787–89.

D22 Morse, Samuel French. "Poetry 1966." *Contemporary Literature*, 9 (Winter 1968), pp. 120–21. Rpt. (abridged) in *Contemporary Literary Criticism: Excerpts from Criticism of the Works of Today's Novelists, Poets, Playwrights, and Other Creative Writers*. Ed. Carolyn Riley and Barbara Harte. Vol. II. Detroit: Gale, 1974, 29.

D23 Perkin, J. C. R. "All Rinsed with Morning." *The Second Mile* [Hantsport, N.S.], Dec. 1978, pp. 24–28.

sunblue

D24 Dudek, Louis. "Poets of Heaven and Hell." Rev. of *sunblue*, by Margaret Avison; and *A Man to Marry, A Man to Bury*, by Susan Musgrave. *The Globe and Mail* [Toronto], 7 April 1979, p. 39.

D25 Johnston, Gordon. "Avison's Temple." *The Canadian Forum*, May 1979, pp. 30–31.

D26 Linder, Norma West. "Starkness and Sensibility." Rev. of *sunblue*, by Margaret Avison; *Poems New & Selected*, by Patrick Lane; *Fall by Fury & Other Makings*, by Earle Birney; and *Intrigues in the House of Mirrors*, by Mike Zizis.

Canadian Author & Bookman, 54 (May 1979), pp. 28–29.

D27 Moritz, Albert. "Stalking the Sacred Asparagus." *Books in Canada*, Aug./Sept. 1979, pp. 28–29.

D28 Lever, Bernice. "Light Under a Bushel." *The CRNLE Reviews Journal* [Flinders Univ., South Australia], 1, No. 2 (Oct. 1979), 61–64.

D29 McNally, Paul. Rev. of *sunblue. The Fiddlehead*, No. 123 (Fall 1979), pp. 100–02.

D30 Scobie, Stephen. "Poetry and Fiction." *Queen's Quarterly*, 87 (Spring 1980), 158–60.

D31 Djwa, Sandra. "Letters in Canada: 1979. Poetry." *University of Toronto Quarterly*, 49 (Summer 1980), 348–49.

D32 Willmot, Rod. "Winning Spirit." *Canadian Literature*, No. 87 (Winter 1980), pp. 115–16.

D33 Livesay, Dorothy. "What Endures." Rev. of *Out of the Violent Dark*, by Gwladys Downes; and *sunblue*, by Margaret Avison. *CV/II*, 5, No. 2 (Winter 1980–81), 18–19.

D34 Guptara, Prabhu S. "A Dark Reservoir of Gladness: Margaret Avison's Third Volume of Verse." *Literary Criticism* [Mysore, India], 16, No. 1 (1981), 42–45.

D35 McColm, Sheila. Rev. of *sunblue. Brick*, No. 11 (Winter 1981), pp. 29–32.

Winter Sun/The Dumbfounding: Poems 1940–66

D36 Adachi, Ken. "Avison's Subtlety Contrasts with Lane's Violent Images." Rev. of *Winter Sun/The Dumbfounding: Poems 1940–66*, by Margaret Avison; and *Old Mother*, by Patrick Lane. *The Toronto Star*, 15 Jan. 1983, p. G12.

D37 Skelton, Robin. "Poetry Selected, Collected, and Resurrected." Rev. of *Earthlight: Selected Poetry of*

Gwendolyn MacEwen, by Gwendolyn MacEwen; *Tarts and Muggers: Poems New and Selected*, by Susan Musgrave; *A Throw of Particles: The New and Selected Poetry of D. G. Jones; A Wild Peculiar Joy*, by Irving Layton; and *Winter Sun/The Dumbfounding: Poems 1940–66*, by Margaret Avison. *Quill & Quire*, Feb. 1983, p. 33.

D38 Garebian, Keith. "Prayers and Sermons." Rev. of *Winter Sun/The Dumbfounding: Poems 1940–66*, by Margaret Avison; and *Digging In*, by Elizabeth Brewster. *Books in Canada*, March 1983, pp. 19–20.

D39 Bemrose, John. "Poetry: Thought, Religion and Passion." Rev. of *Selected Poems: The Vision Tree*, by Phyllis Webb; *Winter Sun/The Dumbfounding: Poems 1940–66*, by Margaret Avison; *Selected Poems 1972–1982*, by Robert Bringhurst; and *As Close as We Came*, by Barry Callaghan. *The Globe and Mail* [Toronto], 28 May 1983, Sec. Entertainment, p. 17.

D40 Djwa, Sandra, and R. B. Hatch. "Letters in Canada: 1982. Poetry." *University of Toronto Quarterly*, 52 (Summer 1983), 343–45.

D41 Berry, Reginald. "Natural & Unnatural." Rev. of *The Beauty of the Weapons: Selected Poems 1972–82*, by Robert Bringhurst; *A Throw of Particles: The New and Selected Poetry of D. G. Jones*, by D. G. Jones; *Winter Sun/The Dumbfounding: Poems 1940–1966*, by Margaret Avison; *A Wild Peculiar Joy: Selected Poems 1945–82*, by Irving Layton; and *Mostly Coast People: Selected Verse* by Hubert Evans. *Canadian Literature*, No. 102 (Autumn 1984), pp. 136–37.

History of Ontario

D42 Coutts, Robin. "How People Lived." *Saturday Night*, 3 May 1952, p. 25.

A Doctor's Memoirs

D43 Cook, Ramsay. "Letters in Canada: 1960. History: Local and Regional." *University of Toronto Quarterly*, 30 (July 1961), 461.

Index to Critics Listed in the Bibliography

INDEX